T0265562

CONTESTED KINGDOM

Contested Kingdom

FAN ATTACHMENT AND CORPORATE CONTROL AT Disneyland

WILLIAM McCARTHY

University Press of Mississippi / Jackson

Publication of this work was made possible in part
due to a grant from Zayed University.

The University Press of Mississippi is the scholarly publishing agency of
the Mississippi Institutions of Higher Learning: Alcorn State University,
Delta State University, Jackson State University, Mississippi State University,
Mississippi University for Women, Mississippi Valley State University,
University of Mississippi, and University of Southern Mississippi.

www.upress.state.ms.us

The University Press of Mississippi is a member
of the Association of University Presses.

An earlier version of chapter 2 ("Disneyland As a Place for Southern Californians")
was published as: McCarthy, W. (2019). "Meet me on main street": Disneyland as
place attachment for Southern Californians." *Tourism Geographies*, 21(4), 586–612.

Copyright © 2024 by University Press of Mississippi
All rights reserved
Manufactured in the United States of America

∞

Library of Congress Cataloging-in-Publication Data

Names: McCarthy, William (William D.), author.
Title: Contested kingdom : fan attachment and corporate control at
Disneyland / William McCarthy.
Description: Jackson : University Press of Mississippi, 2024. |
Includes bibliographical references and index.
Identifiers: LCCN 2024025388 (print) | LCCN 2024025389 (ebook) |
ISBN 9781496854735 (hardback) | ISBN 9781496854728 (trade paperback) |
ISBN 9781496854742 (epub) | ISBN 9781496854759 (epub) |
ISBN 9781496854766 (pdf) | ISBN 9781496854773 (pdf)
Subjects: LCSH: Walt Disney Enterprises. |
Amusement parks—California—History. | Amusement parks—Social
aspects—California. | Online social networks—Social aspects. |
Popular culture—United States. | Fans (Persons)—Social aspects. |
Social media. | Disneyland (Calif.)—Social aspects. | Disneyland (Calif.)—History.
Classification: LCC GV1853.3.C22 M33 2024 (print) | LCC GV1853.3.C22
(ebook) | DDC 338.7/6179106879496—dc23/eng/20240815
LC record available at https://lccn.loc.gov/2024025388
LC ebook record available at https://lccn.loc.gov/2024025389

British Library Cataloging-in-Publication Data available

For Kyawt Kyawt

CONTENTS

GLOSSARY

AP: annual passholder program to Disneyland resort parks from 1984 to 2020

Avengers Campus: Marvel-themed land that opened in 2021 in Disney California Adventure

BBS: online bulletin board systems accessed via dial-up; popular from the late 1970s to 1990s

Cast members: frontline employees at Disney theme parks

DCA: Disney California Adventure theme park, opened in 2001, and only a one-minute walk from the Disneyland front gate

DIG: Disney Information Guide website owned and operated by Al Lutz in the 1990s and hosted by the internet service provider America Online

Disney: media entertainment conglomerate founded in 1923 by Walt and Roy O. Disney

Disneybounding: fan practice of wearing outfits inspired by the appearance of major and minor characters from Disney texts but not so precise a duplication as to be considered cosplay in violation of Disney park policy on visitor attire (such as using Snow White's associated colors and hairstyle reimagined as a 1920s flapper style)

Disneyland: opened in 1955 at Anaheim, California, the only Disney theme park built during Walt Disney's lifetime

Disneyland Resort: Anaheim, California, Disney resort comprising Disneyland theme park, Disney California Adventure theme park, the Downtown Disney shopping district, and three Disney-owned hotels (Disneyland Hotel, Grand Californian, and Pixar Place)

Disney Legend: hall of fame program honoring individuals for extraordinary contributions to the Walt Disney Company; awarded biennially at the D23 Expo

Galaxy's Edge: *Star Wars*–themed land that opened in 2019 in Disneyland

Imagineer: an individual who works in Imagineering

Imagineering: the design and engineering arm of the Walt Disney Company

Magic Key: replacement for the former annual passholder program instituted in 2021

Walt Disney World Resort: Orlando, Florida, Disney resort, opened in 1971, comprising four theme parks, two water parks, and over twenty-five Disney-owned hotels

CONTESTED KINGDOM

CHAPTER 1

Not Just Child's Play

I had always thought of Disneyland and theme parks as commercial, fake, and trite, but when I briefly lived in Southern California in early 2008, the house of Mickey Mouse was hard to ignore for a visit. The region features a multitude of attractions for all ages, including art centers, museums, railway exhibits, air and space museums, aquariums, zoos, parks, beaches, historical landmarks, and so much more. Yet, Disneyland's seeming omnipresence in billboards, local news, television commercials, radio ads, Disney mall stores, Disney branded food in supermarkets, and general topic of local conversation all made a trip feel imperative to undertake. Nevertheless, I was somewhat hesitant to visit. As a young child on the quintessential US family pilgrimage to Walt Disney World (WDW) in Florida, a lasting impression recalls such fear of the Haunted Mansion attraction that I closed my eyes for almost the entire duration of a ride that is more humorous than frightening. Later, as a graduate student, I lived within a one-hour high-speed rail ride to Tokyo Disneyland, but never considered making even a single visit during my two-year residence in Niigata, Japan. In the end, curiosity convinced me to visit the original Disneyland in Anaheim, California, to witness firsthand as an adult the putative notoriety of a Disney theme park.

Since I was neither a fan of nor knowledgeable about Disneyland, I searched the internet for information and advice to plan ahead. Initially, I checked the official Disneyland website and Trip Advisor, but soon found my way onto fan websites with insider tips and discovered people who actually visited Disneyland on a monthly, weekly, and even daily basis. In June 2017, one local fan, Jeff Reitz, was feted by Disney for visiting the park for two thousand consecutive days. In 1986, Italian semiotician Umberto Eco observed Disneyland visitors as akin to robots with little agency shuffling

from ride to ride throughout the park.[1] In 2011, Svonkin noted the regimenta-
tion of park visitors through the design of rides and shows by Disney Imagineers as "their craft of people-moving and audience manipulation."[2] Even
in a recent 2019 study, Morris saw Disney's control as enabling "the park to
operate within rigid guidelines that felt like freedom, but really left us very
little freedom in their use of the park's rides and spaces."[3] However, for over
two decades on Sundays at noon in the park's central hub, a group of mostly
local fans from the MiceChat website have met and enjoyed the park together
on their own terms. The fans, primarily adults, typically lunch, socialize,
and go on a couple rides, or sometimes none at all. Although place scholars such as Cresswell have called Disneyland "the epitome of placelessness
constructed, as it is, purely for outsiders,"[4] I discovered there were numerous local fan-organized meets, events, and clubs in the park every weekend
operating independently of the Disney company's organization or control.
Internet and fan studies scholar Henry Jenkins saw fan participation within
online social platforms as a positive force for user empowerment creating
a participatory culture and as technological extensions of fan communities
that existed before the internet with conventions, zines, and newsletters.[5]
Local Disneyland fans on online social platforms took participation a step
further by creating and organizing regular offline, in-person social activities
at the park. After checking day ticket prices, though, I wondered how so
many local fans could afford to visit Disneyland so frequently.

Like other outside observers, I had always considered Disney theme parks
as tourist destinations that locals might visit once in a while but certainly not
for weekly or monthly trips. In an early study in 1991, before the mass diffusion of the internet, looking at Walt Disney World as a local leisure place,
Milman found Central Florida residents visited less than expected due to a
preference for less time-consuming local leisure activities.[6] Leisure studies
scholars such as Roberts noted that "few people can be more than once-a-
year visitors" to theme parks.[7] In their influential text on remediation, Bolter
and Grusin believed people visited Disneyland only once or twice during
childhood.[8] I also presumed frequent visits would be rare due to prohibitive
expense until discovering Disneyland's annual passholder (AP) program.
The 1984 introduction of APs for US$65 enabled passholders to visit as many
days as desired over a one-year period. Disneyland no longer needed to be a
special occasion trip for locals and instead became, with an AP, as accessible
as a neighborhood park. Prices increased over the years with an equivalent
signature plus AP in early 2020 available for US$1,449, but a lower-tier pass
with more blockout dates (weekends, summer, and major holidays) was
available for purchase exclusively by Southern California residents for only

US$419. In 2023, compared to other regional leisure activities, the lowest price season tickets for the Los Angeles Dodgers were US$1,200 and the Los Angeles Lakers at US$1,500 (courtside was over US$10,000). In addition, Disney has frequently offered promotions broadening economic accessibility such as giving a free ticket on one's birthday in 2009 that could be applied for its face value, US$69, toward a Southern California Select AP then costing US$134, thus bringing down the cost of the lowest-tier AP in 2009 to only US$65 out of pocket for a year of visits. In the mid-1990s, annual passholders were estimated to be less than 100,000 but by the mid-2010s numbered over one million.[9] With so many people able to visit the park regularly and at will, it was perhaps inevitable that local fans would use online social platforms to organize meets and events at Disneyland. The affordability of the AP combined with the affordance of online social platforms to connect people with shared interests turned Disneyland into a common social meeting hub for many Southern Californians. Disneyland became a prominent local place connecting Southern Californians online and in the park.

I visited Disneyland half a dozen times in early 2008 while availing helpful tips posted by local fan experts on the discussion boards of the MousePlanet and MiceChat websites. With each visit I became progressively charmed by the heartwarming park and cast members. Although I departed Southern California in the summer of 2008, I found myself continuing to closely follow various fan forums due to a continually increasing interest in the news, discussions, debates, and history of Disneyland. Plunging into a new fan interest often leads to a deep dive, and Disneyland certainly comprises a vast ocean of lore full of discoveries, stories, and myth.

In the late 2000s, web discussion boards were still the nucleus for online fan interaction and information about Disneyland, but a precipitous decrease in user activity and posting became noticeable by the early 2010s as social media platforms such as Facebook increasingly drew fans away. Smartphones also changed the Disneyland experience by enabling fans to connect with each other easily anywhere, anytime, and even while visiting the park. The concurrent rapid adoption of smartphones and social media gave rise to a networked individualism that focused on an individual's personal network of connections and existing ties (strong, weak, and latent) to be persistently maintained and developed.[10] The networked individualism of social media platforms not only drew traffic away from the shared interest fandoms found on web discussion boards but also transformed governance, content, and usage practices, just as the transition from Usenet newsgroups to web discussion boards had done in the preceding internet era. Facebook, Instagram, YouTube, and Twitter (the original name is used rather than X, because the book predominantly covers the period before the renaming) changed the ownership model from fan-owned websites and discussion boards to corporate-owned platforms. The decade-by-decade succession of platform architectures, from Usenet to web discussion boards to social media, precipitated steady shifts away from the sustained building of shared interest fan social groups to corporate values of generating large volumes of turnover traffic for advertising and marketing purposes at the expense of public social values.

By the mid-2010s, stalwart members of web discussion boards wondered aloud in posts where everyone had gone and why. The common answer was to Facebook, because everyone seemed to be on the platform. There was no longer a need to visit the many shared interest fan websites and discussion boards that had been launched online since the late 1990s and early 2000s. On Facebook, new shared interest groups proliferated rapidly due to being free and easy to create. Fandoms fragmented and scattered across multiple social media platforms into smaller and more exclusive groups. In an earlier era, shared interest web discussion boards had attracted a diverse range of participants across the internet to focus on a particular fandom object such as Disneyland, but social media platforms focused on the individual user as a hub connecting outward to a sundry array of "likes" (friends, family, hobbies, jobs, interests, commerce, and so on). For Disneyland fans, the mid-2010s saw a rapid increase in the number of in-park fan events organized on social media platforms, in addition to the formation of scores of local Disneyland fan social clubs primarily using Facebook groups. Internet and fan studies scholar Nancy Baym has noted that while in-person relationships often turn into online ones through Facebook, Instagram, and Twitter, online connections much less often turn into offline, in-person friendships.[11] However, Disneyland fans in Southern California have taken an inverted approach by rarely using online social platforms to arrange person-to-person meets in the park but rather have used online social platforms to discover events, meets, or clubs to attend in order to mix within a mass gathering of fans to connect and make friends in person at the park. In this book I consider the effects of the different characteristics of the predominant online social platforms of the last thirty years on fan organization and interaction around Disneyland. In addition, I examine the contentious relationship over Disneyland between local fans and a Disney company that has sought to control and regularize fans who assert agency online and in the park. Walt Disney dubbed Disneyland the Magic Kingdom, but the park has been a contested kingdom for the last three decades as local fans and the Disney company have vied over the meaning and purpose of Disneyland through a succession of online social platforms.

I therefore look at two associated phenomena. First is the examination of the fervent sense of place attachment to Disneyland by the approximately one million annual passholders in Southern California through people, place, and process dimensions. Second, in addition to cultural and social factors, the characteristics and nature of the prevalent online social platforms of the last three decades (Usenet, web discussion boards, and social media) are examined to trace the evolution of the interaction, influence, and organization of local Disneyland fans with each other and Disney as corporate owner and place caretaker, and analyze the impact of the online social platforms on the fluctuation of power between local fans and Disney over discourse, commerce, and social formations.

ADULTS ALSO PLAY AT DISNEYLAND

Although often considered a magical place designed primarily for children, Giroux and Pollock found adults at Disneyland also bewitched by "an invitation to adventure, a respite from the drudgery of work, and an opportunity to escape from the alienation and boredom of everyday life."[12] Shortly after opening, Vice President Richard Nixon toured the park with his wife Pat and two daughters on August 11, 1955. Upon boarding Peter Pan's Flight in Fantasyland, Pat Nixon remarked, "Dick's getting a bigger kick out of this than the kids!"[13] French philosopher Jean Baudrillard saw Disneyland as a place for adults to candidly reclaim their childishness.[14] Walt Disney did not design Disneyland just for children but also for postmodern adults that Bernardini termed *kidults*, a portmanteau of "kid" and "adult," who have adopted a lifestyle of childish-at-heart spirit and playfulness.[15] Substantiating Walt Disney's famous declaration that "adults are just kids grown up," both parents and children play in Disneyland, donning Mickey and Minnie Mouse ears. When an ABC television director remarked that the park would be a wonderful place for children, Walt Disney scoffed, citing the economic necessity of appealing to adults: "Don't you know anything? Kids don't have any money."[16] Karis observes Disney theme parks as utilizing a double level of address to appeal to both adults and children with safe, childlike, and child-appropriate spaces in contrast to the adult outside world.[17] Svonkin notes Walt Disney's penchant for incorporating adult themes and tropes into attractions seemingly aimed at children such as Adventureland's Enchanted Tiki Room, which was inspired by the faux Polynesian bars favored by returning World War II Pacific theater veterans and featured female animatronic birds as erotic objects of desire for the show's male avian hosts.[18] For Cross and Walton, a primary appeal of

Disneyland is "the evocation of childhood wonder and the nostalgic longings of the 'child within.'"[19] Disneyland transformed famous Disney texts seen on film and television by adults and children into a spatial, textural, and kinetic spectacle coupled with concomitant merchandising.[20] The pairing of the AP program that started in 1984 along with the rise of online social platforms in the early 1990s provided affordances for Disneyland fans in Southern California to visit, connect, meet, and revel regularly within the spectacle of the park. While Disneyland has been popular with Southern Californians since opening in 1955, the coupling of the AP and online social platforms supercharged the affective, cognitive, and behavioral bonds of attachment for local adults with the park from the 1990s to the 2020s.

This book's study is not a history of Disneyland; many fine accounts have already been written on the subject. I recommend Snow's lucidly written 2020 biography of the park titled "Disney's Land"; the extensive research of Pierce's tome revealing previously untold stories on Disneyland's construction and C. V. Wood, the park's first general manager; Bemis's treatise on US Disney theme parks as evolving places of collective memory and cultural attitudes reflecting the American national narrative with the apt subtitle "mirror, mirror for us all"; and Mittermeier's comprehensive cultural histories of all the Disneylands around the world.[21] For research on theme park fandom, Williams's 2020 book broke important new ground examining fan connections with theme parks through a diverse array of practices including embodied transmedia and spatio-paratextual play through park merchandise, "cult-culinary" objects and diegetic paratexts, haptic fandom, character encounters, and spatial poaching and participatory narratives from the famed Haunted Mansion attraction.[22] In the present book I also look at theme park fandom, but my primary focus is not on fan park practices regarding attractions, characters, food and beverages, and merchandise. Instead, my focal point examines the systemic influence of online social platforms on the three-decade intersection of local fans and Disney at Disneyland as a fandom object and tangible place. The book also comprises the first in-depth longitudinal study of the evolving role and nature of online social platforms on the transformation of fandoms. Furthermore, a model framework is presented for potential application to future longitudinal studies of other fandoms with tangible fandom objects such as a theme park or sports stadium or intangible fandom objects such as a film, television series, or video game.

A fandom arises as individuals follow and identify with a celebrity, brand, team, media text, and so on that provides perceived positive outcomes through membership.[23] But Disneyland fandom differs from other media fandoms because the affective object is a physical place imbued and intertwined with over one hundred years of popular texts, and not centered on a particular person, band, game, film, or television series. In addition, Disney's vast media conglomerate umbrella comprises what Wasko sees as a distinct multiverse including the studios of Pixar, Lucasfilm, Marvel, 21st Century Fox, and the Muppets.[24] Unlike the media fan cultures observed by Hills, Jenkins, and Booth,[25] Disneyland fandom is not characterized by fan fiction or filk music, or cosplay in the park, which is banned at Disneyland for anyone fourteen years of age or older. Instead, adult Disneyland fans devise new practices such as "Disneybounding" in the park by wearing outfits inspired by the appearance of major and minor characters from Disney texts to avoid being considered cosplay. Rowe in a 2022 autoethnography discovered, by Disneybounding at the park, that other guests would stop to chat and cast members would offer complimentary beverages and better access to shows.[26] In this book I focus on online fan practices and their accompanying effects in the park, such as the creation of social formations and activities as well as new ways to engage and resist a corporate owner from literally within the fandom object itself as a physical place. This emergence of a convergence process allowed fans to establish personal identities, narratives, individualities, and positioning within online social platforms and Disneyland.[27] On the other hand, social media influencers, bloggers, and web discussion board owners became coopted to varying degrees to work together with the Disney company to the economic benefit of both parties. Disneyland fans and fannish activities have therefore ranged well within the extremes of resistant "semiotic guerrillas" and consumerist "capitalist dupes."[28]

To understand such a multifaceted research subject encompassing Bennett's four key interconnected areas of fandom (internet communication, creativity, knowledge, and organizational/civic power),[29] in this book I use several theories and concepts to investigate the intersection of Southern California fans and the Disney company at the park and on online social platforms over the last three decades. First, place attachment theory is used to explore the people, place, and process dimensions within the bond between Southern California fans and the park. Second, medium theory and van Dijck's platform analysis model[30] are used to examine the effects of the characteristics and nature of a succession of online media platforms over the past thirty years on the social development, formation, and interaction between local Disneyland fans with each other and Disney. Third, Bourdieu's forms of capital provide a foundation to track and understand the fluid social, cultural, and economic interplay among fans and Disney at Disneyland and on online social platforms.[31] Finally, Foucault's approach to power as being in flux and contested at all levels informs the discussion of the relational ebb and flow between local fans and the Disney company.[32]

DISNEYLAND AND THEME PARKS AS PLACES

Although many post–World War II observers have lamented the loss of informal public life and social commons due to increasing mobility, globalization, cultural homogenization and digitalization, none have considered theme parks as local places of sociality.[33] Even though the decline of Main Streets in small towns has long been cited as a distressing symbol of lost community replaced by automobile-dominated suburbs splitting the social world of residents into disparate fragments without emotional attachment,[34] Disneyland's vibrant Main Street has generally been dismissed as simply a notorious example of Baudrillard's simulacrum. Since the end of World War II, leisure time has become increasingly privatized and individualized in the home, with media technology, particularly television and later the internet, displacing social activities with friends and family.[35] Socializing shifted from the semi-public spaces of cafés, parks, and pubs to the privacy of indoor homes, with people spending less time in public places with friends or meeting new ones.[36] Digital hardware ranging from internet-connected personal computers of the 1990s to the smartphones of the 2000s have been frequently cited as technologies that have isolated and dehumanized individuals. The number of local gathering places sharply declined, including places where young people and adults socialized together.

Amusement and theme parks have long been derided by social, cultural, and intellectual elites and thus not considered places for social commons.[37] As a leisure category, theme parks are associated with out-of-town visitors of the tourism and entertainment industry, and not as intrinsic elements of their surrounding locales. While many people only visit theme parks intermittently, almost all theme parks around the world promote an annual pass program that enables and encourages regular visits by locals. A long-standing assumption holds that people prefer to hang out in real, lived-in, local commercial places rather than in the perceived inorganic and inauthentic commercial spaces of theme parks. Oldenburg's study of third places considers cozy cafés, taverns, bookstores, and hairdressers as local hangouts, but not large physical venues with enormous crowds.[38] Former *New York Daily News* sports columnist Filip Bondy in 2005 wrote a book about a group of New York Yankees baseball fans known as the "bleacher creatures" who inhabited the old Yankee Stadium upper deck seating area known as Section 39.[39] Although the old Yankee Stadium was a cavernous structure capable of holding almost 50,000 fans, a pocket of regulars formed a community from diverse backgrounds around their shared interest. Even the starting Yankee players tipped their caps on the field to acknowledge the "bleacher creatures" who together chanted their names at the top of the first inning at home games. And similar to Disneyland, sports locales such as football stadiums have been treated as hallowed ground by fan groups for "shared emotionalism."[40] However, sports stadiums are designed to separate the spectator and actor, and can only be fully accessed on game days or briefly for tours on selected nongame days, whereas Disneyland opens every day from morning to night for fans to wander through experientially while engaging all senses within "inhabitable text."[41] Kokai and Robson term this kind of experience "immersive Disney" because all the senses get engaged and manipulated, such as the use of forced perspective to shape guest perceptions of park structures, pumping in artificial smells for emotional responses, and reshaping the topography between lands as subtle thematic transitions.[42] Rather than being merely oft-mentioned sites of mindless consumerism, theme parks can be a form of "immersive theater" empowering and providing agency and different modes of reception for visitors to become authors and characters in their own park narratives.[43] Williams uses the term "haptic fandom" to describe this physicality of bodily sensations experienced by each fan differently within the immersive environment of a theme park.[44]

Disneyland's critics have often viewed the park through narrow perspectives such as commercial exploitation, regimented control of visitors, or display of inauthentic and diminished culture. Relph, who saw place meaning as personally constructed through emotional ties and subjective experience, rejected Disneyfied landscapes as holding little meaning for locals due to being "absurd, synthetic places . . . that have little relationship with a particular geographic setting."[45] American historian Daniel J. Boorstin observed Disneyland as a prime example of the inauthentic pseudo-event "with little significance for the inward life of a people."[46] Sorkin saw Disneyland as a completely synthetic "end of public space."[47] Richard Schickel, who wrote an early critical biography of Walt Disney, said Disneyland was mostly a cultural horror with no cathartic release from its symbol-laden attractions.[48] Giroux and Pollock found Disney theme parks "a blend of 'Taylorized' fun, patriotic populism, and consumerism dressed up as a childhood fantasy" that treated visitors as consumers and spectators.[49] French philosopher Louis Marin argued Disneyland was "the representation realized in a geographical space of the imaginary relationship that the dominant groups of American society maintain with their real conditions of existence, with the real history of the United States, and with the space outside of its borders."[50] Bryman defined the "Disneyization" of space as the creation of a ludic atmosphere that masks the true strategy of manipulating the emotions of visitors to open their wallets and consume by inseparably interweaving the theme park with shopping, hotels, food, and beverages.[51] Cross and Walton believed Disneyland's

simulation of enchantment did not generate a sense of playfulness; Jones and
Wills considered Disneyland a disciplined ordeal with visitors directed on
how to behave and where to walk.[52] The assumption has been that theme park
visitors, particularly to Disneyland, spend most of the day rushing through
rides, shows, and shopping with little time to socialize and play.

While Disneyland's critics have issued pointed criticisms, particularly
regarding the company's focus on consumerism, the critiques have primarily derived from an etic (outsider) perspective that has overlooked the emic
(insider) perspective of fans and locals. Humanistic geographer Yi-Fu Tuan felt
cultural critics who dismissed Disneyland as mindless entertainment were not
observant enough and were unable to bear the park's sunny optimism.[53] Francaviglia noted that academics in general were reluctant to publicly admit any
positive influences from Disneyland due to habitual Disney-bashing within
academia.[54] Warren and Lukas argued that much of the postmodern criticism of Disneyland lacked in-depth ethnographic investigation and empirical
observation of visitor behavior in the park.[55] For example, Fong and Nunez in
2012 concluded that Disneyland was a "world of strangers" after only spending nine hours in one day at the park.[56] Eco saw Disneyland visitors as robots
herded from one ride queue to the next without considering the potential for
socializing while waiting in line.[57] Etic critics have generally not scratched
below notions of out-of-town tourists holding park maps wide open to orient
themselves while puttering around the park. By contrast, savvy local Disneyland regulars are often aware of "tricks" such as the opportunity to make a
free improvised sandwich in Disney California Adventure (DCA) by taking
fresh sourdough bread samples at the Bakery Tour to the free toppings bar
with lettuce, tomatoes, pickles, onions, and sauces at Smokejumpers Grill in
the Grizzly Peak land. The fan practice ended when the toppings bar did not
return when the park reopened from the pandemic in April 2021. And until
early 2019, the gratis meal could be topped off with dessert courtesy of free
chocolate squares handed out at the entrance of the Ghirardelli Soda Fountain
and Chocolate Shop across from The Bakery Tour. The failure to differentiate
between the park experiences of tourists and locals has led critics to neglect the
extraordinary cultural and social milieu created by Southern California fans at
Disneyland. Only recently have observers (such as Sparrman in 2022) noted
visitor agency in Disneyland as "when walking down Main Street, children
and adults do not necessarily behave like pre-programmed robots in ways that
follow the intention of the designers."[58] In a comprehensive forty-year review of
place attachment literature, Lewicka in 2011 wondered whether entertainment
sites were capable of fostering place attachment since the possibility had not
been explored.[59] The present book rectifies this long-standing research gap.

Critiques of Disneyland often become outdated as the experiential media of the park continuously and significantly changes from decade to decade and even year to year. For example, criticizing Disneyland for sanitizing and promoting American history presumes that history-based attractions still predominate in the park. The Walt Disney era of Tomorrowland attractions that lionized American progress in science and space has long been replaced by the corporate marketing synergy of rides featuring Buzz Lightyear, *Star Wars*, and *Finding Nemo*. Frontierland has steadily shrunk in size in recent decades with the 2007 reskin of Tom Sawyer Island into Pirate's Lair (a commercial tie-in with the Pirates of the Caribbean attraction and film franchise) and the 2016 truncation of the Rivers of America and bulldozing of Big Thunder Ranch to clear room for the new *Star Wars* themed Galaxy's Edge land. The Abraham Lincoln attraction on Main Street was displaced for most of 2019 by Disney film previews. DCA's original lands and attractions have been largely scrubbed of California history, which was the park's raison d'être upon opening, and replaced by popular Disney texts. The Golden Dreams theater attraction, celebrating the contributions and recognizing the hardships of immigrants to California, was replaced in 2011 by a Little Mermaid dark ride. The Pacific Wharf area representing the waterfronts of Monterey and San Francisco was rethemed in 2023 to the alternate history San Fransokyo of the 2014 animated Disney film *Big Hero Six*. The flying theater attraction Soarin' originally highlighted the landscapes of California but now showcases global destinations including the Eiffel Tower, Taj Mahal, Great Wall of China, Iguazu Falls, and Sydney Harbor. Disney has removed many symbols and references to California at DCA attractions as Superstar Limo became Monsters Inc., Orange Stinger changed to Silly Symphony Swings, Mulholland Madness turned into Goofy's Sky School, California Screamin' transformed to The Incredicoaster, Sun Wheel into Pixar Pal-A-Round, and Hollywood Tower of Terror morphed into Guardians of the Galaxy Mission Breakout. The first primary reason for the wave of replacements has been commercial, with merchandise based on Disney texts outselling items based on American history. The second is that visitors to playful places throughout history have always preferred attractions focused on popular entertainment rather than elite edification.[60] Tomorrowland's two-story Innoventions attraction building that showcased futuristic technology in partnership with major corporate sponsors including Honda, Microsoft, and Hewlett-Packard shuttered in 2015 to make way for *Star Wars* exhibits and meet and greets. Cast members at the Lincoln attraction, the only Disneyland attraction devoid of humor, informed me that the theater show generally plays to sparse audiences even on crowded days at the park. And as for criticism of the notoriously long queues for attractions, Disney and Universal theme parks have been increasingly switching to virtual queues and timed reservations using smartphone and wristband apps, though these digital changes have arrived with new fan complaints of significant upcharge pricing and more crowded park walkways.

Place is usually cited as areas where people live, such as neighborhoods, towns, and cities, so Disneyland is indeed placeless in the sense that no person other than Walt Disney in his apartment above the Main Street Fire Station has ever actually resided at the park. However, a non-lived-in place such as Disneyland can still be imbued with meaning and value through sentiment and experience for local fans. Fan groups have long found meaning in what others characterize as frivolous or insignificant, and their production of meaning is not solitary and private but necessarily social and public.[61] Contemporary research has expanded the concept of place to illustrate how car drivers "inhabit" roads and vehicles for a sense of place,[62] owners of second homes develop a bond with another domicile,[63] and mobile workers create a sense of home in cars, airports, trains, and hotel rooms.[64] Place attachment has increasingly been observed in leisure and recreational environments, including lakes, forests, and mountains,[65] neighborhood parks,[66] national parks,[67] rail trails,[68] and wild, scenic streams for trout anglers.[69] The traditional conceptualization of place and attachment requires adaptation to a more protean approach.

PLACE ATTACHMENT

Besides approaching place in the traditional sense of a bounded neighborhood of homes and buildings, people can also identify and feel a sense of place with a regularly visited proximate venue. For Tuan, a place is a space evolved and imbued with meaning and value attracting people through the "steady accretion of sentiment" and experience with meaning deriving from the senses (smell, vision, touch, hearing, and taste) or mediated by symbols understood through one's range of experience or knowledge.[70] Relph sees places sensed as a "chiaroscuro of setting, landscape, ritual, routine, other people, personal experiences, care and concern for home, and in the context of other places."[71] Tuan refers to this acutely personal and profound attachment as topophilia or love of place.[72] Studies of place attachment have run the gamut from planets, continents, countries, islands, towns, neighborhoods, streets, buildings, and specific rooms to spiritual and imaginary locations.[73] And place-making can be constructed through the association of particular social activities to a locale.[74] When routines become focused on a specific location, Seamon sees the formation of a "place-ballet" evoking a sense of belonging to the locale through the rhythm of everyday life.[75] For theme parks, Lukas sees total immersion within their premises as affording new senses of place and perspective for novel forms of sociality and world vision.[76] Correspondingly, Carlà and Freitag distinguish theme parks as "'hybrid' environments that combine architecture, music, landscape design, language, film, and performing arts with kinetics in order to provide an entertaining experience for visitors by immersing them into a multi-sensorial themed environment."[77]

The early twentieth-century amusement parks at Coney Island in Brooklyn, New York, and Blackpool in Northwest England featured immersive thematic attractions that offered relaxation and distraction for industrial urban workers. These early twentieth-century playful places emanated from a remediated lineage of Roman Saturnalia, medieval festivals and carnivals, pleasure gardens, and world's fairs.[78] Lukas saw these immersive worlds as places where people wanted to spend time and get lost; and for theme parks to be immersive worlds, the storytelling needed to be fully incorporated into every detail, because under- or unutilized spaces would fail to create a persuasive atmosphere instilling a consistent mood and coherent theme in visitor minds.[79] Alexander et al. in 1977 presented the concept of "pattern language" as the purposeful design of meaningful places with balanced physical interrelationships that reduce entropy and increase place attachment.[80] This type of purpose-designed establishment informed Oldenburg's third places and Benedikt's leisure experiences at, for example, huge bookstores with espresso machines and vintage-inspired décor.[81] However, until recently, research on the intersection between theme parks and visitor sociality and attachment has been minimal. A study on the Wizarding World of Harry Potter presented Universal Creative's reproduction of the milieu of the *Harry Potter* films with a highly detailed experience as fostering a sense of fan connection to the thematically immersive land, but sociality among the fan visitors was only briefly alluded to.[82] Among non-Western theme parks, Bollywood Parks Dubai was found to provide a sense of belonging for South Asian visitors to connect and celebrate Indianness but did not recognize or explore in-park sociality or local attachment.[83] Mitrašinović's influential book on global theme parks regarded the social realms within their bounds as purposely and skillfully limited by design and production.[84] Aziz et al. examined Malaysian theme parks with a survey to determine visitor satisfaction and revisit intention by measuring perceived quality, and arousal-based and pleasure-based experiences,[85] but, as with almost all studies on theme park visitors, lacked the exploration of in-park sociality and local attachment I address in the present book.

Scannell and Gifford propose a tripartite organizing framework of place attachment that examines people, place, and process.[86] Person looks at attachment between individual and collective meanings. Places with important individual memories often conjure strong attachment, build a sense of self,[87] and derive from personal milestones, experiences, and realizations such as meeting a partner or achieving a goal.[88] Group level attachment encompasses the symbolic meanings of a place shared by fellow members for the historical preservation of culture or religious locales.[89]

Process examines the psychological aspects of place attachment pertaining to cognitive, affective, and behavioral elements. Manzo and Perkins consider cognitive as "place identity and community identity"; behavioral as "participation in community planning, preservation, and development efforts"; and affective as "one's emotional relationship to the neighborhood or specific places within."[90] Cognitive attachment often derives from memories of a place such as events connected to and representative of oneself.[91] Affective attachment entails a love of place and people therein accrued through emotional investment.[92] Behavioral attachment is exhibited by actions taken to maintain proximity to a place[93] or simply long length of residence, which has often been cited as a particularly important factor in place attachment.[94] Behavior is also observed in participation through group planning, preservation, and development efforts focused on a place as well as engaging in social activities such as celebrations.

Place looks at the size, scale, and nature of socially and physically bound characteristics of attachment. Kaplan noted that attachment also derived from the scale, enclosure, and spatial diversity of a physical place,[95] which at a theme park can correspond to the intimate architecture, berm surrounding the park, and themed lands. Attachment is not only to the physical characteristics of a place but to the symbolic meanings that the physical features represent to an individual or group.[96] Repeated place use consists of social and physical goals leading to place dependence as individuals value a place for specific activities, particularly recreational.[97] Studies generally divide communities into those of interest and of place, with the former omitting reference to a physical place (such as online, professional, and religious groups) and the latter rooted in a physical place (such as neighborhoods and coffee shops).[98] A theme park is therefore a rare hybrid community of interest and place.

In Scannell and Gifford's person-process-place framework, place attachment examines "a bond between an individual or group and a place that can vary in terms of spatial level, degree of specificity, and social or physical features of the place, and is manifested through affective, cognitive, and behavioral psychological processes."[99] This framework is used to determine the attachment by Disneyland fans in Southern California to a place so often termed, and appearing from the outside, as placeless.

MEDIUM THEORY AND PLATFORM ANALYSIS

Medium theory operates on two levels by looking at the micro/individual situation level to determine the effect of choosing one medium over another for an environment or interaction and at the macro/structural level for the effect that adding a new medium to an existing matrix of media can have on social interactions and structures.[100] A medium does not simply pass information between environments but can shape the social environments. As a new medium, the internet initially afforded many-to-many social engagement on platforms such as Usenet and bulletin boards, and subsequently on web discussion boards and social media such as Facebook, Twitter, Instagram, TikTok, and YouTube. Gillespie defines a platform as an "online content-hosting intermediary" that affords communication, interaction, and commerce.[101] Within the internet medium has emerged a succession of online social platforms each with specific characteristics fostering social change. The internet is often distinguished from previous forms of media as being the most interactive, with characteristics producing different impacts on social participation.[102] The internet extended the conversational interaction and participation by consumers beyond what was possible with electronic and print mass media. Mass media producers, distributors, and marketers still endeavored to maintain their established dominance over media content as was enjoyed under the pre-internet media environment, so there has been a struggle between corporations and consumers over the social implications of participation from the rise of the internet and smartphones.[103]

The internet enabled media fandoms to build communities and share fan labor online in novel ways compared to predigital mediums.[104] Over the past thirty years, the online social platforms of Usenet, web discussion boards, and social media emerged and allowed fans to interact not only with each other but also the corporate media owner of the fandom object. Each platform in turn impacted discourse, social formations, and commerce at the micro and macro levels during its prevailing decade. The tension between structure and agency can be observed as macro-level patterns at the medium level shaping, along with social and cultural factors, the micro-level actions of the company and fans regarding Disneyland.

In this study I use José van Dijck's platform analysis model to examine three decades of shifts in technology, ownership, governance, business models, users/usage, and content for each platform's impact online and in the park on local fans and Disney.[105] By tracing the history and political economy of connective (van Dijck's preferred term over social to emphasize the technology itself) media using actor-network theory, the platform analysis model consists of two parts, each with three elements. First are the techno-cultural constructs of technology, users, and content. *Technology* is not only how sociality is facilitated, but also the way that code shapes the performance of sociality through design. *Users/usage* analysis looks not only at engagement with the platform and technology, but also intended and actual practices. *Content* refers to the media objects produced and disseminated through the technological capacities of the platform that are then subjected to rigid and uniform formats and layouts for presentation. Second are the socioeconomic structures of ownership, governance, and business models examined under the perspective of political economy. Van Dijck sees the major social media platforms as forming an ecosystem of connective media that corporatizes sociality by normalizing the coopting of social terms such as "sharing" and "friending." To "like," "share," and "repost" not only constitute a form of user expression but also facilitate rankings, recommendations, and data analytics for the platforms.[106] These kinds of metaphors permeating social media often serve to mask their corporate ownership.[107]

Van Dijck argues that the rise of social (connective) media eroded the earlier idealization of online sociality as a public sphere because the underlying business interests of the corporate owners prioritized and stressed profit and control (that is, governance) as users accepted or acquiesced to commercial objectives and a "locked in" ecosystem, or even adopted corporate values as influencers. The term *influencer* in this book refers to fans who have become well-known for often visiting the park to share opinions, news, and information about Disneyland and the Disney company to their followers on online social platforms that in turn earn them an income. Although scholars such as Cunningham and Craig prefer the term *content creator*[108] and Kiriakou prefers *lifestyler*,[109] this book uses influencer as not only the most commonly used and recognized label but more importantly to signify the powerful role that influencers have assumed as promoters of viewpoints and policies favorable toward Disney and other corporations to their fan audiences. Since the photos, captions, videos, and narrations ostensibly are produced by the influencers, social media advertising often obscures the corporate involvement to be perceived as authentic by fans. The interests of corporations such as Disney are served through the exploitation of fan users providing free labor content as "prosumers" within the commodification of networks, contacts, user profiles, and user-generated content.[110] Social media standardized and commercialized fans into being primarily "users" and fan activities as "user-generated content."[111] Fans no longer needed to figure out how to code, maintain, and protect their own websites or discussion boards since the social media companies provided the code, maintenance, and security for free while fans provided content without remuneration from platform owners (notably excepting YouTube). Social media platforms regularized and commodified fan interaction with sharing between users as a resource to be tapped. As Tim O'Reilly proclaimed in the opening remarks of the first Web 2.0 conference in 2004, "customers are building your business for you." Many fandoms, including Disneyland fans in Southern California, were early adopters of the first online social platforms such as Usenet that afforded the development of new discourses, practices, and social formations. However, the nature of subsequent online social platforms enabled corporations to reset the discourse and coopt and commercialize fan media, practices, and events. My examination of the evolving intersection over the last thirty years between Disney and local fans around Disneyland employs a new model framework, introduced later in this chapter, that can be used in future longitudinal studies looking at fandoms and corporate media owners on online social platforms.

FORMS OF CAPITAL

The establishment, accretion, and fluctuation of status that fan studies scholar Matt Hills observes "as a social hierarchy where fans share a common interest while also competing over fan knowledge, access to the object of fandom, and status"[112] are examined in this book using Pierre Bourdieu's forms of capital[113] to highlight the interplay and exchange online and in-park of social, cultural, and economic capital between local fans and the Disney company. These forms of capital are transformed, or parlayed, from one form to another across online and offline domains.[114] Economic capital consists of resources such as money and assets that can be used to obtain the other two forms of capital. Social capital is a network of personal connections that can potentially be converted into economic capital. Cultural capital is the knowledge of texts and works important to fans that can be converted into economic and social capital. This kind of knowledge rewards the holder with a subcultural authenticity that cannot be learned or certified at conventional educational institutions.[115] These "big name fans" in their subcultural communities gain wide recognition and even celebrity status that can in turn be commodified.[116] The fans with cultural capital become a fandom's "core members" who carry out much of the community building and maintenance such as moderating discussions and forums.[117] In addition, cultural capital can be institutionalized by a fan-recognized authority that bestows its imprimatur to an individual or group as credentialed to undertake specific activities. Cultural capital can accrue within fan cultures by simply knowing more than others about the fandom object, thus giving a fan expert more prestige within the group.[118] Hills proposes: "Following Fiske's coinage of 'fan cultural capital' (the knowledge that a fan has about their object of fandom), I would suggest that 'fan social capital' (the network of fan friends and acquaintances that a fan possesses, *as well as* their access to media producers and professional personnel linked with the object of fandom) must also be closely investigated in future analyses."[119]

Fiske, writing in 1992, saw popular culture capital as not generally convertible into economic capital outside of a few exceptions such as fan artists at conventions.[120] However, soon after the publication of Fiske's article, early online social platforms gradually started to afford fans new ways to establish hierarchies of cultural and social capital to parlay into economic capital. By 2006, Malaby observed social capital online as "not only a resource for social action but also one that can be leveraged to cultivate market capital."[121] The production, use, and transformation of Bourdieu's forms of capital across the intersecting domains of fans, online social platforms, and the Disney company at Disneyland are tracked and noted throughout this book's study.

POWER/KNOWLEDGE

The Disney company has been notable, some observers would say notorious, for wielding and using power to maintain order and control in its theme parks.[122] Hobbs sees a range of Disney control "from the strict dress and conduct codes of its employees, protection of the Disney brand, and its expected behaviors of the guests."[123] Michel Foucault's genealogical viewpoint on power as being in continuous flux and negotiation, and not a deterministic system of constraints,[124] provides an apt approach to delineate the thirty-year fluctuation of power between the Disney company and Southern California fans over Disneyland. For Foucault, power is omnipresent and exercised at every level of the social body, not just by the higher echelons of a large corporation such as Disney but by fans and lower-level employees as well. Power is diffused, not concentrated, discursive rather than coercive, and constitutes agents rather than tools to be wielded. Power is relational with an unstable network of practices, techniques, and procedures that necessarily generate resistance. Power is not centralized with an owner or location, and nor is resistance, as power is not a thing that is "acquired, seized or shared, something one holds on to or allows to slip away."[125] Foucault sees sovereign, or juridical, power of top-down forms of social control with physical coercion as relenting to a disciplinary, or capillary, power of diffused social surveillance. The normalization process is accomplished through the organization of space and/or time that impacts behavior and activity so people discipline themselves without the need for overt coercion. Compared to previous eras of traditional top-down systems of sovereign power, everyone now participates and reproduces knowledge through everyday actions and perceptions that are in constant flux. Conduct is perceived and internalized by people within their own situations to become normalized and embodied in cultural norms as a new dominant discourse. Power is then constituted as accepted forms of knowledge and "truth" produced by discourse and institutions that are reinforced by the media and ideological shifts. Power produces reality and cultural norms with associated social discipline and conformity. Since power and knowledge are then inherently integrated, Foucault formulated the concept as power/knowledge.

Foucault's conceptualization of power as fluid and contested at all levels complements the examination of the succession of online social platforms over the last three decades on the contested relationship between local fans with each other and with Disney. The flow of power through early online social platforms benefited local fans who constructed knowledge through discourse on Usenet and websites to produce resistance to the Disney company regarding Disneyland. Later, local fans used social media platforms to build a discourse conducive to an environment online and in the park for the creation of events, meets, and clubs. Disney has seldom used sovereign coercive power against fans in Disneyland, and in the rare instances when employed the results have been generally ineffectual. Instead, Disney gradually grasped the nature of the new social platforms and constructed methods to shape online discourse using the characteristics of the platforms, as well as systematically coopting fan practices, media, and activities to foster a knowledge environment precipitating the fan internalization of company authority in all regards except fan-organized social formations in the park.

MODEL ANALYTICAL FRAMEWORK

The contest in the park and online over the past three decades between local fans and Disney over the meaning and purpose of Disneyland transformed substantially with each wave of technology and platforms, and strategies and practices. To examine this contestation through the decades, a model analytical framework has been created to visually explicate the intersection

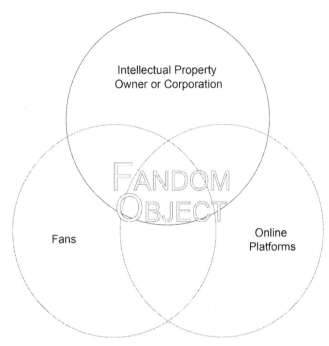

Figure 1.1. The three domains of fans, online platforms, and intellectual property owner or corporation intersecting around a fandom object.

of the three domains of fans, corporation, and online social platforms at the place of Disneyland as well as to use van Dijck's platforms as microsystems and Bourdieu's forms of capital for analysis.[126]

Over the past three decades, the domains of corporate intellectual property owners and fans have intersected around fandom objects through a succession of online platforms. Figure 1.1 illustrates this new model to analyze and understand the intersection of the three domains encompassing the fandom object. Malaby defines a domain as "a semibounded arena for action where certain conventional expectations apply and certain resources may be available."[127] Thus, the domain of fans is comprised of practices and presumptions along with a particular set of affordances, constraints, market pressures, and social conventions. The different forms of capital are accrued, parlayed, and transformed within and between corporations and fans often owing to the nature of the prevailing online social platforms of each decade.

Media fandoms customarily do not have physical places for ongoing congregation because the milieu of their fan object is intangibly experienced through mediation via film, television, books, audio, software, etc. By contrast, the tangibility of theme parks has afforded local fans a regularly available physical place to congregate and interact directly with each other, the fandom object, and corporate owner. Disneyland is especially distinct by being open every day of the year from morning to night since 1985 unlike most theme parks such as Six Flags, Cedar Point, and Dollywood, which shut down completely during the winter months and open only for weekends and holidays during the spring and fall. Parks in warmer climates, such as Knott's Berry Farm, LEGOLAND, and Six Flags Magic Mountain, generally close for Christmas Day, inclement weather, and/or one or two days per week during the off-season. While Disney must contend with fan discourse online just as any other corporate owner of a media fandom object, the nature of Disneyland as a continuously evolving physical place accessible every day in person by over one million annual passholders (by the mid-2010s) presents an exceptional fandom object for in-depth study. The model framework is applied in chapter seven to each of the predominant online social platforms (Usenet, web discussion boards, and Facebook groups) to analyze the thirty-year evolution of the intersection between fandom object, corporation, online social platforms, and fans.

DATA COLLECTION

This book's longitudinal study of Disneyland fans in Southern California over the last thirty years encompasses a parallel look at the evolution and interplay of fans and corporation on both online social platforms and at the park. The regional nature of the study has entailed a scope limited to Southern Californians in order to focus on Disneyland as a local place. Building significantly on Bury's 2016 article on participatory culture and community from a broad spectrum of media fandom on online social platforms from Usenet to Tumblr with thirty-three fan interviews,[128] this study of Disneyland fandom collected a significantly more comprehensive range of data using multiple methods, including internet documents from fan websites and online social platform groups; an online survey of 637 Southern California fan participants; over two months of on-site fieldwork and participant observation at Disneyland; and eighteen in-depth interviews with web discussion board owners, fan event and club organizers, Disneyland cast members, and social media influencers. The same multiple methods were also used in a 2023 study of De Efteling theme park fans in the Netherlands.[129] Since there is now a very large number of Disney theme park social media influencers, vloggers, and bloggers, a set of criteria was established in order to be selected for the study's interviews, including residency in Southern California for at least one decade in the last thirty years and status as an organizer of meets, events, and clubs, web discussion board owner, or social media influencer. The full list of interviewees can be found in appendix 1. Website owners and social media influencers based in Central Florida focusing primarily on Walt Disney World or the global theme park industry, such as the Tim Tracker, Paging Mr. Morrow, WDW News Today, Tom Bricker's Disney Tourist Blog, AllEars, DISboards, and many others were therefore not approached for interviews for this book's specific focus on Southern California but would be ideal for future research on the interplay of Orlando theme park fandom and online social platforms. Despite requests via email, an interview with a current representative in Disney corporate or Disneyland guest relations was not obtainable. Instead, to understand Disney's perspective, the study consulted pertinent articles from periodicals, Disney publications, and web documents as well as interviews with former and current cast members, longtime observers of the Disney company, and a retired Imagineer. Qualitative content analysis was conducted on the interview transcripts through a process of open, axial, and selective coding.[130]

The online survey probed within Scannell and Gifford's tripartite framework of people, place, and process for place attachment.[131] Surveys have long been a popular method for researching place attachment.[132] Survey respondents were delimited to those who had visited Disneyland at least once, were at eighteen years of age or older, and resided in one of the ten counties comprising Southern California. Survey respondents were solicited through posts to nine online venues focused on Disneyland fans and word-of-mouth during participant observation and fieldwork at the park. The nine online venues for survey recruitment included seven Disneyland Facebook fan groups, the Meetup.com group for Disneyland fans, and the MiceChat website. Group and website administrators permitted the researcher to post the survey link and often encouraged member participation. The survey was open from October 1, 2017, to December 5, 2017, and the complete list of questions is available in appendix 2.

Fieldwork and participant observation at Disneyland was conducted in October and November 2017 and February 2018. The qualitative and quantitative content analysis of social data documents, including Usenet, website discussion boards, club and event websites, social media presences, podcasts, and vlogs of the many Disneyland online fan groups were investigated for their diverse forms and practices.

OVERVIEW OF CHAPTERS

This book is based on two associated arguments. First, Disneyland constitutes a special place of attachment for many Southern Californians. Second, the online social platforms of the past three decades, in addition to cultural and social factors, affected not only the close relationship that local fans hold with the park but also their interactions with each other and the Disney company. While each chapter of this book examines a specific aspect and/or time period concerning these two connected arguments, the chapters are interrelated within the overall examination of the intersection between local fans, Disney, and online social platforms at Disneyland. Each succeeding chapter is tied together through the concepts and theories discussed in this chapter along with the model framework to understand this intersection.

Anchored by place attachment theory, chapter 2 looks at Disneyland as a special local place for Southern Californians through cognitive, affective, and behavioral processes. Most locals did not visit on a regular basis during the park's first few decades of operation, but the advent of the AP program in 1984 enabled regular visits. The diffusion of online social platforms in the 1990s enabled fans to connect and organize with each other not only for knowledge and information but also to establish social formations in the park without the permission or involvement of the Disney company. This chapter challenges the assertion by etic observers that Disneyland is asocial and placeless by demonstrating the particular cultural and social factors behind the special connection between local fans and the park. Understanding this bond is crucial to the explication in subsequent chapters of the contestation between local fans and Disney over discourse, commerce, and social formations online and in the park over the past three decades.

In chapters 3 and 4, I examine the development and evolution of Disneyland fandom online by dividing the internet era into two periods: before and after the rise of social media platforms. In the first period, from 1990 to 2005, the early online social platforms of Usenet and website discussion boards affected, in different ways, the relationship between local Disneyland fans with each other and the Disney company. This period was primarily characterized by Disneyland fandom's unity and resistance to the company, while Disney sluggishly struggled to understand and react to the new medium and platforms used by fans. However, the second period, from 2006 to 2020, saw the popular rise and eventual dominance of social media, with fandom fragmenting into countless groups across platforms. This fragmentation often occurred along generational lines as younger fans preferred the visually oriented platforms of Instagram and YouTube with coeval content creators and tastemakers known as influencers, while older fans migrated to a multitude of fan groups on Facebook. This fragmentation of the fandom across platforms and groups led to a decline in resistance to Disney and an increasing resignation to corporate authority.

Disneyland was designed and constructed in the 1950s under the assumption of infrequent visits by locals with no conception of fan-organized events, clubs, and meets in the park. Chapter 5 charts the rise in fan social formations at Disneyland from only a few in the 1990s to a multitude by the end of the 2010s, as shaped in large measure by the characteristics of the online social platforms of the last thirty years. The high transaction costs of early online social platforms inhibited the creation of fan social formations in the park, but the low transaction costs of social media platforms, particularly for creating groups on Facebook, enabled many fans for the first time to organize their own Disneyland events, meets, and clubs. This chapter demonstrates that fans are inherently a challenge to control by continually organizing in-park play activities and social experiences that Disney, for the most part, has been unwilling to offer.

The previous three chapters illustrate that online social platforms from the 1990s to 2010s played significant roles in transforming the relationship between local fans and the Disney company. Chapter 6 uses Foucault's concept of power/knowledge to examine the contestation of fan and Disney power online and in-park as influenced, to a considerable degree, by the nature of each decade's predominant online social platforms. I conclude that the social patterns affecting the flow of power online have often negatively correlated with the power situation in the park.

Chapter 7 uses the book's new model framework underpinned by van Dijck's platform analysis to illustrate the interplay and exchange of Bourdieu's forms of capital around a fandom object by fans, corporations, and each internet decade's predominant online social platform. In addition, the present and future challenges to Disneyland as a persistent place of attachment for Southern Californians are discussed, including the changes and issues faced by local fans and Disney since the park reopened in April 2021 after being closed for over a year due to the pandemic.

This book's central focus explores the intersection between online social platforms and a fandom object as a physical place. My conclusion in chapter 8 reflects on the gradual process of commodification of both leisure places and online social communities during their histories. The generalizability of the study to other theme parks and leisure places worldwide is also considered, as well as future directions for research. In the final section I contemplate the future of Disneyland as a persistently meaningful physical (and probably irreplaceable as virtual) place for local fans who continually adopt and adapt new online platforms for their social purposes while Disney pursues strategies of commodification, co-option, and control.

CHAPTER 2

Disneyland as a Place for Southern Californians

Unlike playful places throughout history, such as Saturnalia, festivals, carnivals, fairs, pleasure gardens, and amusement parks, Disneyland launched in 1955 as a theme park open year round for all seasons from morning to night. In the first few decades of operation, most locals did not go to the park on a regular basis; visits were considered special occasions and the cumulative cost would be prohibitively expensive.[1] Until 1982, Disney charged not only for park admission but also per attraction with a ticket book that once depleted had to be repurchased. The 1982 conversion to a passport-style ticket enabled visitors to enjoy an unlimited number of attractions for a day. Then, the 1984 start of the annual passholder program enabled locals to visit the park as much as desired over the course of a year. The early online social platforms of the 1990s plus the AP program supercharged the relationship between locals and Disneyland by enabling fans to connect and organize online with other locals to exchange knowledge and information, establish social formations in the park without Disney's involvement or permission, and dissent against Disney's management of the park. During the 2010s, the AP program grew to over one million passholders. Similar to the pleasure gardens and mechanical amusement parks of past leisure eras, Disneyland has often been cited by etic observers as vacuous, antisocial, and placeless, but in this chapter I challenge those observations by examining the particular environmental, cultural, business, and personal factors behind Disneyland's development and evolution that have helped foster and shape a special connection between locals and theme park. I use Scannell and Gifford's framework of affective, cognitive, and behavioral processes for place attachment to analyze the bond of Southern California fans to Disneyland's social and physical features.[2] This special bond underlies the discussion in subsequent chapters of the struggle between local

Disneyland fans and the Disney company for power and influence online and in the park over the past three decades.

THE PROBLEM OF PLACE IN SOUTHERN CALIFORNIA

In contrast to the tall buildings and noticeable downtown areas of East Coast US cities, the lack of distinct downtowns in post–World War II Southern California led to criticism, similarly faced by Disneyland, of being place-less. Rather than creating density within an urban core, Southern California spread outward, annexing adjacent farmlands to produce a continuous expansion of suburbs. The amorphous shape and enormous size of the Los Angeles metropolis induced a sense of placelessness amongst its denizens, impeding a sense of stable attachment and shared identity.[3] In 1964, urban architect Victor Gruen regarded Los Angeles as "seventeen suburbs in search of a city,"[4] as the design of Los Angeles faced criticism as inhibiting public social life.[5] Gruen warned of a crisis within subcityscape, the liminal space that linked but threatened to swamp both urban and suburban areas:

> Subcityscape features gas stations, repair shops, shacks and shan-ties, used-car lots, billboards, dump heaps, roadside stands, highway stores, rubbish, dirt and trash. It grows like a weed in all directions. . . . Subcityscape drags all other urban elements down to its lowest level, hampering their functioning, disrupting communications between them, and converting every attempt to reach landscape or nature from cityscape or suburbscape into a nightmare. Its existence is the most obvious indictment of laissez-faire planning, or non-planning.[6]

By contrast, Disneyland's Main Street featured a traditional town square that was missing among the vast sprawl outside the park.[7] Gruen noted approvingly of the cellular planning concept of Disneyland's layout and variety of accompanying transportation systems within the park.[8] Architect Charles Moore, who famously stated, "you have to pay for the public life," cited Disneyland as providing the public environment of play and of watch-ing and being watched that was missing in Los Angeles.[9] Gruen lamented the difficulty of convincing merchants and banks to allocate funds for fea-tures and functions and design and decorative elements unrelated to the sale of merchandise.[10] Businesses feared flower beds would be targeted by thieves, kids would fall or swim in fountains, outdoor eateries would lead to litter, sculptures would get tarnished or defaced, brightly painted colors would turn dirty (therefore grayish green paint was preferred since it already appeared unclean), tree roots would crack pavements, planters would make snow removal cumbersome, and maintenance and cleaning costs would be exorbitant.[11] However, in an outdoor urban project where Gruen added the aforementioned flourishes: "maintenance people discovered to their great surprise that flowers were not stolen, that trash was not thrown around, but that, on the contrary, the 70,000 persons who visited the center on an average day took possessive pride in the beauty offered them."[12] Gruen believed people enjoyed sharing life experiences within crowds such as at parades, baseball games, concerts, and other gatherings for work or leisure.[13]

Disneyland was an orderly place compared to the sprawl of Los Angeles as Walt Disney emphasized the park would "be a place for California to be at home, to bring its guests, to demonstrate its faith in the future."[14] In the years before his death in 1966, Walt Disney took inspiration from Gruen's writings on urban architecture and eventually came to believe Disneyland could be an antidote to the twentieth-century urban malaise isolating the individual.[15] By the 1970s, Southern Californians also saw Disneyland as the antithesis of Los Angeles and a potential model for urban transportation, innovation, and community.[16] In a 1963 speech at the Harvard Graduate School of Design, architect and community builder James Rouse said Disneyland's technological approach to solving human problems made it "the greatest piece of urban design in the United States."[17] Moore said Disneyland "engaged in replacing many of those elements of the public realm which have vanished in the featureless private floating world of southern California, whose only edge is the ocean, and whose center is otherwise undiscoverable."[18] And at Disneyland "everything works, the way it doesn't anymore in the world outside."[19] As public space contracted throughout the twentieth century, communion within a crowd of strangers at an amusement or theme park provided opportunity to feel part of a community and society.[20] Southern California residents came to appreciate Disneyland as a regional landmark and symbol to feel ownership as part of their lives.[21] Perhaps channeling Baudrillard's famous comment that "Disneyland is presented as imaginary in order to make us believe that the rest is real, when in fact all of Los Angeles and the America surrounding it are no longer real, but of the order of the hyperreal and of simulation,"[22] a writer at the local *OC Weekly* periodical wryly observed: "In an era of carefully manicured plants choking out native grasses, Spanish-revival condos replacing old-style architecture, and planned communities substituting for real ones, Disneyland is about as authentic a SoCal landmark as you could ask for."[23]

To be sure, Walt Disney did not intentionally design Disneyland to be a model answer to the urban issues facing Southern California, and only in retrospect did observers note contrasts between the park and region, and possible prescriptions Disneyland could offer for urban maladies. In the last few decades, the local governments and companies of Southern California have made progress opening new public spaces and transportation options. Still, the park features a singular urban environment whereupon just the evocation of the name Disneyland can summon a quasireligious state of mind.[24]

DISNEYLAND AS PLACE IN SOUTHERN CALIFORNIA

"Disneyland has a soul," proclaims Todd Regan, the founder and CEO of MiceChat, one of the oldest and largest Disneyland fan groups in Southern California.[25] Regan echoes many fans who see the original 1955 park as distinct compared to any other Disneyland or theme park around the world. Disneyland in Southern California is not just the first Disney theme park but also the only one developed and built during Walt Disney's lifetime. The park's relatively small footprint, less acreage than any other Magic Kingdom–style Disney park except Hong Kong, fosters a more intimate feeling for visitors as attractions often come into close proximity to the narrow pedestrian pathways and occasionally interlink, such as the park railroad cutting through the big show scene of Splash Mountain (rethemed to Tiana's Bayou Adventure in 2024), Jungle Cruise captains cracking jokes about the adjacent Indiana Jones attraction, and the interweaving of tracks and waterways among the Casey Jr. Circus Train and Storybook Land Canal Boats. The latter two attractions are also present at Disneyland Paris but lack the intimacy of Disneyland's originals; the Paris train runs on a tubular track as a standard powered roller coaster and the boats along an underwater wire without human guides, while the Southern California train runs on wooden tracks as an internal combustion–powered railroad and the boats feature on-board motors and Fantasyland-costumed human guide narrators. The earthen berm surrounding the park keeps sightlines to the outside world obscured. In 1963, Walt Disney received a guarantee from the city of Anaheim that no building that could be seen from within the park would ever be approved for construction in the area surrounding Disneyland. Even the sky above Disneyland within a three-mile radius has been a designated no-fly zone since 9/11, leading to a knock-on effect preventing Disney from using drones for shows over the resort.[26] Disneyland is atemporal as the year-round temperate climate of Southern California produces a "perpetual spring"[27] as a kind of American Eden.[28]

Although some fan scholars caution about conflating fandom with religion,[29] some leisure scholars compare Disney theme parks to a religious pilgrimage where familiar stories and symbols manifest in a place to allow the faithful to trace divine steps.[30] Hutchins proposes Disney fans as a "cult of mouse" engaging in beliefs and rituals such as holding "the superiority of the brand above others, proselytizing to others about the brand, perpetuating the company's origin myth and sacred texts, being devoutly faithful and loyal to all products."[31] In addition, traditional religion is conspicuously absent from Disneyland with no church on Main Street USA even though Christian religious signs would have been thematically accurate to the milieu.[32] At Disney theme parks, "magic and fantasy, not religion, reign."[33] Ken Pellman, a former cast member in the custodial department and cohost of the popular Disneyland fan podcast *The Sweep Spot*, points out numerous symbolic religious parallels to Disneyland including annual passes as tithing, Sleeping Beauty Castle as the central temple, Disney films as holy texts, passholders as congregants, and Imagineers as high priests.[34] The exclusive members-only Club 33 restaurant and lounge above the Pirates of the Caribbean attraction could be said to comprise "the innermost sanctum of Walt Disney worshippers"[35] with Walt Disney as the park's "founder-prophet."[36] Disney even offers a guided walking tour of the park called "Walk in Walt's Footsteps" featuring, on most days, the highly coveted fan experience of a trip to Walt Disney's apartment above the Main Street Fire Station.

Visits to the physical sites of fandom have been described in religious terms as pilgrimages or rituals.[37] However, Disneyland enthusiasts differ from other media fandoms in two important ways. First, their affective object is tangibly imbued and intertwined with over one hundred years of myriad Disney texts (in addition to the Muppets, Pixar, Marvel, Lucasfilm, and Fox). Second, most fandom communities exist outside of fixed territorial space.[38] While fandoms embrace sites peripherally important to their cultural texts for visits such as production locales on Vancouver streets for *The X-Files*,[39] Manchester for the *Coronation Street* set,[40] or Graceland for Elvis Presley enthusiasts,[41] fans usually visit just once as a pilgrimage since the primary fandom object remains the music, film, or television show itself. The pilgrimage is symbolic as the sites are often ordinary. Hills describes the Vancouver shooting locations of *The X-Files* as "banal: a back-street alleyway, a university building, a shopping precinct escalator."[42] Brooker sees a psychological leap of faith as necessary for many geographical media pilgrimages such as "when a fan visits Union Station, Los Angeles, it takes significant imagination and investment to transform this busy, modern railway hub into the dingy police headquarters of *Blade Runner*."[43] Doss recounts that Graceland is a "mundane mansion" and "Elvis's guitar-shaped swimming pool is awfully teeny."[44] Popular media fans must adopt a liminal position to make "the intangible tangible by achieving a proximity to the 'real' Kent Farm (a private dairy farm in the Fraser Valley outside the city) if you are a *Smallville* fan or a 'real' Caprican building (the Vancouver Public Library downtown) if you are a fan of *Battlestar Galactica*."[45] The real-world locations inspiring fan pilgrimage incorporate local utility and residents and are not designed for fan usages and gratification, so fan visitors must "actively make these places special—either through physical transformation of the space (adding familiar objects) or performance in that space (costume and cosplay)."[46] While popular media tourism has targeted fandoms of films, television shows, and books to make the trek to their production locales as a rare pilgrimage,[46] Disneyland is an elaborately staged physical spectacle of imaginary places as a fandom object visited by local fans on a regular basis. "Being there" within the physicality of the park allows an "interlinking of place, authenticity and experience"[47] that most other media fandoms can never enjoy in the same way.

By the mid-2010s, there were over one million Disneyland annual passholders able to avail weekly and monthly meetups (MiceChat, Facebook groups, meetup.com, homeschooling, and social clubs) and annual and biannual fan-organized special events (Gay Days, Bats Day, Lolita Day, MiceChat Gumball Rally, and dozens more), making Disneyland a popular local hangout for Southern Californians. Since the 1970s, up to two-thirds of Disneyland visitors have been said to be California residents.[49] Many passholders visit weekly or monthly, and one local, Jeff Reitz, gained fame and almost 30,000 Instagram followers by 2019, visiting Disneyland every day starting from January 1, 2012. Disneyland as a fan object is open to visit in person every day of the year, whereas fans in other media fandoms typically only attend one or two conventions annually.[50] While fan conventions can "blur the line between fiction and reality, bringing the text to life through immersive fan practices, such as fan fiction, cosplay, and gaming,"[51] the experience is short-lived as all signs of the fandom are torn down on the final day to make way for the next event on the convention center calendar. Disneyland's architecture of reassurance[52] attracts locals to visit the park regularly to experience a sunny optimism often missing from their lives and the Southern California region. Jones and Wills opined that Walt Disney built a twentieth-century Versailles for all people, not just the king,[53] though Marling retorted that it was a "Versailles for middle class Americans in plaid Bermuda shorts."[54] Over successive generations, Disneyland's popularity has endured by consistently ranking second in attendance among theme parks worldwide, behind only Walt Disney World's Magic Kingdom Park in Florida,[55] and first in 2017 as the most Instagrammed place on the planet.[56]

Since almost the beginning, Disneyland has staged special events to appeal to Southern California locals who have constituted the majority of park visitors. From 1957 to 1968, Date Nite featured pop music and dancing for young couples. According to then Disneyland executive Jack Lindquist, after spending the first two operating years in the red, Date Nite finally made Disneyland profitable by appealing to local area teenagers.[57] On weekend evenings starting in 1965, swing bands (including Tommy Dorsey, Duke Ellington, and the Glen Miller Band) have played at the stage and dance floor next to Sleeping Beauty Castle. Since 1967, the Tomorrowland Terrace stage has periodically featured concerts by local Southern California rock bands. Starting in 1961, Grad Nite has allowed graduating high school students in Southern California to party all night at Disneyland. In 1984, Disney initiated the AP program with a US$65 pass granting daily admittance to Disneyland for a year. In its first few decades, Disneyland was open all year from morning to night but closed for one or two weekdays every week for maintenance. However, since 1985, Disneyland has been open every day of the year except for severely inclement weather, 9/11, and the pandemic from March 14, 2020, to April 30, 2021. By the early 2000s, Disney instituted a multitier system with an option for less expensive passes blocked out during typical peak attendance days such as Saturdays, summer months, and the Christmas to New Year's interval. Disney also started offering discount passes exclusive to Southern California residents in order to increase park attendance during the off-season. The popularity of these nonpremium annual passes led to record attendance along with complaints of overcrowding. Since 2006, select evenings in September and October have been reserved for Halloween costume parties requiring a separate hard ticket, even for annual passholders. In 2018, Disney started a new series of hard-ticket night events called After Dark featuring popular themes such as *Star Wars*, Valentine's Day, and 1950s fashion. From almost the beginning, Disneyland has used special events to appeal to Southern California locals to generate higher levels of attendance and revenue.

Since the 1990s, Southern Californians have used online platforms to organize their own annual themed events such as Gay Days and Bats Day, weekly meetups, and scavenger hunts at Disneyland. In the 2010s, the rise of social media platforms, which required almost no transaction costs in terms of technical knowledge or financial resources,[58] enabled any local to establish a Disneyland social group with a presence on Facebook, Instagram, Twitter, YouTube, and other online platforms. In addition, smartphones allowed locals to take their online social groups into the park to connect, organize, and meet. This confluence resulted in the flourishing of hundreds of events, clubs, and meet-ups initiated and nurtured by locals with Disneyland as their place of choice to hang out and socialize in Southern California. The assumption that theme park visitors simply spend most of their day rushing to rides and shows has been a conventional view by observers who considered Disneyland a highly regimented visitor experience.[59] Not only did these etic critics not consider the potential for sociality at the park, but also failed to recognize the shared identity and attachment of locals to Disneyland as a distinctive place in a Southern California lacking a community and social focal point.

THREE PROCESSES OF PLACE ATTACHMENT TO DISNEYLAND FOR SOUTHERN CALIFORNIANS

Cognitive Attachment

Place identity often begins from a young age on a cognitive level with a locale and community.[60] In this study's survey, most respondents first visited Disneyland as preteens, with 89 percent reporting their initial visit before turning thirteen years old and 66 percent before turning six. During participant observation and interviews, many local visitors could recall park trips during childhood with siblings, parents, and grandparents that instilled a deep attachment to Disneyland. Koren-Kuik distinguishes the physical Disneyland environs as the spatial level of diegetic narrative from the individualized interactions that create personalized spatial narratives located within the hyperdiegetic level of "musing about related past experiences, feelings of nostalgia, [and] particular familial dynamics."[61] Thus, specific locations in the park can often hold powerful individualized meanings, such as a bench in DCA where one local woman often reflected as the last place she laughed and smiled with her then cancer-stricken mother. When Disney in 2018 rethemed Paradise Pier in DCA to Pixar Pier, the woman was very upset the view enjoyed with her mother from that bench would be altered forever. Indeed, Jeanette Lomboy, a vice president overseeing the Disneyland resort, noted in a 2021 *Los Angeles Times* article: "you can't move a bench without touching someone's memory. Maybe that bench was where a kid took their first steps or where someone proposed."[62] A couple years later, the same woman got engaged at the park and planned for a Disneyland wedding. Marriage proposals occur practically every day in front of Sleeping Beauty Castle, though some fans choose other personally meaningful places to pop the question since a castle proposal is sometimes considered a bit cliché. Sandvoss and Kearns observed that "the personal, affective bond between fan and fan object is thus underscored by the construction of the fan object as a process of personalization as fans select between different texts to create fan objects that correspond with their expectations and experience."[63] The fan object "is intrinsically interwoven with our sense of self, with who we are, would like to be, and think we are."[64] Disneyland fans signify their identity through clothing (from attraction T-shirts to Disneybounding) and a vast array of paratextual products (produced by Disney or fans) that create a cognitive sense of self that is reflective of their local theme park.

In interviews and participant observation, many fans noted a greater identification and fondness for Disneyland the place than the oeuvre of Disney media texts. Repeatedly, I heard fans proclaim being foremost a Disneyland fan and then secondly a Disney fan. The park is a living and tangible manifestation of not only favorite Disney films but also many stories endogenous to the park. At park opening in 1955, only Fantasyland was full of attractions inspired by Disney intellectual property, while Frontierland's only Disney media connection was Davy Crockett; the remaining lands of Tomorrowland, Adventureland, and Main Street USA contained practically no direct Disney textual association. Although most of the world's most popular theme parks, including Universal, Warner Bros., and LEGOLAND, produce attractions based on well-known media texts, some of Disneyland's most popular attractions have had no prominently associated Disney text as inspiration or association. These fan favorites include the Haunted Mansion, Big Thunder Mountain Railroad, Space Mountain, "it's a small world," and the Enchanted Tiki Room. Pirates of the Caribbean opened in 1967 and remained a park-exclusive text until 2006 when music and characters from the Johnny Depp film franchise that debuted in 2003 were added to the dark ride attraction. Jungle Cruise has been a fan favorite since opening in 1955, with a Disney film based on the ride only released in 2021. The Haunted Mansion has a very active and vocal fan base with fan-organized events (Bats Day, Haunted Mansion Dress Up Day) and social clubs (Hitchhikers, Ghost Keepers, Mansion Militia, and many more) revolving around the attraction. However, the two *Haunted Mansion* films released in 2003 and 2023 based on the famed attraction underperformed at the box office and no story elements from the films have been added to the ride. Sandvoss cites Relph's concept of "other-directedness" to describe the visitor experience at Disneyland as transpiring through the absent codes and symbols of Disney entertainment media,[65] but several of the most popular attractions are actually immanent to the park.

The surveyed Southern California fans visit Disneyland frequently with 69 percent having logged one hundred or more lifetime visits and 28 percent topping five hundred. They visit regularly, with 15 percent going at least once per week and 74 percent going at least once per month. Besides cast members (who receive a number of free passes from Disney to enter with family or friends), 87 percent reported having an AP. To be able to socialize with family and friends and participate in fan events, meets, and clubs at Disneyland throughout the year essentially requires the purchase of an AP to make regular visits. Survey respondents were less likely to own an AP to other Southern California theme parks with only 20 percent holding a Universal Studios Hollywood pass, 16 percent for Knott's Berry Farm, 7 percent for Six Flags Magic Mountain, 7 percent with SeaWorld, and 4 percent at LEGOLAND. Annual passes at these parks can often be purchased for less than US$200 with fewer, if any, block-out dates, while the least expensive Disneyland pass for Southern California residents was US$399 in 2019 with nearly two hundred blockout dates (only 7 percent of respondents had this minimum-level access pass). Knott's even offers an AP with a meal and beverage plan so anyone can visit the park and receive two complimentary meals with unlimited soft drinks every day of the year for only US$323.99 (as of January 2024). However, Disneyland remained the most popular choice for survey respondents to have a local park annual pass. In addition, due to the legal age of alcohol consumption being twenty-one years old, some Southern California university students cited Disneyland as a common place to socialize and hang out as an alternative to the legally prohibited bars and nightclubs. Fans credit Walt Disney's legacy of meticulous attention to detail and the ongoing place-making magic of Imagineering for rewarding repeat visitors with new discoveries. Interactions with specific aspects of a place create one's personal identity and most cherished values.[66] And Disneyland possesses an evolving and tangible display of particulars, fostering a large band of Southern Californian devotees.

Affective Attachment

Place is also constructed through emotional connection. The affective is the core for a sense of community and place attachment that strengthens social relationships and collective action.[67] When interviewees were asked whether other Southern California theme parks could fulfill the same social role as Disneyland, the answer was emphatically negative. Social club and fan event organizers and participants all agreed that Disneyland offered a singular environment in the region, if not anywhere worldwide. The word "magical" was used repeatedly to differentiate Disneyland from any other place in Southern California. Noah Korda, the founder and organizer of Bats Day, an annual fan event since 1999 celebrating goth subculture, considered Knott's Berry Farm's Ghost Town as a potential event location but

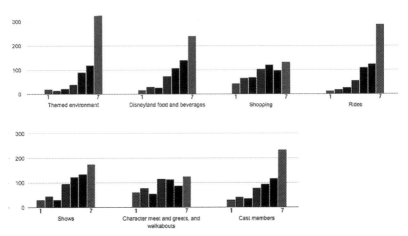

Figure 2.1. For the social atmosphere at Disneyland, how important are each of the following (1 Unimportant—7 Very important)? (n=637).

concluded the lack of a focal point at Knott's (such as Disneyland's castle) and the fervent fan affection for New Orleans Square and its Haunted Mansion attraction were both persuasive factors mitigating against changing venues.[68] Even though Dr. Who is a non-Disney text, hundreds of Whovians come to Disneyland to celebrate Galliday, a fan event started in 2014 with activities including ride takeovers and a group photo in front of Sleeping Beauty Castle. Amy McCain, the founder and organizer of Galliday, selected Disneyland to celebrate Whovian fandom, even though the park holds no attractions or connection to Dr. Who, because in Southern California "no other place has the magic of Disneyland."[69]

Disneyland was the favorite place outside of home to socialize with family and/or friends for 74 percent of survey respondents. Media fandoms often function as alternative social communities,[70] and for Disneyland fans the park was often their primary social community. The themed environment was cited by 51 percent of respondents as very important to the social aspect of Disneyland, followed by rides, food and beverages, and cast members. The oft-expressed importance of theming by interviewees and survey respondents affirms Baker's findings that among seventy-seven analyzed across North America, Asia, and Europe the most popular parks were the ones with the deepest thematic and narrative features.[71] The interviewee and survey responses also affirm Milman's view that theme park guests favor a fantasy milieu with safety, cleanliness, and helpful frontline employees.[72] Often cited as unimportant to the social aspect were character meet and greets and shopping (see Figure 2.1), even though Disney famously foregrounds consumerism at the park.

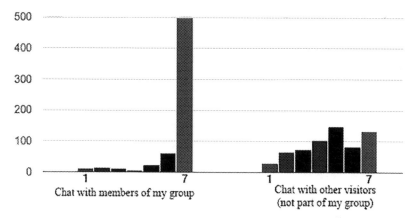

Figure 2.2. While you are in line for an attraction at Disneyland, how likely are you to do the following (1 Never—7 Very Often)? (n=637).

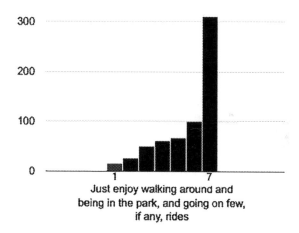

Figure 2.3. On a typical visit to Disneyland, how likely are you to do the following (1 Never—7 Very Often)? (n=637).

Disney research has indicated that visitors only spend 3 percent of their time on rides and at shows and instead enjoy "the precise commodity that people so sorely lack in their suburban hometowns: pleasant, pedestrian-friendly, public space and the sociability it engenders."[73] Belying the image of robots ushered from ride to ride and standing silently in lines, 94 percent chat very often with other members of their group while in queues (see Figure 2.2), and 49 percent very often stroll around the park on a typical day going on few, if any, rides (see Figure 2.3). Regular park visitors from Southern

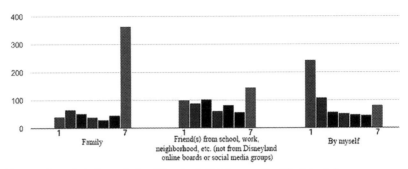

Figure 2.4. Do you typically spend a day at Disneyland with (1 Never—7 Very Often): (n=637).

California do not consider going on rides an essential trip activity because they can easily return another day and have already experienced the rides innumerable times. Just being present at Disneyland is emotionally satisfying.

Walt Disney designed Disneyland to be a place for multigenerational families to enjoy rides together without the need for older or younger members to sit out attractions due to extreme motion or scary show scenes. Going to Disneyland with family very often, the highest level, was reported by 57 percent of survey respondents, and 69 percent answered five or higher out of seven as often visiting with family (see Figure 2.4). When asked why people went swing dancing at Disneyland on Saturday nights instead of Los Angeles lounges and clubs, the administrator of the Disneyland swing dancing Facebook group said the restricted alcohol policy at Disneyland made for an inclusive and pleasant atmosphere allowing children to dance with adults.[74] As for visiting with friends from school, work, or neighborhood, 44 percent responded with a five or higher for often spending time with friends on a typical Disneyland visit. Families and friends of all ages use Disneyland as a local place to connect and socialize together.

Though most visit with family or friends, 13 percent very often spend the day at Disneyland alone, and 27 percent responded with a five or higher for often going solo. Unlike home or other places such as the mall, being alone at Disneyland is to be within the crowd and community of other like-minded fans. Solo trips are not uncommon, with only 38 percent reporting never going to Disneyland alone. Almost a third, 31 percent, strongly agreed, and 70 percent agreed with a five or higher, as feeling trust and camaraderie in the company of other Disneyland fans while in the park (see Figure 2.5). A sense of community develops around feelings of membership in a group with shared history, interests, and concerns,[75] so Disneyland can provide comfort when going through tough times. When the grandmother of MiceChat's Regan passed away in Kansas, Regan went to the park alone and took the Disneyland

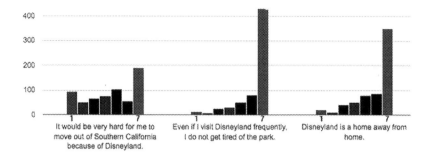

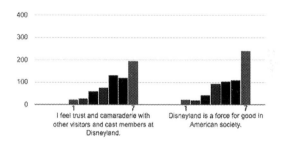

Figure 2.5. Do you agree or disagree with the following statements (1 Strongly Disagree—7 Strongly Agree)? (n=637).

railroad around the park for hours nonstop. The train had been a source of comfort for Regan since childhood park trips, so a day circling Disneyland provided a soothing place to reflect, decompress, and, at the end of the day, go home feeling better.[76] Regan believed, and other fans informed me, that locals have commonly used Disneyland as an escape to a safe fantasy world to deal with stressful life issues from childhood to adulthood including bullying, legal troubles, marital woes, career anxieties, body image, and self-identity.

Disneyland is an escape from the outside world with some visitors even shedding a few tears upon entering Main Street as a cathartic release. Wasko sees Disneyland as representing the unreal, escapist, and romantic.[77] This need for escape is also evident within other media fandoms, as Jenkins notes, fans "inhabit a world where traditional forms of community life are disintegrating, the majority of marriages end in divorce, most social relations are temporary and superficial, and material values often dominate over emotional and social needs."[78] A fandom object can fulfill a profound need in a fan's life but most media fandoms can only provide an escape to a screen for reading, viewing, and listening, while Southern California Disneyland fans can tangibly access and experience the object of their fandom on almost any day and socialize in person. The tangibility of Disneyland, such as throwing coins into Snow White's Wishing Well at the grotto next to Sleeping Beauty Castle, creates a powerful affective connection for fans. While being in Disneyland, 55 percent have made friends with a stranger, which is especially commonplace at meets, clubs, and events. Besides chatting within one's group, 57 percent reported five or higher as chatting often with strangers while waiting in attraction queues, which were purposely designed by early Imagineers in a switchback style rather than single file to encourage sociality among park visitors.[79] During two months of participant observation in the park, and primarily doing so alone, I often chatted with other visitors and cast members while in lines, shops, rides, and walkways. Being in Disneyland can be a social experience with not only one's group but also with strangers.

An unwillingness to move away has often been noted as a leading indicator of place attachment. Leaving Disneyland behind would not be easy for the 30 percent who strongly agree, and 55 percent agreeing with a five or higher, that moving out of Southern California would be difficult due to attachment to Disneyland. Regan specifically moved to Southern California from Kansas in the early 1990s to be close to Disneyland after being smitten during early childhood family trips.[80] Other fans similarly relate stories of migration from across the United States to Southern California for the express purpose of making a home near Disneyland with one informing me of purposely moving into a residential development within easy walking distance of the park. And living nearby does not necessarily lead to Disneyland fatigue; 68 percent strongly agreed that even after frequent park visits, they do not tire of Disneyland, and 88 percent rated this sentiment five or higher. This echoes Sandvoss's view of fandom as comparable with "the emotional significance of the places we have grown to call 'home' because it offers us a 'physical, emotional and ideological space' and a sense of 'security and stability.'"[81] Disneyland as a home away from home was strongly agreed upon by 55 percent, and 81 percent agreed with a five or higher. This personal connection is so affirmative and earnest that 38 percent strongly agreed that Disneyland is a force for good in American society, and 71 percent agreed with a five or higher. The affective connection of local fans to Disneyland as a place is quite profound.

Behavioral Attachment

On the behavioral level, people participate in place planning, protection, improvement, activities, and celebrations for the construction of place.[82] Disney promotes participatory fandom by offering "the consumer/fan a spatial platform which brings all the elements together in the experience of walking or

Figure 2.6. MiceChat Gumball Rally gamebook, February 2018. Photo: Author.

riding through narratized space. The land of Disney relies on two elements to ensure its success: a particular kind of utopia and a special type of fandom."[83]

Since the 1990s advent of BBS group scavenger hunts, Gay Days, and Bats Day, fans have been creating their own events in Disneyland without the explicit permission of the Disney company. Fan-organized events were attended by 62 percent of survey respondents and spanned a thematic spectrum including Dapper Day (fashion and style), Steam Day (steampunk), Lolita Day (Harajuku fashion), MiceChat Gumball Rally (scavenger race) (see Figure 2.6), Awareness 4 Autism, Tiki Day, Maynard Appreciation Day (honoring a popular cast member), Lyme Disease Awareness, and many more on almost every weekend of the year. Some events, such as Gay Days (see Figure 2.7) and Dapper Day, attract thousands of participants. Others attract only a handful such as Alive in Our Hearts for couples to commemorate pregnancy and infant loss through commiserating about their experience, taking a group photo in front of Sleeping Beauty Castle, and riding the children-centered "it's a small world" attraction.

Schiffler records 2013 as the beginning of the Disneyland social club phenomenon as cited from an interview with a club leader,[84] but in 2012 the Neverlanders social club formed and is believed to have been the first to wear the customary matching jean jacket vests with back patches.[85] The first known public reference to social clubs at Disneyland was a post to the MiceChat discussion board on April 17, 2013, titled "does anyone know the name of this Disneyland crew??," which sparked a discussion of the Neverlanders. By the summer of 2013 and throughout 2014, many fans rapidly established new

Figure 2.7. Gay Days group photo in front of Sleeping Beauty Castle, Disneyland, October 2017. Photo: Author.

social clubs with their own denim vests and patches to identify affiliations as White Rabbits, Mice with Attitude, Wonderlanders, Big Bad Wolves, and dozens more formations. Potential recruits found clubs through group websites, social media pages (primarily Facebook), or by approaching a member with a club vest in the park. The social clubs can sometimes convey a sense of ownership of the park, with specific spots for group check-ins and selfies though they have no official affiliation or recognition by Disney.[86] Since being a social club member is an ongoing time commitment (minimum thresholds for attendance and activity) and money (for denim vests and patches, and a few clubs charge dues), only 22 percent of respondents reported being a member of a Disneyland social club. The primary reason members joined was social, to meet other Disneyland fans and be part of a family-type group to enjoy the park together. They also formed bonds outside the park for barbecues, sports, and community. Members of social clubs built social capital through networking, cooperation, and trust within their "families of choice."[87]

A sense of community and place attachment manifest behaviorally in participation and practice through "feelings of mutual trust, social connections, shared concerns, and community values."[88] Members often feel an obligation to protect against perceived internal and external threats to their community through collective action.[89] Disneyland fans in Southern California see the park as a community space with actions that reflect a sense of joint responsibility. Almost all respondents, 99 percent, reported having helped another visitor at Disneyland with directions, information, or photo-taking. With community cleanup linked to strong feelings of place attachment,[90] 87 percent of respondents reported picking up and throwing away the trash of strangers while at the park. In addition, 72 percent have found and reported lost property, 51 percent have assisted a cast member, and 22 percent have tipped or bought a gift for a cast member. In a place-attachment practice specific to Disneyland, 79 percent of respondents gave a valid Fast-Pass ticket (essentially a front-of-line attraction pass with a limited number available from Disney every day) to a stranger. It was also not uncommon for valid FastPasses to be left on park store shelves and benches for other visitors to find and use. This practice ended in June 2017 when Disneyland switched to a digital FastPass system that eliminated the paper passes that were easily transferrable between unrelated visitors. Some fans enjoyed making their own Disney-like magic by giving toys and gifts to other people's children in the park. Two event organizers said they sometimes came to the park with small toys in their backpacks for this purpose.[91] The MouseWait mobile app was developed by a fan couple to allow other Disneyland fans to crowd-source attraction wait times, but users devised social practices for the app unforeseen by the developers. Members used MouseWait to give gifts surreptitiously to anyone using the app at Disneyland by stashing cookies, chocolates, or small toys in a Main Street locker and then sharing the locker number and code with all other app users to go partake of the free gift. MouseWait also allowed members to propose spontaneous meetups and ride takeovers in the app's lounge while in the park.

In interviews with fan organizers of Disneyland events, meets, and social clubs, all mentioned how Disneyland afforded them a place to develop a vibrant social circle filled with other Disneyland fans. The three coorganizers of Lolita Day have strengthened their fellowship over a decade running their annual event, as well as the friendships made with participants who return year after year. For the fifth anniversary event in November 2017, the coorganizers distributed a specially made pin to honor participants who came with event pins from the four previous years (see Figure 2.8). Organizers of events with less than a few hundred participants (Galliday, Lolita Day, Steam Day) often lose money by not charging for pins, material, and mementos associated with the event, in addition to the substantial time spent on planning and promotion.

Organizers of larger, more established events (MiceChat anniversary, Gumball Rally, and Bats Day) report barely breaking even with their events. Dapper Day and Gay Days are exceptions generating profit for organizers. Social club leaders generally report breaking even financially due to

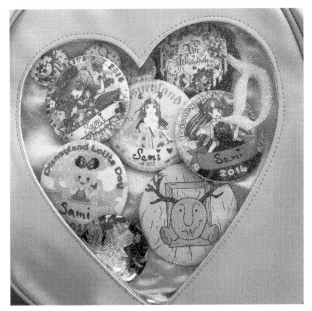

Figure 2.8. Lolita Day event pins, October 2017. Photo: Author.

revenue derived from paid social events outside the park and the sale of club vest patches. MiceChat's Regan has met Disneyland fans at the central hub in front of the castle (see Figure 2.9) on Sundays at noon for over twenty years. Sometimes a few dozen people showed up, and other times only a handful. When asked the reason for organizing and attending meets for so long when there was no profit and the number of participants was tiny compared to Mice-Chat's large online following, Regan replied that the simple joy of meeting fellow fans at the shared cherished place of Disneyland made it worthwhile. Regan even became ordained to perform wedding ceremonies because of all the couples who have met through the MiceChat community.[92] Jenkins, citing Sennett's work on the competing regimes of value on labor, observed that fan work is not just about economic rewards but also affective and social rewards.[93] Indeed, few fans in any fandom earn more than a small profit from their fan labor.[94] Instead, fans often derive satisfaction from creating and sharing within a larger community in spite of potential restrictions and tradeoffs with the corporation that owns the intellectual property.[95] Benkler also cites the attainment of social status within a community as a nonmonetary reward for nonmarket production.[96] For most fan event, meet, and social club organizers, the accrual of cultural and social capital is not converted or convertible into economic value. Throughout the participant observation of events, meets, and clubs, the common thread was a labor of love to foster a sense of local place at Disneyland.

Figure 2.9. Disneyland's central hub where the MiceChat community meets on Sundays at noon, October 2017. Photo: Author.

DISNEYLAND AS A CONTESTED PLACE

Rather than being the placeless nonplace full of strangers that Disneyland's critics have declared for decades, Walt Disney's original park exhibits numerous cognitive, affective, and behavioral characteristics of place attachment. As Disneyland is not a lived-in place such as a house, neighborhood, or city, Southern California fans have used Disneyland in a manner similar to dropping in at a neighborhood park on a regular basis. These locals are at Disneyland to be social at events, meets, and clubs, and in queues, walkways, and benches with friends and family, as well as strangers. They are active with scavenger hunts, dressing up, singing, and strolling through the park. They celebrate birthdays, holidays, weddings, engagements, and friendships, and commemorate loved ones who have passed away. Disneyland holds more meaning for these Southern Californians than simply being an ersatz space with iron rides, fast food, and tchotchke shopping. Many Southern Californians are deeply attached to Disneyland as an extraordinary place in their lives.

According to Bob Gurr, a retired Imagineer and Disney Legend who worked closely with Walt Disney for twelve years on many early attractions, Walt Disney never intended Disneyland to be a neighborhood park with frequent visits by locals.[97] To ensure his animated films would be a recurring family event enjoyed by successive generations, Walt Disney instituted a seven-year cycle for each film's rerelease to build pent-up demand and preserve the film's mystique. Gurr sees Disneyland as similarly conceived as a place to be enjoyed as a dressy outing every couple years because frequent visits would make the place too familiar and prosaic and thus shatter the park's unique magic. Gurr feels contemporary fans have focused too much on trying to figure out and nitpick the inner workings of every attraction to the point that the joy of the ride journey itself has become lost.[98] Similarly, in Baym's study of musicians and audiences, "the last shards of mystique" dissipated as fans online discovered all the behind-the-scenes details of pop star lives and music production.[99] The enigmatic aura of music icon David Bowie in the 1970s would be difficult to reproduce in today's media environment. In addition, Gurr believes some passholders have become socially addicted to one another with Disneyland as a convenient escape valve to avoid addressing real-life problems.[100] Muniz and O'Guinn found similarly that members of brand communities are often more tightly connected to each other than to the brand itself.[101] When asked what Walt Disney would think of Southern Californians regularly visiting Disneyland, Gurr gazed skyward and said, "I'm sorry Walt, this place is now a social hangout."[102]

However, Jenkins, echoing Roland Barthes on the death of the author, maintained that fans do not simply recover an author's meaning but rework the material to suit the context of their lived experience by inventing something different from authorial intent.[103] Barthes pointed out that rereading is generally counter to the business and ideological customs of society, and thus texts are constructed to hold our attention only for the initial reading to uncover the story's conclusion.[104] Rereading for Barthes shifts reader interest away from resolving primary narratives and instead toward thematic elements, character relations, and social knowledge since a reread book still has the same words but reveals new story elements during each subsequent reading.[105] Barthes therefore distinguishes between readerly (meaning is solidified by the author) and writerly (meaning is under constant reader reinterpretation) texts.[106] For Barthes, Disneyland would be in the perpetual present as Disney Imagineers constantly update the park to keep the experience fresh for repeat visitors and then fans produce new meanings after every modification.[107] Other media fandoms ossify, as with no new Elvis Presley or Michael Jackson recordings. Brooker noted that until the 2016 reboot, *The X-Files* fans expressed temporal regret "that the most vibrant and rewarding period in the show's fandom was now lost in nostalgic memory."[108] Bielby and Harrington noted that the object of a media fandom often comes to an end with the death of a celebrity, conclusion of a television series, or no new installments in a film franchise,[109] but Disneyland as a real physical place lives on and continues to evolve every day. Walt Disney famously said Disneyland would never be finished while incessantly tinkering with the park's attractions to tell more compelling stories and entice return visits.[110] Disneyland therefore is a superlative example of a writerly text. Indeed, the seeds of Disneyland as a text to be frequently reread were being planted and even recognized by the Disney company as early as 1956 with at least some Southern Californians using the park in a manner not intended by Walt Disney. In the official Disney publication, *The Complete Guide to Disneyland*, published only a year after the park opened, a page called Disneyland Data relates the following tidbit, "A 63-year-old lady from Redlands, California, has visited Disneyland once a week every week since opening date, July 18, 1955."[111] When this was pointed out, MiceChat's Regan cheekily exclaimed, "she was the first MiceChatter!"

The Disney company has made changes to Disneyland that have not always been in accordance with the wishes and practices of fervent local fans. Sandvoss states the reason people go to Graceland or other fan sites is to find "physically manifest places of fandom: a search for authenticity, a search for the real . . . a search for unmediated experience, of putting oneself, literally, in the place of the fan text and thus creating a relationship between the object of fandom and the self that goes beyond mere consumption and fantasy."[112] However, unlike other media fandoms, Disneyland fans in Southern California regularly visit a constantly reimagined and reinvented fan object populated with a vast array of texts since the company was founded in 1923. The popular emergence of the internet in the 1990s not only unlocked the potential for Southern California Disneyland fans to create activities in the park beyond the official Disney ones but also enabled local fans to protest company plans perceived as lackluster or harmful to the park. The following two chapters investigate this contest over Disneyland in the discourse between the Disney company and Southern California fans on online social platforms before and after the rise of social media.

CHAPTER 3

Disneyland Online Fandom, 1990–2005

Unity and Resistance

Before the era of Facebook, YouTube, Instagram, and Twitter, early internet social platforms gave rise to fan groups and activities online and at the park. Usenet, which was ungoverned, unowned, and unmoderated, became the primary early online social platform for fans to share knowledge and information about shared interests and hobbies. As Usenet declined in usage, fans migrated to website discussion boards, which still centered on shared interests and hobbies but, unlike Usenet, were owned, governed, and moderated by a small coterie of highly motivated fans. Later, the rise of social media shifted fans away from shared interest websites with discussion boards to personal social network media owned, governed, and moderated by big technology companies. This chapter examines the period from 1990 to 2005, when the novelty and nature of Usenet newsgroups and web discussion boards shaped an evolving relationship between local fans and the Disney company, as well as the relationship of fans to one another and the park as a local place. During the 1990s, the Usenet newsgroup alt.disney.disneyland afforded fans social capital to organize as a voice of resistance to Disney. In the early 2000s, the eclipse of Usenet by web discussion boards divided online fans into just a few distinct websites, but fans still came together to support the Save Disney campaign that eventually ousted CEO Michael Eisner in 2005. Usenet and the early years of web discussion boards enabled fans to speak out and organize on issues important to the fandom, while Disney in this formative internet era was slow to understand and effectively react to fans on the new digital medium.

PRE-INTERNET PRINT-BASED DISNEYLAND FANDOM

Coppa sees "the mission of fandom, in fact, is to make mass media social."[1] Before the wide diffusion of the internet, the principal medium fans used to regularly interact and exchange information was official and unofficial print periodicals distributed through postal mail.[2] The official Disney-produced publication for fans was the subscription-only *Disney News* magazine, which started in 1965 as a quarterly, covering Disney media and Disneyland.[3] In 1994, the magazine was rebranded for sale on newsstands as the *Disney Magazine* but ceased publication in 2005 with a special issue celebrating the fiftieth anniversary of Disneyland. A popular fan-produced unofficial periodical was the *E-Ticket* magazine published from 1986 to 2009 with a total of forty-six issues. Other fan-produced periodicals included the *Duckburg Times* (1977–92), *StoryboarD* (1987–95), the *Mouse Club* (1980–92), and *Persistence of Vision* (1992–98).[4] The print newsletter of the Disneyana Fan Club (originally known as the National Fantasy Fan Club) started in 1985 and was still being published as a quarterly as of early 2024. Many fan-produced print periodicals folded as the internet became increasingly popular with Usenet newsgroups, listservs, bulletin boards, and ISP discussion boards as platforms for fan interaction.[5] Audience communities organized around a text and online communities organized through a network integrated for interpersonal uses as communities of practice with habitualized ways of acting.[6] Duffett observed the ability to interact online "turned the fan community from a network of local cultures or periodic rituals into a non-stop process of social effervescence."[7] The development of shared rituals and traditions becomes a way to publicly demonstrate association through shared behaviors and values.[8]

DISNEYLAND FANS ON BBSES

From the late 1970s until the mid-1990s advent of the World Wide Web and browsers, BBSes (bulletin board systems) were a popular way to connect with like-minded hobbyists and fans by logging into a computer server to upload or download software and data, and exchange news and information. Kollock and Smith described these early communities as "groups of people who meet to share information, discuss mutual interest, play games, and carry out business."[9] Many of the communities formed through fan attachment to media properties and became active cultural agents in the reading and appropriation of favorite texts.[10] The range of groups became so vast and varied that people could "shop" for their community based on narrow affinities. Participants in early online communities often established relationships due to shared homogenous interests despite potential heterogeneity in social background such as age, ethnicity, and class.[11] Participants were often local to each other due to the cost structure of dial-up access at the time, thus discouraging expensive long-distance calls to log in to far-flung BBSes.[12] Thus, due to their technological nature, BBSes often combined a shared fandom interest such as Disneyland with a specific locality such as Southern California.

Mouse Ears was an early popular Disneyland-focused BBS that was text-based and centered on information exchange.[13] At a time when few people had internet access, the people you met online were different from the people you met offline because the two worlds rarely overlapped. However, Ken Pellman recalled being a teenager on Main Street waiting for the early morning rope drop and having a conversation with a family who recognized his ideas and opinions as similar to posts they had read on Mouse Ears. The family asked if he was *the* Ken Pellman who had posted to the BBS, to which Pellman answered affirmatively while being taken aback at being recognized solely through online postings.[14] The early forums made fans realize they were not alone in their passion, with so many other like-minded people posting ideas, information, and opinions. In addition, any fan with internet access could build social and cultural capital by communicating with many other fans in an ongoing and evolving mass conversation without the gatekeepers of fan print periodicals. Posters on BBSes often used their real names but not photos or other personally identifying information. Mouse Ears faded away to be replaced by the Mouse House BBS, which was similar to Mouse Ears except Mouse House organized official meetups and scavenger hunts in the park.[15] Launched in 1993, The Castle was another BBS focused on Disneyland that attracted, at its peak, almost six hundred users.[16] Board administrators organized meets for the opening and closing of attractions, park history tours, screenings of Disney films, and King's Challenge as the group's big annual event in the park with competitions attended by nearly sixty members in its peak year.[17] One attendee quipped on the board after the event, "it was good to put a face to your names, even if you all looked nothing like I expected."[18] In the late 1990s, The Castle eventually dissolved as a social meltdown that Ackerman and Star define as a phenomenon of people no longer coming to a space because they believe others will not show up anymore.[19] The owners of The Castle realized a move to the web was necessary for survival but would entail considerably more technical and financial resources than they had on hand.[20] While the print-based fan clubs Disneyana and Mouse Club had previously organized annual meets in the park in the mid-1980s through their print publications, Mouse House and The Castle were probably the first to use the internet to organize in-person Disneyland meets and events, thus auguring the social media platform era of the 2010s that enabled the creation of hundreds of meets, events, and clubs in the park for local fans to participate in (as detailed in chapter 5).

Internet service providers (ISPs) in the 1990s, such as America Online (AOL), Prodigy, and CompuServe in the United States, lowered the economic and technological barriers for getting online by providing users with an easy-to-use graphic user interface for navigation and ubiquitous discs (at first 3.5-inch floppies and later CD-ROMs) with large blocks of free service hours. The ISPs also provided discussion boards and chat rooms exclusively for member use. MiceChat's Regan recalled picking up the free discs to get access each month under different usernames to explore the Disney discussion boards and chat rooms.[21] Regan eventually settled on the online handle of Dusty Sage as a nod to growing up in Kansas (and the migration to California in the 1930s of poor tenant farmers due to the Dust Bowl) and status as a Disney savant since childhood. Regan's Dusty Sage moniker has persisted to the present day as friends and business associates still use both his handle and real name. On the ISP boards and chat rooms, Regan discovered not only other passionate Disneyland fans but also a large contingent of gay Disney fans.[22] Regan embraced a technology that allowed for the amplification of an individual fan voice to a large potential audience to discuss Disneyland but lamented the ephemerality of the public conversations that disappeared after logging off chat rooms or thirty days after posting on the ISP boards.[23] Regan enjoyed cultural capital as a Disney expert, and eventually used the boards and Usenet newsgroups to establish social capital by organizing social Sunday meets at the Disneyland hub. Due to structural scalability to accommodate the increasing number of fans coming online, readability by enabling threaded posting, persistence of posts through archiving, interconnectivity across systems, and wide accessibility via complimentary access offers provided by ISPs, early online communities of interest flourished on Usenet newsgroups.

RISE OF USENET

Usenet was an early noncentralized digital network for topical discussion and file sharing via newsgroups. Established in 1980, Usenet existed well before the appearance of the World Wide Web. In early research on Usenet, Baym observed individual users posted to the discussion boards known as newsgroups mainly for social interaction on topics that were of personal rather than professional interest.[24] During the "Great Renaming" in 1987, Usenet groups were divided into seven large hierarchies, including society (soc.) and recreation (rec.), which became the most popular.[25] Within the hierarchies, there were categories such as culture and arts, and then further subcategories. For more niche and alternative topics, an eighth hierarchy was implemented in 1986 called ".alt," which became the most popular by number of posters, posts, average line count, replies, repliers, and newgroups.[26] By 1996 there were 17,000 groups and approximately three million users globally, though the total number of users was probably higher due to the undercounting of lurkers, who browsed but rarely, if ever, posted. Lurkers comprised the majority of members in online groups and often felt a sense of community even without posting.[27]

The characteristics of Usenet as an online social platform shaped how users interacted, perceived, and utilized newsgroups. Most newsgroups were unmoderated and conversations were infamous for devolving into rants and flame wars fanned by a cloak of anonymity enabled via junk and spoofed email addresses.[28] As a decentralized system, Usenet had no corporate or super-organizational oversight. Newsgroups did not contain information about the number of subscribers, members, or other demographic information, which contributed to a lack of social context for users. In an influential early book on online social platforms, *The Virtual Community*, Howard Rheingold dubbed Usenet "an anarchic, unkillable, censorship-resistant, aggressively noncommercial, voraciously growing conversation among millions of people in dozens of countries."[29] Usenet differed from web forums and bulletin boards by featuring neither administrators nor a central server for storage. Some newsgroup denizens accrued cultural capital as regulars who often compiled and published FAQs (frequently asked questions) to guide new posters in group norms. Usenet was a place for publication and conversation that Rheingold likened to "a giant coffeehouse with a thousand rooms."[30] Online communities formed as internet-connected collectives of users interacting over time with a shared purpose, interest, or need.[31] Outside of designated marketplace newsgroups, commercial posts were not tolerated in the belief of the time in the 1990s that "if Usenet were to become exploited as a marketing arena the character of the net would be so dramatically altered that it might lose its appeal entirely."[32]

Disneyland Fans on Usenet

Fan reception has always been shaped through interaction with other fans, and through culture and society writ large.[33] Internet communication not only afforded amplification of individual fan voices but also saw the formation of fan groups previously unable to experience regular interaction due to expense, hassle, and geographical disconnection.[34] As early as 1990, in newsgroups such as alt.tv.twinpeaks, fans engaged in online social interaction to pool intellectual resources toward common goals that previously might have remained private meditations.[35] Usenet provided multiple newsgroups for Disneyland discussion including rec.parks.theme for general theme park fans, rec.arts.disney.parks for all Disney theme parks, and rec.arts.disney. announce for announcements of new Disney company projects including those related to the theme parks. The most active for Disneyland fans became alt.disney.disneyland since the focus was exclusively on Walt Disney's original Southern California park. In addition, while posters on rec.arts.disney.parks maintained a relatively positive perspective on Disney theme parks, alt.disney. disneyland became well-known for fan critiques of the park.[36] Jenkins sees these types of fan critiques as not unusual considering organized fandom's penchant for engaging in criticism "where competing interpretations and evaluations of common texts are proposed, debated and negotiated."[37] Many posters were local annual passholders who enjoyed pointing out anything in the park during weekly visits that was not seemingly up to the high standards originally set by Walt Disney. Since newsgroup posts were archived for back reference by many newsreaders, and then by web services such as Deja News, fans could easily go back and trace any issues or concerns about the park over time. With alt.disney.disneyland as a unifying focal point of sociality, fans could engage in many-to-many group discussions to exchange knowledge and information, and critique the Disney company's management of their beloved park. The affective attachment of local fans to Disneyland fostered a sense of ownership that often clashed with the overriding commercial objectives of Disney as the legal corporate owner of the park.

Disneyland Fans on Websites

The graphic user interface browsers of the World Wide Web, such as Mosaic in 1993 and then Netscape Navigator and Internet Explorer, enabled fans to create websites devoted to their hobbies and interests. One of the first and most popular fan websites was AintItCoolNews started by Harry Knowles in 1996. Though its primary focus was films, Jim Hill wrote articles for the site on Disney and Disneyland.[38] At the time, the few Disneyland-centric websites created by fans focused on niche subjects such as the thematically distinct trash cans of each park land or the ADA (Americans with Disabilities Act of 1990) at Disneyland for advice to enjoy the park in a wheelchair.

However, one fan decided to create a website to provide general Disneyland fandom with a voice that would gradually harness the fan collective to

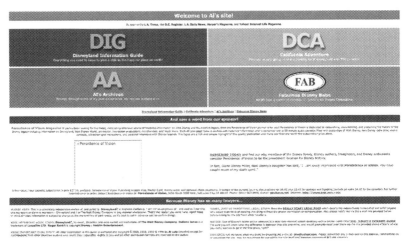

Figure 3.1. Screenshot of April 27, 1999, Disneyland Information Guide from Al Lutz's AOL members space. Source: https://web.archive.org/web/19990427090252/http://members.aol.com:80/alweho/index.htm.

challenge the Disney company. Al Lutz was a prolific Disney newsgroups poster who got tired of repeatedly answering the same questions about start times for park shows, so Lutz took over the moribund Disneyland newsgroup FAQ consisting only of park hours and basic information, and transformed it into a comprehensive guide expanded to seven sections. In 1996, Lutz started a companion website on AOL members space called the Disneyland Information Guide, popularly known as DIG (see Figure 3.1). Doobie Moseley, cofounder of the longstanding Disney fan site Laughing Place (http://www.laughingplace.com), said, "all of us, and I mean all of us, go back to Al Lutz and the Disneyland Information Guide; that's really the thing that started all of this."[39] At a time when Disney only had a limited web presence, the hundreds of webpages that comprised DIG were an unofficial but comprehensive website for information about Disneyland.[40] Together, DIG and alt.disney.disneyland formed what Gee would call an online "affinity space" focusing on a common endeavor (not race, class, gender, nationality, and so on) as paramount, newbies and savants sharing a common space, fans creating and sharing new content and encouraging and enabling the acquisition and spread of knowledge, different levels of participation and status achievement, and leaders as resources and not absolute authorities.[41]

Lutz's news columns became famous among fans for spoilers and rumors leaked by informants within Disney's corporate offices of new attractions opening and old ones closing as well as photos of park construction sites. This type of fan practice of Disneyland news reporting has since become perennial, with entire YouTube channels and social media accounts dedicated to inside-baseball–style coverage of the park as a prime example of Hills's pretextual poaching in an extension of Jenkins's textual poaching of already completed, published texts.[42] In addition, unlike some fan websites that provided only positive and/or descriptive coverage of Disneyland, DIG, in a section called Disneyland Blues, was unafraid to criticize park management by name for cutbacks to maintenance, costuming, food services, attractions, and any other perceived shortcomings. Disgruntled Disney employees including Imagineers, managers, and cast members emailed Lutz with insider information for the website and columns not only to highlight issues in the park but also to sway internal Disney corporate battles.[43] Lutz was also known for a biting humor targeting Disney's shortcomings in the park, such as after a renovation dubbing the Fantasyland Theater the WonderBra Theater because the makeshift overhead tarps resembled a brassiere. Still today, many fans and cast members from the Usenet era refer to the Fantasyland Theater as WonderBra theater. For Disneyland fans online, Lutz became a prominent influencer in an internet era before the term had been coined, but instead of being a pliant brand ambassador for Disney, Lutz's online website and columns aimed to hold Disney accountable to fan expectations and wishes. On alt.disney.disneyland, a user with the handle NWC started a thread on May 9, 1999, with the title "My Compliments to Al Lutz":

> I personally believe that Al Lutz is actually motivating Disney to clean up Disneyland! . . . I was worried I might not see Disneyland at its best when I go this month but now I hear that Pirates of the Carribean [sic] is completely fixed, Mark Twain is getting a good clean up, and various classic attractions are getting rehabs. In fact, I am hopeful I will be able to hear the Space Mountain music when I go! I gotta thank Al Lutz because without his webpage and constant vigilance over Disneyland's maintenance, things that are fixed right now would still be rotting. Thank you Al, and keep up the hard/good work.

A user with the handle the Fabulous Disney Babe responded: "not bad for a 'fan site.'" However, the newsgroup also included dissenters who did not believe Lutz had much impact on Disney's park actions, such as user K.E.R. responding in the Al Lutz compliments thread on May 10, 1999: "So you are saying that it's his doing that the park is so clean now, correct? . . . I don't think he had anything to do with current park conditions. People in management often get printouts of things, but that doesn't mean they (the webmaster or author) actually has [sic] anything to do with what's being done in the park."

Still, most newsgroup posters believed Lutz's effort had at least some impact on Disney to make improvements; as user JENinSoCa responded on May 10, 1999: "Disney does read the fan sites. And no, we don't know for sure, but it seems highly likely that Al's site does play a part in there somewhere. I'm not saying it's the only reason stuff gets fixed, I'm just saying it sure looks like they use it. (i.e. the trash cans being moved to hide some disrepair)."

DIG lit an initial spark of online dissent that would later eventually spread as a call-to-arms among fans to support the ouster of Paul Pressler, president of Disneyland from 1994 to 1998 and Chair of Walt Disney Parks and Resorts from 1998 to 2002, and Michael Eisner, CEO and Chair of the Board of Directors of the Disney company from 1984 to 2005.

After participating on alt.disney.disneyland and discovering DIG through Lutz's FAQ, Doobie Moseley started a website called Doobie's Disneyland in 1996 with trivia and trip reports. In 1999, Moseley and wife Rebekah initiated a more ambitious project, Laughing Place, in an attempt to create a portal similar to Yahoo! but exclusively devoted to Disney-related websites, which, at the time, included 196 sites.[44] Due to being self-employed and often going to the parks, Moseley saw an opportunity to try to turn the cultural capital accrued from running a popular personal website into economic value during the fervor of the dot-com era by launching a general Disney fan website and directory.[45] Beyond serving as a directory to other Disney-related websites, Laughing Place quickly evolved to become a popular news and information hub covering not only the theme parks but all aspects of Disney.

Fan Resistance to Disney in the 1990s

Fandoms have a tradition of forming bases for consumer activism by talking back to producers, organizing to lobby, expressing opinions, and engaging in criticism.[46] Early fan discussions on BBSes and newsgroups were generally positive toward Disney and Disneyland as many fans were simply excited to discuss their fandom with so many like-minded people. However, soon thereafter, a critical eye toward the company and park developed on alt.disney.disneyland with Al Lutz as one of the most instrumental in the fandom's change of perspective through his newsgroup posts and DIG website. Fans, whose only recourse in the past was filling out complaint forms at City Hall on Disneyland's Main Street, could now vent with fellow fans on the newsgroup. And fans who were also cast members could tip off the newgroup about park shortcomings. Kevin Yee, who would become a prolific fan poster and author of books on Disney theme parks, reported on the newsgroup as a lead cast member in New Orleans Square in late 1996 that Disney had replaced the metal cutlery and melamine plates at the French Market and Café Orleans restaurants with plastic utensils and paper plates. The report of the switch caused an uproar among the newsgroup fans who criticized Disney for prioritizing profits over the environment and "good show" (a Disney term for park elements that imbue fully immersive storytelling within the themed milieu). After forty-five days of complaints at the park and online, Disney reversed the change and brought back the metal and melamine.[47] One reason Regan's Sunday meets in the park became popular was because online fans wanted to meet in person and connect with Lutz as the writer of gossipy and critical articles about Disney. On alt.disney.disneyland, user Mr. Liver stated in a post on May 10, 1999, that due to meeting Lutz at the park: "He's earned my trust. I've known him for quite awhile now, and the few encounters where I have spent the day with him have always been pleasant ones."

Lutz was a prolific and vivid writer but not necessarily comfortable as the center of attention in crowds of people, so Regan became the host and social glue for the Sunday meets. Regan recalls the early Sunday meets as the "internet's big bang" for Disneyland fandom as "MiceAge, MiceChat, MousePlanet, Laughing Place, Jim Hill Media, Yesterland—all those Web sites were built by that first group in the hub."[48] This big bang in the park established the social structure and power hierarchies of early internet Disneyland fandom with identifiable core members that Ren et al. observed in other online communities as performing the majority of community building and maintenance.[49]

The mid-1990s saw two major turning points in fan use of the internet to challenge a Disney corporate management that had yet to figure out a strategy to deal with online fans at the beginning of the internet age. The first flashpoint was the cancellation of the long-running Main Street Electrical Parade in 1996 and its replacement by a new night parade called Light Magic in 1997. Initially rolled out in 1972, the Electrical Parade had become a beloved Disneyland institution, so Disney celebrated the parade's "glowing away" forever by selling commemorative display boxes with light bulbs from the presumably soon-to-be retired parade floats. Anticipation was high for the new Light Magic parade, so Disney offered a US$25 private preview event for annual passholders. Perhaps anticipating hiccups, then Disneyland president Paul Pressler announced before the parade's start that the paid event visitors were about to witness was only a dress rehearsal and not an actual premiere. From the start, the parade was visibly unready for audience previews with audio and projector failures, missed cues among performers, and technical features highlighted in promotional material but not yet fully operational. Passholders, who were already wary of the change away from the beloved Electrical Parade, angrily lined up at City Hall to demand refunds and stinging reviews soon thereafter hit alt.disney.disneyland, dubbing the parade "Light Tragic." After receiving withering criticism from fans online and disinterest among parkgoers, Disney officially put Light Magic on hiatus only a few months later, with the *Los Angeles Times* summing up the failed parade as the "$20 million dud."[50] Though Disney officially said the parade was on hiatus until 2000, Light Magic never returned. Instead, Disney raised the ire of fans, especially those who had bought commemorative display boxes when the Electrical Parade supposedly bowed out in 1996, by resurrecting the previously "glowing away" forever parade for nightly performances in DCA from 2001 to 2010, and again at Disneyland in 2017, 2019, and 2022. The hasty torpedoing of "Light Tragic" by Disney gave fans a sense of empowerment with online interaction to bring real change in the park and contest Disney's attempts at public relations spin control.[51]

The second flashpoint in fan power and resistance was the campaign to have Paul Pressler removed as president of Disneyland. After longtime Disneyland president Jack Lundquist stepped down, CEO Michael Eisner moved Pressler from chief of Disney stores to the head of Disneyland in 1994, even though Pressler had no theme park management experience and was the first Disneyland president who had not been a protégé of Walt Disney. With a retail management mindset, Pressler set out to make the theme park more akin to a huge Disney mall store. Fans started to note maintenance cutbacks such as burnt-out light bulbs not being replaced on Main Street, where fan lore holds sacred Walt Disney's rule that every light bulb should be cataloged and replaced at 75 percent of life expectancy so Main Street always appears perfect and pristine. Before the mid-1990s, most fans were unaware of the professional backgrounds of the people running the park as business school MBAs, artists and creatives, or cast members who steadily climbed up the corporate ladder. However, fans on alt.disney.disneyland started to collectively research Disney corporate executives to trace the retail mall sensibility taking hold at Disneyland to Pressler's history as head of Disney stores. At the same time, many longtime Disneyland executives from the film studios, Imagineering, or cast member ranks were being pushed aside by the MBAs.[52] Park merchandise began to become homogenized across stores and specialty items vanished from shelves. Third-shift maintenance staff who worked overnight to maintain the park's rides, shows, and stores underwent budget cuts to save money. Park paint chipped and flaked away without refurbishment. The cutbacks increased park profits but fans online cried foul at witnessing the magic of Disneyland being seemingly erased by the "sharp pencil" staff (as disdainfully dubbed by Walt Disney) with accounting and finance degrees.

Fans on alt.disney.disneyland grew increasingly incensed with the perception of Pressler's mismanagement of the park, so Lutz decided in 1996 to make an ancillary page to DIG satirically called "Promote Pressler!"[53] The idea was to encourage Disney to promote Pressler away from Disneyland to any other part of the huge corporation and thus stop negatively affecting the park. In addition, Lutz felt anger against Pressler was running too hot on the newsgroup, so the site was also intended as a humorous release valve for fan anger.[54] Unlike the crafting of fan outrage sometimes found on today's online social media platforms to generate the clicks, views, followers, subscribers, and engagement for high metrics on Social Blade with attendant advertising revenue,[55] Lutz's campaign against Disney management was based on a fervent fan belief of the need to save Disneyland, not to generate outrage for personal economic benefit, as such remuneration did not exist in this early internet era. Ken Pellman recalled being at a company presentation for cast members where Pressler introduced on stage a Disney Studios animator who replied to Pressler's introduction, "well, thank you, I haven't ever been introduced by somebody who has their own webpage before." The reference was to Lutz's "Promote Pressler!" page, as having a personal webpage was still a novelty in 1996.[56] The animator apparently thought Pressler had created and posted the page calling for his own promotion. Pressler appeared taken aback by the comment but presumably discovered the page in his "honor" shortly thereafter, since the web of 1996 had a relatively limited number of sites for search engines to index. The *Los Angeles Times* ran a front-page story on September 12, 1996, about the "Promote Pressler!" campaign and online Disneyland fan resistance, and a brief article on the campaign also appeared in the January 1997 issue of *Harper's Magazine*. The *Times* story interviewed "cyberrebel" fans who "rode into cyberspace sounding the charge to 'take back Walt Disney's Disneyland'" due to the "crass merchandising, lax maintenance, rumored changes to long-standing attractions and the encroachment of corporate greed on Walt Disney's legacy."[57] Rides opened later and closed earlier to save on operating costs. Pressler hired the management consulting firm McKinsey and Company, who recommended a 25 percent budget cut and elimination of 42 percent of the jobs in the park's facilities, engineering, and construction divisions.[58] On Christmas Eve, 1998, a thirty-three-year-old park visitor was killed while waiting to board the sailing ship *Columbia* on the Rivers of America when a heavy cleat loosened, became a projectile, and struck the unfortunate man in the head. An investigation revealed the cleat's fastener had been improperly replaced with a substitute material for financial reasons and the cast member in charge had received insufficient training.[59] The death was the first in the park's history due to the negligence of the Disney company and not to visitors disobeying park rules, such as the man who stood up and fell out during a ride on the Matterhorn roller coaster in 1964. Many fans online cast blame for the death at the Rivers of America attraction on the cutbacks to maintenance and training under Pressler.[60]

Fans initially thought their wish was granted in 1998 when Pressler was finally promoted out of Disneyland. However, Pressler was given even more power over Disneyland with a promotion to head of all Disney parks world-wide, and his protégé, Cynthia Harriss, took over as Disneyland president. The fan relationship with the park was complicated at the time as Regan recalls:

> It's a love-hate relationship, it started off as a hate-hate relationship because we saw Disney falling apart. We loved the history of Disney. We did not like what Disney had become, and Disney was terrified of us because there was this burgeoning online thing. They weren't even on the internet. They didn't even have a web page when we started and they didn't know what to make of it and they didn't like it.[61]

In the 1990s, the internet emerged as a new medium allowing fans to shock and challenge the powerful Disney company in defense of their beloved park. Usenet was an early seed of Bruns and Burgess's calculated publics of Twitter and modern social media that provided the digital affordances to circulate protest activities in real time, potentially reaching a wide public audience with technological and communicative structures for convergence, collaboration, and participation.[62] By using one platform, Usenet, that was freely accessible to essentially anyone online and one newsgroup in particular, alt.disney.disney-land, for many-to-many discussion and organizing, and one website, DIG, as a persistent information clearinghouse, Disneyland fans congregated around the same few online venues to organize, protest, and attempt to influence Disney. As a fan leader Lutz garnered considerable cultural capital through his DIG website and posts on the Disneyland newsgroup, which led to significant social capital with online fans, but none of this capital was cashable for economic benefit in that internet era. Even though not all fans on alt.disney.disneyland necessarily agreed with each other, there was unity as to the common online venue for vigorous fan critique. If one was not on alt.disney.disneyland, then that fan was not a part of that internet era's collective Disneyland fan debate and critique. The early internet of the 1990s did not offer each shared-interest fandom a choice of many different sites to congregate. Disney management was similar to other corporate media executives of the time as generally indifferent and even hostile to fan opinion while assuming the most vocal fans were not representative of general public sentiment and not a reliable basis for decision-making.[63] Media companies of the time saw the internet mostly as a means of promotion rather than connection with the audience.[64] In the first half of the next decade, fans would become even more involved in Disney management issues when they sided with Roy E. Disney, son of company cofounder Roy O. Disney and nephew of Walt Disney, in the Save Disney campaign to oust CEO Michael Eisner and his team, including Paul Pressler.

Decline of Usenet

Usenet provided a popular early online platform for fan discussion, but the flame wars and pervasive spam drove some fans to new internet social platforms with moderators to filter out abusive, off-topic, and commercial posts. In addition, Usenet's ASCII character set could not visually compete with the web's display of color graphics. With a new alternative for sociality and knowledge exchange, ISPs, which were often a division of media conglomerates, started discontinuing support and access for a Usenet that had always been dreaded for its pirated intellectual property (music, movies, and software) and pornography.[65] America Online, one of the biggest ISPs in the United States at the time, cut off Usenet access for its twenty million subscribers in 2005, with other large ISPs following suit. Smaller ISPs often cut off access to the .alt hierarchy due to the binaries groups teeming with pirated intellectual property. After losing direct access to alt.disney.disneyland through ISPs both large and small, some fans migrated to rec.arts.disney.parks; but most abandoned the Usenet platform for the then newly emergent shared-interest web discussion boards of the early 2000s. Usenet's nature as an ungoverned, mostly unmoderated, unmonetizable, simple text-based platform led to its eventual demise as a popular platform. Furthermore, legacy and digital media companies could neither control nor monetize Usenet, so both were pleased to witness its demise. Online communities depend on active member commitment, participation, and interaction for maintenance and vibrancy, or otherwise fade away. Usenet still persists today as a platform, but with scant posting activity.

RISE OF WEB DISCUSSION BOARDS

Forums and bulletin boards based on hobbies, interests, culture, technical support, politics, and localities were popular within the space of ISPs such as AOL, Prodigy, and CompuServe from the late 1980s through the 1990s. The boards were exclusively gated to the subscribers of each service with no opportunity for cross-participation between services. Each topic board was text-based, multi-threaded, and attributed to the subscriber's member name. Posts were ephemeral and often purged from the system thirty days after initial posting. After Mosaic was released in 1993 to become the first popular web browser, users of different ISPs could share and view content with each other in an accessible and convenient manner. The earliest web discussion board goes back to 1994 from the W3C.[66] Website boards were differentiated from chat as a form of asynchronous discussion with longer posts saved within an accessible archive. The boards were generated by a web application with a variety of functions available as a package by a hosting service or an outside provider. The app was coded using one of a variety of server-side programming languages including PHP, Java, and Perl, but could be installed and run by a website administrator unfamiliar with web languages by using a WYSIWYG design editor. The code behind the boards enabled photo posting, avatars, colors, typefaces, font styles, and a community mailbox, and had a treelike structure organized with many categories and subcategories for topic discussion. The participants in web-based discussion boards engaged in a threaded sociality that was a public, recorded, polylogical (relying on multiple conversation partners) discourse displayed in a sequential order.[67] Threaded sociality stood in contrast to the organic, fluid, private, and usually unrecorded nature of typical in-person conversations. Ease of use and functionality made the boards popular with numerous interest-based websites that wanted to create a community while holding ownership and governance rights. Though sometimes the priorities of administrators and users conflicted,[68] discussion boards exhibited community as "a group of people who share social interaction, social ties, and a common interactional format, location or 'space.'"[69] However, when users ran afoul of the rules set by site owners or board moderators, they could be banished with limited, if any, alternatives of other sites and boards with the same shared interest. Web discussion board owners, and moderators to a lesser extent, accrued cultural and social capital through governance of one of a limited number of venues for fans of a specific shared interest. Usenet's decline led to fan migration to websites with discussion boards in search of conversation, participation, and community.

Disneyland Fan Website Discussion Boards

The creation of fan owned websites and discussion boards provided a venue for enforced civil discussion via moderators, while owners had visions of dotcom boom–era riches. The dream plan was to parlay the considerable social capital accrued from owning a popular fan website into economic value. In 1999 a group of regulars on alt.disney.disneyland decided to start a website in the hopes of making millions of dollars as a Disney theme parks vacation advice and planning hub.[70] The group ultimately decided on the name

MousePlanet, subsumed Lutz's DIG, and launched on July 17, 2000, with columns by founding members such as Lutz, Adrienne Vincent-Phoenix, Jim Hill, and others. Todd Regan, another founding member, recalled, "we were sure we were going to start this site and we would sell it out and we would all be rich and be able to go to Disneyland for the rest of our lives and not have to work ever again."[71] MousePlanet organized weekend meets and occasional scavenger hunts in the park. In July 2001, MousePlanet launched a discussion board for Disneyland and other Disney theme parks around the world.

However, the expected riches of owning a dot-com never materialized, just as many other web-based ventures discovered during the dot-com bust of the early 2000s. Despite entreaties to Disney to advertise on the site to reach fans, the media conglomerate never bought a banner ad and instead opted to build and market an official Disneyland website. MousePlanet was unable to generate much income as the founders eventually realized that a business model predicated on the hope of attracting substantial online advertising revenue was not viable in that internet era. The early 2000s was still a premature time to convert online social capital into economic value. Clashes over personality, finances, and site vision led to the exit of some site founders. Adrienne Vincent-Phoenix remained and took over as CEO of MousePlanet. Jim Hill left to write for Laughing Place for a time, then started his own website, JimHillMedia.com, and wrote for the *Huffington Post* covering Disney. In 2002, Al Lutz started MiceAge.com to continue writing popular columns filled with gossip and criticism of Disney and Disneyland. The new site also featured a number of other former MousePlanet writers, including Kevin Yee, but Lutz no longer wanted to deal with fan bickering and drama, so the site incorporated no discussion boards.[72] In January 2005, Regan started MiceChat.com as a website composed only of discussion boards focused mainly on Disneyland. Regan's goal was to bring home to MiceChat an online Disneyland fan community still deciding which fan website discussion board to join after the abandonment of the rapidly emptying newsgroups and ISP forums.[73]

In January 2001, Laughing Place launched discussion boards coded from scratch by Moseley. The community board for members to discuss weekend and holiday activities, personal matters, and park meets was the second most popular by number of posts after the Disneyland board. The first in-park event for Laughing Place readers was held in 2000 for approximately seventy-five fans. However, after the launch of the discussion boards in 2001, event attendance grew much larger and an annual awards program commenced with nominations and recognition for members considered the kindest, most helpful, most uplifting, and other positive attributes. The site users dubbed the awards the Golden Doobies in honor of the cofounder of Laughing Place,

Doobie Moseley, who was not involved in the administration of the awards program. A dinner for the Laughing Place community was held annually in Southern California on Disneyland's anniversary with a few Disney voice artists and animators in attendance as honored guests. When the winners of the Golden Doobie Awards were announced, some recipients broke down crying due to their deep emotional investment in a site where they read and wrote messages every day not only about Disneyland but also to discuss personal issues, triumphs, and tragedies with online friends.[74] Moseley says the event still "makes me very, very happy to this day to know something I created became a vehicle for all these people to become friends."[75] The annual meets on Disneyland's anniversary continued with fan organizers after the Moseleys left Southern California in 2003 to live near Walt Disney World in Central Florida. The Moseleys flew back every year for the event until the last one in 2009.[76] The Moseleys would not be the only fan website owners and bloggers to make the move to Central Florida in the early 2000s; the Alveys of Theme Park Review, Kevin Yee, and others also migrated east to live close to the largest assembly of theme parks in the world.

Fan Resistance to Disney in the Early 2000s

As past and present Disney managers, creatives, and cast members became alarmed by the perceptible decline of the park and company through cutbacks and changes, company insiders started to see popular fan website columnists as a channel to leak unflattering information about Disney's inner workings. Traditional print news media organizations that usually covered Disney, such as the *Los Angeles Times* and *Orange County Register*, were reluctant to report leaks perceived as unsubstantiated gossip, but fan columnists had less inhibition reporting such disclosures and rumors.[77] The internet afforded amateur fan websites a voice that could compete with professional publications by not necessarily adhering to the ethics and constraints of traditional journalistic reporting. After leaks were published on fan sites, professional news media outlets often picked up the disclosures to become stories for publication. This arrangement between amateur fan columnists and professional journalists created a symbiotic relationship as the former received recognition from traditional media outlets and the latter could publish rumors that would ordinarily not be fit to print.[78]

Disney suffered a repeat of the "Light Tragic" passholder preview fiasco with the opening of Disney's California Adventure (DCA) in 2001 on the former space of the Disneyland parking lot. The company offered preview days to passholders before the new park's official premiere, thus allowing fans once again to post reviews online in advance of opening day. The park was themed as a simulation of California icons and destinations even though visitors were already in the state and thus proximate to the real thing before setting foot in the park. As a former retail executive, Pressler concentrated on merchandising and dining services at the expense of attractions, which were comparatively few, especially for children. Unlike Disneyland, DCA lacked a berm so the nearby hotels, power lines, and Anaheim Convention Center were visible from within the park. The attractions eschewed practically all Disney texts, including Mickey Mouse, in favor of California references and theming. The reviews posted to online boards by passholders were nearly unanimous in scorn and derision of the new park. The special sense of magic that local fans felt with the original Disneyland was not so easy to transfer to another newly produced Disney theme park. John Hench, who was a Disney Legend, Imagineer, Walt Disney confidant, and the official portrait painter of Mickey Mouse, summed up popular sentiment best at a Disney staff preview by famously roasting the new park with the curt declaration: "I liked it better as a parking lot."[79] The word of mouth was so poor that only ten thousand visitors showed up on opening day,[80] even though Pressler and Harriss anticipated DCA would be filled to capacity every day and thus disappoint visitors who would have to settle for the outmoded Disneyland instead.[81] As chief of the resort, Harriss assumed the new park would be so crowded that passholders were blocked out for the first few months after opening day and numerous cast members were shifted from Disneyland to DCA in anticipation of enormous crowds. The shockingly poor attendance at the park became the target of jokes in popular culture as a television episode of *The Simpsons* in 2003 featured Homer suggesting a place to hide with his mother with no one around—Disney's California Adventure. Unlike the disparaged Light Magic parade, the new theme park just across the esplanade from Disneyland could not simply be canceled and replaced with a mothballed but beloved attraction. Opening day ticket prices were set the same as Disneyland, but Disney quickly slashed prices to the new park after dismal initial attendance, and still, visitor numbers did not increase. Surveys indicated only 20 percent of visitors in the first year were satisfied with their park visit.[82] Publicly, Disney CEO Michael Eisner still proclaimed the park a success even with lackluster attendance, revenue, and reviews.

Though regarded by Eisner as a potential future CEO of Disney, Pressler left the company in September 2002 to become CEO of clothing retailer The Gap, Inc. In September 2003, a twenty-two-year-old man died from blunt force trauma on the Big Thunder Mountain Railroad attraction when the rollercoaster derailed due to improper upkeep.[83] Although Pressler had already been gone from the company for a year, some online fans still blamed the former park president's legacy of maintenance cost-cutting for the second death in Disneyland history due to park negligence. Harriss stepped down as Disneyland president in October 2004 to join Pressler at The Gap, Inc. Online fans rejoiced at the end of an era still referred to as the dark times of the Pressler/Harriss years at Disneyland. In October 2004, Matt Ouimet succeeded Harriss as Disneyland president. Ouimet immediately won over fans by ordering an extensive refurbishment of the park in time for Disneyland's fiftieth anniversary celebration in 2005. In addition, the Ouimet family visited the park on weekends and waited in the regular stand-by queues to chat with other visitors. Ouimet revived this practice from Walt Disney who stressed the importance of understanding firsthand the visitor perspective to obtain direct actionable feedback. Walt Disney required other park executives to follow his lead so they would not become remote from the visitor experience at the park they managed. Fans saw Ouimet as a kindred spirit with a sincere attachment to the park, unlike other modern Disney executives for whom Disney historian Jim Korkis says, "the memory of Walt Disney is often considered an impediment to operating the business for the greatest profit."[84] Ouimet's tenure lasted only three years and many fans, including MiceChat's Regan, believe Disney executives were envious of his success and popularity with fans and forced him out.[85]

Roy E. Disney, the son of Disney company cofounder Roy O. Disney and nephew of Walt Disney, had grown increasingly troubled with CEO Eisner's management of the company founded by his family. Eisner forced Roy E. Disney to resign from the company's board of directors, but in a resignation letter dated November 30, 2003, Roy E. Disney addressed seven failures at the company, including, much to the approval of fans, the decline of the theme parks: "3. The timidity of your investments in our theme park business. At Disney's California Adventure, Paris, and now in Hong Kong, you have tried to build parks 'on the cheap' and they show it and the attendance figures reflect it."[86]

After resigning, Roy E. Disney started the Save Disney campaign to oust Eisner and his team. Since institutional shareholders and business executives were unwilling to challenge Eisner directly, Roy E. Disney turned to the internet to gain traction for his campaign by launching a website, SaveDisney.com, that linked to numerous fan websites that, in return, linked back to SaveDisney.com to spread the word and show support (see Figure 3.2).

Since the death of the founders of the Disney company, Walt Disney in 1966 and Roy O. Disney in 1971, Roy E. Disney had become the most public Disney family member still directly involved in the company and the public

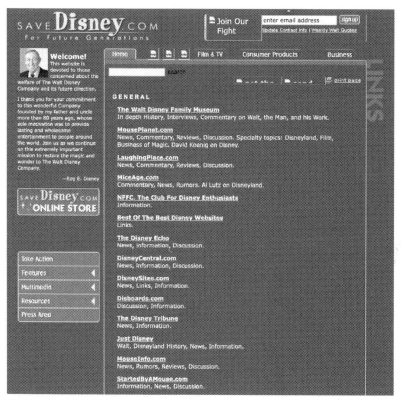

Figure 3.2. Screenshot of February 6, 2005, SaveDisney.com links page. Source: https://web.archive.org/web/20050206103259/http://savedisney.org/links/.

face of the movement. Online fandom on websites and discussion boards rallied to the Save Disney cause by providing a vocal base of supporters. In the book *Disney War* recounting the downfall of Eisner as CEO, Stewart saw the internet-based campaign of SaveDisney.com as "the first dissident shareholders to attempt to use the internet to democratize the notoriously unresponsive system of corporate governance."[87] The internet afforded fans a voice not only to join and support the Save Disney campaign but also to gain recognition for their efforts by a prominent member of the Disney family. On the website Roy E. Disney shared an open letter to shareholders:

> Now is the time for all Disney shareholders to take the first step in bringing needed change. . . . Join us in voting NO on the re-election of Michael Eisner, George Mitchell, Judith Estrin, and John Bryson as directors. . . . By just saying NO you will send a message the Board of

Directors cannot ignore . . . you will force the Board to recognize the widespread conviction that serious changes in both senior management and the Board are necessary.[88]

The next day Eisner was rebuked by 43 percent of shareholders at the annual company meeting. Theme park industry observer Niles reported: "Bolstered by an online echo chamber of support, Roy's message of dissent spread, attracting the attention of stockholders, analysts, fund managers and, eventually, journalists who could no longer ignore the growing dissatisfaction with what the Disney Company was producing."[89]

A little over a year later, in March 2005, Eisner stepped down as CEO. Bob Iger ascended to the top position with the baggage of being Eisner's lieutenant but moved in the first few years to mend fences with fans, investors, and corporate partners with major new investments. In 2007 Lutz scooped traditional media outlets and thrilled fans by reporting on Disney's planned investment of US$1.5 billion for a major overhaul and expansion of DCA. Iger repaired Disney's relationship with Pixar Studios after clashes between Eisner and Steve Jobs almost led to the end of the Disney/Pixar partnership. Iger later completed the purchase of Pixar in 2006, followed by Marvel in 2009, Lucasfilm in 2012, and, finally, 21st Century Fox in 2019.

THE DECLINE OF USENET AND WEB DISCUSSION BOARDS, AND FAN UNITY AND RESISTANCE

During the 1990s, the alt.disney.disneyland newsgroup became the most popular venue for Disneyland fans to congregate and debate since Usenet was freely accessible to all regardless of ISP, ungoverned so no one could get booted from the group, and the text-based content suited ongoing threaded discussion. On a micro level, an individual fan could suddenly feel empowered through connecting and commiserating with many other like-minded fans. On a macro level, Usenet as a platform afforded the creation of an organized collective of individual fans to form a powerful voice to challenge a huge corporation such as Disney in a manner unimaginable before the popular emergence of the internet in the early 1990s. The unity of the fandom on one newsgroup on the Usenet platform enabled fans to organize and resist the Disney company. Over time, Usenet's lack of governance became a fatal flaw as flame wars, commercial spam, and pirated intellectual property inundated the newsgroups, thus triggering ISPs to cut off access and fan migration to web discussion boards during the early 2000s. Three boards emerged as the most popular for Disneyland fans to congregate—MiceChat, MousePlanet, and Laughing Place. Although not united within one venue as before on the newgroup, Disneyland fandom on the web discussion boards still played an important role in the Save Disney campaign that ousted Eisner as CEO in 2005. Some fans kept accounts on more than one board because each site had a somewhat different character and governing style reflective of the site owners and their relationships with members. On the micro level for discussion boards, individual fans could still interact within a huge gathering of fans, but only under the governance and permission of the few fans who owned the boards. On a macro level, unlike the anarchic spirit of Usenet that Disney could never negotiate or tame, web discussion boards were owned by fans with financial constraints that Iger-era Disney would be able to capitalize on to quell fan resistance (as discussed in chapter 6). During this early internet era, fans who procured cultural capital through prolific posting to Usenet and/or ownership of web discussion boards were initially uninterested and then unable to figure out a way to convert their considerable social capital into economic value. The subsequent internet era would see the rise of social media platforms that caused steady declines in traffic and posting to all three popular Disneyland web discussion boards as fans migrated en masse to the new platforms, particularly Facebook. The unity provided by Usenet and web discussion boards that afforded Disneyland fans the ability to organize collective resistance against the Disney company until 2005 faded away with the fragmentation of the fandom due to the nature of the newly popular social media platforms.

However, the unity derived from only one Usenet group and a few discussion boards had other impacts on the fandom. Unity during this era meant the creation of only a limited number of in-park fan-organized social activities. Even though Usenet and web discussion boards were accessible to anyone with an internet connection, many were simply unaware or uninterested in seeking out like-minded fans on the early platforms or attending fan activities in the park. Usenet newsgroups and web discussion boards could be intimidating platforms for newcomers to introduce themselves and join the conversation after observing the insider banter and practices of regular denizens. Due to the ever-looming threat of banishment through the governance of site moderators, the nature of web discussion boards served to normalize fans into a narrow set of social and content restrictions. While the unity of the fandom was pivotal for resisting Disney, the limited number of groups to choose from prevented some fans from finding a congruent social group until the rise of social media platforms in the 2000s, as discussed in the following chapter.

CHAPTER 4

Disneyland Online Fandom, 2006–2020

Fragmentation and Resignation

The unity and resistance of local Disneyland fans observed in the previous chapter manifested in large part due to the nature of early online social platforms up to 2005 and Disney's sluggish development of an online presence and engagement strategy. This chapter examines the evolution of Disneyland online fandom from the start of the rise of social media platforms in 2006 until 2020 when the park shut down in March due to the pandemic (and did not reopen until April 2021). During this fourteen-year period, the online fandom experienced increasing fragmentation across numerous platforms and gradual resignation to a perception of Disney's authority and expertise over park operations. However, the numerous new fan group formations created due to the affordances of the new social media platforms also allowed any fan who previously felt excluded by the limited social options available during the Usenet and web discussion board eras to find or create more personally satisfying new groups, particularly on Facebook. This fragmentation also split by generation. Younger fans were more receptive to park changes by Disney and preferred the visually oriented platforms of Instagram and YouTube used by coeval social media influencers; older fans displeased with Disney's plans for the park could only reluctantly resign themselves to change and migrate to Facebook groups as web discussion boards steadily declined in posting activity. The rise of social media also exerted market pressure on the fan owners of web discussion boards to maintain a high level of cultural capital within the fandom by competing for the views and attention of fans increasingly enamored with the newly emergent platforms and influencers. This chapter looks at an era of

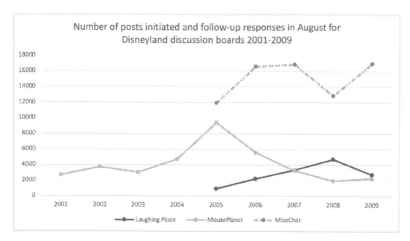

Figure 4.1. Number of posts initiated in August and follow-up responses from 2001 to 2009 for the Disneyland section of the Laughing Place, MousePlanet, and MiceChat web discussion boards.

fragmentation and resignation that occurred in large measure due to the nature and low transaction costs of social media platforms, particularly Facebook.

THE SHIFT AWAY FROM WEB DISCUSSION BOARDS

By 2006, web discussion boards had become a popular type of online social platform for many fandoms. The three major websites with discussion boards primarily devoted to Disneyland were Laughing Place, MousePlanet, and MiceChat. Discussion boards were launched in February 2001 for Laughing Place, July 2001 for MousePlanet, and January 2005 for MiceChat. Todd Regan used social capital accrued from participation in Disneyland newsgroups and forums, involvement in the early years of MousePlanet, and Sunday meets in the park to shift the fan audience from MousePlanet and other forums over to MiceChat's discussion boards after the site launched online in January 2005. MousePlanet's Disneyland forum achieved peak posting activity in 2005 with 9,407 posts in August, but that same month during its initial year of operation, MiceChat surpassed MousePlanet with 11,929 posts (see Figure 4.1). In August 2006, MousePlanet's posting activity dipped by 40 percent compared to the same month in the previous year to 5,603 posts, while MiceChat's increased in the same time frame by 28 percent to 16,594. Unfortunately, Laughing Place suffered a backup server failure in 2004 that irretrievably deleted most board messages posted before that time. By the end of the first decade of the new millennium, Laughing Place and MousePlanet both saw significantly less posting activity compared to MiceChat.

As the number of users quickly grew over the first few years, Regan expanded offline activities beyond Sunday afternoon meets to group trips to Walt Disney World in Florida, Disney cruises, theater shows and musicals, and photography tutorials. Lutz fell chronically ill, so Regan relieved the burden of website maintenance from Lutz by fully incorporating MiceAge within MiceChat by 2008. With Lutz and other MiceAge columnists aboard, MiceChat became the online site for the most popular articles and discussion boards devoted to Disneyland. Although Lutz retired from regular column writing in 2012, the infrequent but highly anticipated MiceChat gossip column disclosing rumors of new Disneyland attractions and developments continued to be branded the MiceAge Update as an homage to Lutz. In February 2013, the MiceChat community presented Lutz with a custom stenciled and designed window pane in the same manner as the ones Imagineers and other Disneyland dignitaries receive on Main Street at Disneyland. The window proclaimed Lutz as "The Main Street Tattler."

Unlike Disney fan website owners without a technology background, as a computer programmer Doobie Moseley enjoyed adding technical features to Laughing Place, such as a custom-built discussion board that allowed users to directly post phone camera photos to threads in an era before the mass diffusion of social media and smartphones. However, Laughing Place's technology-based competitive advantage dissipated as social media platforms such as Facebook and Twitter became widely popular in the late 2000s for any nontechnical fan to develop an online presence and drew audiences away from shared-interest websites. Laughing Place's Disneyland forum saw a 43 percent decrease in posts in August 2009 compared to August 2008. Moseley admits that while Laughing Place was early with discussion boards at the beginning of the decade, the site was late to adopt and adapt to new digital media trends at the end of the decade:

> We've been late to so many games. We started Laughing Place early. I did a good job with discussion boards. We did a lot of things early on. I was right on top of things early on. Somewhere along the way we started using Facebook. Late to Twitter. Late to podcasting and eventually it all caught up to Laughing Place and it became a much smaller place than it was. We're not the first internet site not to see a trend. But we're definitely not one of the first podcasts, we were very late to that game. We were extremely late to putting video on YouTube and that hurt too.[1]

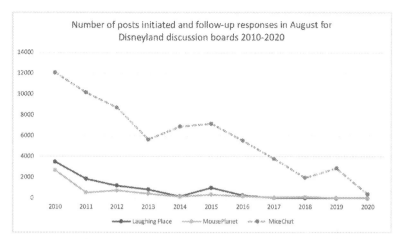

Figure 4.2. Number of posts initiated in August and follow-up responses from 2010 to 2020 for the Disneyland section of the Laughing Place, MousePlanet, and MiceChat web discussion boards.

Not all web discussion boards saw as sudden and steep a decline as did Laughing Place and MousePlanet. MiceChat's boards still enjoyed robust posting numbers at the end of the decade as many fans were just beginning to dabble with the new, at the time, online social media platforms. In Moseley's defense, some older fans were slow not just to adapt to social media but even to adopt any kind of digital media. The Disneyana fan club enlisted Regan to set up a Facebook page for the venerable group that was still relying on a print news-letter to reach all members well into the 2010s.[2] The administrator of the swing dancing Facebook group recalled in the 2000s that one participant would email the monthly schedule of bands to the group's regulars but that some did not even have email accounts so schedules still needed to be printed and distributed by hand.[3] Almost every interview with discussion board owners and event organizers from the 1990 to 2009 era mentioned being "old" when conversation turned to the challenge of adapting to the emergence of social media during that period. As Moseley conceded in 2017, "we're not using them (social media) as well as we should be, and we would still like to be a major Disney website, but it's not going to be me because I'm just old."[4] Being able to adopt and adapt to the new online social media platforms also opened a generational divide within the fandom as discussed later in this chapter.

By the end of the 2000s, social media had become increasingly popular, especially with younger fans, and by the early 2010s, the adoption of social media platforms at a mass level effected the displacement of web discussion boards as the primary online outlet for fan interaction. Figure 4.2 illustrates the decline in posts for the discussion boards of all three major Disneyland fan websites over the course of the 2010s.

Laughing Place experienced a 99 percent drop in Disneyland posts over the decade as the board became moribund from 2016 onward. In an early 2018 site redesign, Laughing Place removed the link to the discussion boards on the home page's primary navigation bar. Instead, the link was relegated to the final item of a third column submenu within a drop-down menu subsection called More Disney (see Figure 4.3). The Disneyland submenu did not even contain a link to the boards. One member in a February 22, 2018, post wondered of the site administrators, "before they pull the plug, I hope they at least say . . . bye." Laughing Place co-owner Moseley assured the few remaining stalwarts in a March 2, 2018, post that the discussion boards were not going anywhere and a more prominent link to the boards was under consideration. However, as of early 2024, that link did not materialize, and, instead, the discussion boards were organizationally relegated on the website to a subdomain labeled "old" (http://www-old.laughingplace.com/discussion/) and displayed as unavailable due to a server error. Laughing Place by 2013 was no longer a full-time job for Moseley, who considers the site, outside of marriage and having a child, to be his greatest life experience.[5] MousePlanet has consistently featured a link to its Forum (along with Articles, Walt Disney World Guide, and Disneyland Guide) in the site's primary navigation bar, but posts to the Disneyland board still dropped 99 percent between 2010 and the end of the decade. MiceChat's forums link has also consistently remained in the site's primary navigation bar, but the Disneyland board suffered a steep 84 percent drop in posts between 2010 and 2018, rebounding a bit in 2019 to a 77 percent drop from 2010 due primarily to heightened fan interest and discussion of the then new Galaxy's Edge land that opened in July 2019. In the initial year of the pandemic in 2020, posts to the MiceChat Disneyland forum fell 97 percent from 2010 levels. The steady year-on-year trend throughout the 2010s was the displacement of fan activity from website discussion boards to social media platforms.

As a website and forum dedicated to connecting disparate fans with a common shared interest, MiceChat's Regan was caught off guard by the rapid rise in popularity of social media and its focus on preexisting personal networks:

> I didn't really understand it immediately. It seemed like something that young people were doing and it seemed like something that was counterintuitive to what we were trying to accomplish because we really wanted people to post trip reports and have Disney community. And Facebook was the opposite of that because you really are only communicating

Figure 4.3. Laughing Place home page with drop-down submenu navigation to the discussion boards link. Screenshot taken on June 17, 2018.

with your friends and family and we are the antithesis of that. We're putting people in touch with other fans, whether you know them or not.[6]

After getting a better handle on the upstart social media platforms, Regan saw success drawing a sizable audience to the MiceChat accounts on Facebook and Twitter, but did not find as much traction parlaying his long-standing cultural and social capital among Disneyland fans into large numbers of followers and subscribers on platforms such as Instagram and YouTube where the allure is visual, not textual. Table 4.1 comparatively illustrates a snapshot of this divide in the subscriber and follower standings for Disneyland fan websites, influencers, and events at the close of the decade in March 2019, just a year before the pandemic shut down the park in March 2020.

RISE OF THE DISNEYLAND INFLUENCERS

The social media stars of 2010s Disneyland fandom, such as Leo Camacho, Sarah Sterling, Patrick Dougall, Tiffany Mink, and Francis Dominic, were all under-thirty-year-old millennial and Gen Z personages, while Regan and Moseley were middle-aged members of Gen X. Although Regan adapted MiceChat for the new platforms, most of the under-thirty fans I

Table 4.1

Number of subscribers or followers on social media platforms for Disneyland fan websites, influencers, and events, as well as the official Disneyland and D23 accounts in March 2019.

	Facebook (group)	Instagram	YouTube	Twitter	Other
Laughing Place	10,560	2,467	hidden	24,400	--
MousePlanet	25,126	10,700	2,506	44,400	--
MiceChat	66,875	12,200	7,273	55,100	reddit (119)
Sarah Sterling	21,078	79,800	78,202	17,400	--
Leo Camacho	18,762	123,000	40,180	18,700	--
Francis Dominic	*	76,400	6,223	15,500	--
Gay Days Anaheim	50,218	3,662	5**	2,755	--
Bats Day	10,496	4,350	--	3,262	--
Galliday	4,760	609	14	461	Tumblr
Lolita Day	3,108	963	--	--	--
Steam Day	1,167	--	--	--	Flickr (325)
Disneyland (official)	17 million	7.2 million	71,374	1.34 million	Tumblr Pinterest (54,401)
D23 (official Disney fan club)	817,910	802,000	54,673	495,000	--

* Private personal page only

** Inactive since 2010

spoke with during my fieldwork in 2017 and 2018 had only vaguely heard of MiceChat, if at all. With the proliferation of so many Disneyland fan groups enabled by Facebook and other social media platforms, MiceChat was no longer one of only a few rarefied groups for fans to congregate and instead became merely one among a multitude vying for the attention of millennials and Gen Z fans online and in the park.

To launch and maintain a website has always required a fair amount of money and know-how to obtain and manage the domain name, hosting service, and underlying technology. For MiceChat, the hosting service alone can cost US$2,000 per month due to security needs from being a frequent target of distributed denial of service (DDOS) attacks after then video columnist Sarah Sterling became involved in Gamergate in 2014.[6] Although Sterling only posted views about Gamergate on personal social media accounts, any Google search at the time quickly revealed Sterling's work as a video columnist for MiceChat, so the site was hit by DDOS attacks as a much easier target to take down than corporate-owned social media platforms with high-level security systems. To start and maintain a social media presence requires little technical knowledge and costs nothing for the usernames, hosting, security, and technology provided by the platforms. Since the transaction costs, not only in terms of money but also time, effort, and attention, to form new groups collapsed, young fans, including social media influencers, were able to compete and siphon off audiences from established fan websites.

Disney also created official social media accounts for Disneyland to connect directly with fans and easily surpassed the number of subscribers and followers of fan websites, influencers, and events. The YouTube account of influencer Sarah Sterling was the sole exception, with more subscribers than the official Disneyland channel in 2019 (though the official Disney Parks account, which covers all global Disney theme parks, had more than ten times the subscribers of Sterling). The older fan websites saw more success reaching fans, on Facebook looking for information and discussion and on Twitter to disseminate news. Influencers primarily reached fans through YouTube and Instagram. Event organizers (discussed in detail in the next chapter) mainly reached participants using Facebook. Influencers used social media platforms as the most effective means to establish and display cultural capital while building social capital with young followers just as Regan and Moseley from the previous internet era had used, in a similar manner, web discussion boards as the most effective online platform. Emerging in a new internet era allowed influencers to brand themselves by choosing the most effective new platform(s) of the day, while older fans who started websites with discussion boards were stuck with an expensive and technologically cumbersome platform from an earlier internet era. When some fans over thirty years old were asked whether being a social media influencer would be of interest, they reported feeling too old for that young person's game, but if they suddenly found themselves twenty years old again they would love to give it a try. The time of having a very limited choice of online venues for fan discussion ended with the advent of a new internet era with a multitude of choice among hundreds of online fan groups. This shift affected not only fans interacting with each other but also interaction between Disney and fans.

Anyone, though primarily young people, could take advantage of the low transaction costs of social media platforms to create accounts and try

Figure 4.4. Thingamavlogs members, from left, Camacho, Mink, Sterling, and Dougall, Twitter account with October 5, 2017, farewell post. Screenshot taken on June 17, 2018.

to build an audience. Some, such as Sarah Sterling, posted YouTube video content in conjunction with fan websites such as MiceChat before striking out on their own after gaining exposure to the longstanding site's audience.[8] Sterling originally focused on Harry Potter fans but there already existed a large crowd of content creators for the J. K. Rowling oeuvre. So, instead, Sterling built cultural capital within the then underserved content niche of being a Disneyland cast member, as well as offering pro tips and advice for visiting Disneyland, and then, notably, for Disneybounding, after the practice was originated by Leslie Kay in 2012. Disneybounding provided a good reason to turn the camera on oneself to showcase one's Disney-inspired style rather than the park's attractions, and was particularly suited for the visual orientation of Instagram and YouTube. Unlike the substantial costuming of cosplay that can sublimate or conceal personal identity, Disneybounding does not obscure one's identity and is thus better suited for influencers aiming to foreground themselves. The practice also afforded a reason to create content in locales outside of Disneyland, such as at the mall to shop and assemble an outfit or at home to try on different ensembles. A *Wired* magazine article in 2014 saw dressing up as a favorite character at work such as Disneybounding as a form of "stealth cosplay."[9] Young influencers banded together to form content creation groups such as Thingamavlogs, which included Leo Camacho, Tiffany Mink, Sarah Sterling, and Patrick Dougall (see Figure 4.4). Their YouTube channel chronicled the Disney adventures of four young fans in a manner somewhat reminiscent of the classic television sitcom *Friends*. Thingamavlogs disbanded in October 2017, even though the channel had nearly 100,000 YouTube subscribers at the time, so the four members could concentrate on their individual channels and careers while still at times getting together for collaborations.

Another popular influencer occasionally appearing with the former Thingamavlogs members was Francis Dominic, who built cultural capital on Instagram by chronicling the experience of being an intern in the Disney College Program. Dominic's popularity continued to grow even after finishing the program. Social media content creators became influential as tastemakers for fashion, photography, and dining at Disneyland, particularly with young fans. Sterling was known for Disneybounding and commentary, Camacho for Disneybounding and cosplay, and style was a signature for Dominic, who even started a clothing line. Other influencers concentrated on the park's food and drinks, such as the YouTube vloggers Magic Journeys. After first noticing the online influencer trend with blogs focused on Disney, family, and travel, the company in 2010 initiated an engagement strategy with its first weeklong Disney Social Media Moms Celebration with behind-the-scenes parks access and special events. The event was not free as attendees still needed to pay a discounted fee, but an invite was considered quite coveted among fans blogging and posting about Disney.[10] In 2019, the name of the event was given an inclusive updating to Disney Creators Celebration along with requirements by the company that attendees post about the event beforehand, during the event, and after returning home.[11] Being an online fan influencer for the Southern California theme parks became so popular and widespread that a fan-organized conference focused solely on the topic was held for the first time at the Knott's Berry Farm resort hotel in March 2019.[12] Sessions included tips on photography, writing, monetization strategies, and getting noticed by theme park and hotel operators. In 2017, the short-lived company Disflix was started by a few Disney influencers to instruct new fans, for a fee, in building and making money through their social media accounts—but quickly was met with criticism by many fans for overtly and explicitly monetizing and selling the cultural capital of popular influencers. The site shut down before even launching and the term "Disflix" and hashtag #disflix came to represent failure, inauthenticity, and avarice to Disney fans.[13] By the early 2010s and continuing through the decade, the influencer phenomenon took hold and changed the relationship not only among Disney and fans but also fans with each other.

Young aspiring influencers were not the only ones to take advantage of the low transaction costs, as any fan now had a free and easy way to reach an enormous potential audience on social media platforms. And anyone who felt out of place or had interests dissimilar from those of meet-up participants of established groups such as MiceChat could form their own new Facebook groups to connect with suitably like-minded fans. One founder of a social club recalled attending a couple of MiceChat meets in the late 2000s but not clicking socially with the other meet members, so the fan was elated when the concept of Disneyland social clubs became popular in the early 2010s on Facebook groups by allowing the fan to find a small special group of people to hang out with at the park.[14] As Mike Marquez, the coordinator of many small-scale Disneyland fan events, remarked: "Disneyland is the happiest place on earth. The Disneyland social community is not the happiest place on earth . . . so many different types of people."[15]

Disneyland fandom is not unusual in this regard. Jenkins notes that fan communities are often rife with feuds, divisions, and personality conflicts.[16] Young fans in particular started to find each other on Instagram and YouTube instead of Facebook and the older discussion boards. Disney under CEO Bob Iger also led a broadening and expansion of overall Disney fandom as the company acquired popular intellectual properties such as Marvel in 2009 and Lucasfilm in 2012, which were then incorporated into Disneyland as lands, attractions, merchandise, and meet and greets, and by fans through Disneybounding.

Fragmentation of the Fandom Due to Social Media Platforms, Mostly Facebook

"And then Facebook killed us off," Moseley concluded after contemplating the evaporation of the Laughing Place web discussion board community.[17] Before social media platforms there were a limited number of active web discussion boards to talk about Disneyland online. Just as in Usenet newsgroups, debates on the boards could get heated and turn into flame wars, but the boards retained moderators to ban the unruly and delete divisive posts. Unlike unmoderated Usenet newsgroups, a user banned by a moderator from a web discussion board was essentially exiled from that online fan community. Regan referred to the spiral of invective posts leading to banishment as a YAGE—"yet another grand exit."[18] Moseley observed that some fans could not abide the negativity of the web boards, so the establishment of Facebook provided a way to associate only with existing friends and avoid heated debates with strangers. Many fans enjoyed self-selecting socially into smaller Facebook groups that provided environments more conducive to convergent thinking; members could agree on a point of view and interact more closely with better conversational environs because the social density was easier to support.[19] Just as Meyrowitz saw electronic media leading the individual to subdivide into narrower groupings, the affordances of social media platforms accelerated the fragmentation of online groups into ever finer distinctions.[20] The social media platforms also lowered the discovery cost for anyone looking to join a like-minded group; as Fraade-Blanar and Glazer noted, "a few clicks of a mouse can inform anyone, anywhere, about membership opportunities at any time, instead of relying on word of mouth or traditional advertising campaigns."[21] As Moseley explained: "And so people who initially come to the website to talk Disney and have friends, over time realized I don't want to argue about Pirates of the Caribbean (the ride) one more time. I just want to get in touch with my friends. Well, it's much easier to keep in touch with my friends on Facebook than on our discussion boards. That was the natural evolution of things."[22]

Community was the second most popular board section, after Disneyland, on Laughing Place, but Facebook was an easier platform to keep in touch with all one's friends and groups in one free, convenient, and easy-to-use website and app. In addition, people grew weary of registering and logging in on numerous web discussion boards to leave comments to strangers and instead preferred to do so on a very limited number of social media platforms with people they already knew.[23] Korda experimented with boards on the Bats Day website (http://www.batsday.net) and then Yahoo! Groups without seeing much traction with either in the early 2000s. However, Korda saw immediate success with MySpace and then even more so with Facebook, which became the dominant way of interacting with fans as the event website logged less traffic every year.[24] For the five fan-organized events analyzed in Table 4.1 above, the number of members in event Facebook groups was considerably more than their corresponding Instagram, YouTube, and Twitter presences. None used YouTube extensively, if at all, two did not use Twitter, and one did not even use Instagram (opting for Flickr instead). According to this study's survey respondents, 75 percent named Facebook their favorite online platform for connecting with other fans in the late 2010s (see Figure 4.5). Whereas Bury et al. reported media fandoms in the early 2010s as reluctant to use Facebook due to privacy concerns and not being perceived as a "fannish space,"[25] Facebook by the late 2010s for Disneyland fans was seen as the primary online social platform to connect with the fandom. Facebook was most popular because respondents said the platform was easy to use, convenient, nearly universally adopted, and the only social media platform some friends used. The structure of relational dynamics on Facebook also promoted symmetrical relationships between fans as "friends" rather than asymmetrical relationships, often with celebrities and other public figures, as "followers" or "subscribers" on Twitter, Instagram, and YouTube.[26]

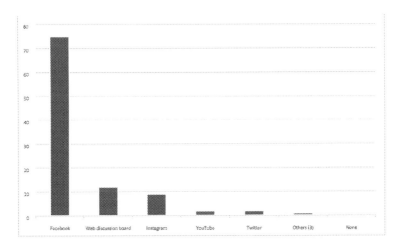

Figure 4.5. Favorite platform to connect online in the late 2010s with other Disneyland fans (n=637).

When asked in the survey to indicate the online platforms local fans had ever used to interact with other Disneyland fans, 92 percent named Facebook, followed by Instagram with 51 percent, and web-based discussion boards at 50 percent (see Figure 4.6). A majority of surveyed fans also named Facebook as the first online platform used to connect with other Disneyland enthusiasts (see Figure 4.7). During the 2010s, web discussion boards faded away as almost everyone joined Facebook to discover they could create and/or join a multitude of Disneyland groups suited to their particular social needs and desires.

Mike Marquez credited the organizers of early events such as Bats Day for paving the way for the creation of so many new events in the park.[27] Soon after discovering Facebook groups, Marquez created the "Unofficial Disneyland Events and Gatherings" group to promote fan events in Disneyland. With over 3,000 followers by the late 2010s, some members hailed from around the world but Marquez believed most were local passholders.[28] Marquez has witnessed fans start all kinds of Disneyland Facebook groups including "family-friendly groups, parent groups, teenage groups, you have dark groups, you have 18 and over groups, you have dirty Disney groups, if you have any type of group you can think of and Disney from bad to good, it's there."[29] Almost anything associated with Disneyland has a dedicated Facebook group or even multiple groups.

At first, Regan thought Facebook would be similar to Friendster and MySpace by burning brightly for a brief period and then fading away.[30] However, as Facebook kept growing in popularity, Regan noticed that community-based discussions about dinner plans, weekend outings, crafts, and so on started to disappear from the MiceChat forums. In an attempt to

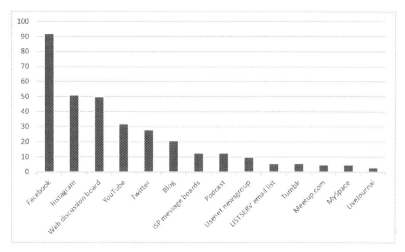

Figure 4.6. Online platforms ever used to connect with Disneyland fans (n=637).

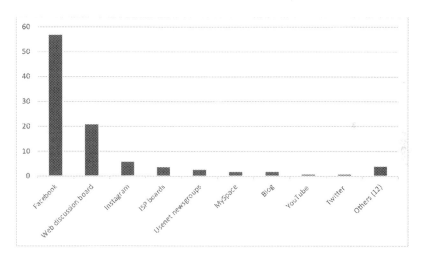

Figure 4.7. First online platform used to connect with other Disneyland fans (n=637).

appeal to the MiceChat members migrating to Facebook, as well as attract new fans, Regan created not just one catch-all MiceChat group but several MiceChat umbrella groups on Facebook to cover a variety of interests such as Sunday meets, Gumball Rally, Mice Trips, news, and fan discussions. Regan tried to fashion Facebook into a marketing funnel by placing article teasers on MiceChat Facebook groups with concomitant links back to the full content on the MiceChat website. Facebook became the number one driver of traffic to the MiceChat website, followed by Google searches and then

Twitter, although 50 percent of visitors still arrived directly from the address bar or bookmarks.[31] When MiceChat was solely a website, the audience was all in one place on the site, but the proliferation of social media platforms dispersed fans to such an extent that some were not even aware of the original website and only knew of MiceChat through its Twitter, Facebook, or podcasting presence.[32] Compared to the in-depth and protracted conversations on website boards, Regan lamented Facebook's discussion system for not indexing and displaying in a manner conducive to extended interaction and instead encouraging people to ask the same questions repeatedly because the platform's search functionality was so cumbersome and inefficient.[33] Bury et al. noted in 2013 that Facebook functioned more akin to a mailing list with updates than a forum with engaging social discussion.[34] Unlike posts on Usenet newsgroups and web discussion boards composed within spacious text boxes encouraging multi-paragraph responses to new thread topics, replies to Facebook group topic posts use the structural contours of thought bubbles that discourage long-form feedback in favor of brief retorts consisting only of a few words, emojis, or an animated GIF. In a 2016 podcast interview, Rheingold, who coined the term *virtual community*, criticized Facebook groups as being so disorganized that the platform degraded even the concept of a forum and speculated that a business reason must have been responsible for the muddled group threading because those issues had already been resolved with online forums such as discussion boards a long time ago.[35] In-depth, persistent user discussion within a topic thread does not provide economic value to Facebook, so the platform structurally strives to discourage users from focusing on a particular thread in favor of encouraging users to continually scroll through their timeline filled with the periodic posts of sponsored advertising that generate huge revenue for the company.

Regan believes the overnight success MiceChat had in 2005 would be nearly impossible to replicate in the social media era of the 2010s due to the difficulty of standing out with so many Disneyland fan groups and accounts spread across so many platforms and more constantly emerging. Holding first-mover status was advantageous, though other sites among the first, such as Laughing Place and MousePlanet, were unable to keep up as well in the 2010s with all the new fan groups on social media platforms. Regan wondered if only reaching a few hundred views, followers, or subscribers was worthwhile to the fans who started new groups, and though some folded after only a short while, many persisted in the hopes of catching fire with fans or simply derived satisfaction from sharing their passion regardless of low traffic and little chance of financial remuneration. In the end, for fans who used to feel ill-suited in outlook, interests, or relations within the limited ecosystem of online fan venues in the Usenet and web discussion board era, the affordances of social media platforms such as Facebook to create and/ or join a multitude of groups was a great personal benefit and opportunity.

Market Pressures

Moseley fondly recalled the days before social media of going to a park event, returning home, doing a write-up with photos, posting the report on the Laughing Place website, placing a link on the newsgroup alt.disney.disneyland, and then thousands of fans clicking through to read the article the following day.[36] In the 2010s, waiting until returning home from a park event to write and post a report would have been way too late when almost anyone could not only post but broadcast live from the park using Facebook, Periscope, and YouTube. And with so many fans getting involved in content creation, standing out from the crowd became much more challenging. Some individuals and groups visited the park almost every day to make videos for tens of thousands, hundreds, or just dozens of views. When Pirate's Lair on Tom Sawyer's Island reopened in June 2017 after being closed for over a year due to nearby construction on Galaxy's Edge, the first rafts of the morning from Frontierland to the island were full of YouTube vloggers, Instagram influencers, and fan website staff making social media posts and doing live video reports. Their "big" collective discovery was nothing had actually changed on the island during the long closure. Conceivably, almost every nook and cranny of Disneyland could be viewable online at the same time via fan livestreaming. Moseley wondered, "where are we going to differentiate, and can we actually make money at this, in this point in life with all the competition?"[37] Many fans created and posted content from their day-to-day Disneyland trips without any expectation of economic reward, and thus created a challenging environment for anyone trying to make money from content creation alone.[38] On the other hand, the restrictive ecosystem of the previous era's web discussion boards had meant fewer voices could reach fans. With social media platforms enabling almost any individual or group to post photos and videos online, fans could finally choose from a plentiful array of perspectives.

Since Facebook afforded the creation of so many new groups catering to Disneyland fans, event organizers had to choose judiciously which groups to include to promote their events because Facebook would suspend user accounts that posted essentially the same message to many groups within a twenty-four-hour period. Marquez's personal Facebook page was suspended for seven days after posting an event promotion to more than five groups in one day.[39] While organizers generally needed to market their events widely to reach and persuade enough fans to participate, they also ran the risk of Facebook flagging and suspending their accounts as spam. Since organizers in the 2010s were quite dependent on Facebook for fans to discover events, groups, and clubs, competition among organizers for followers and shares on the platform became quite keen. One way to stand out from the pack was through paid promotion, which Facebook instituted in 2012, but Disneyland fan events and clubs make little, if any, money even if able to attract many new participants. While paid promotion could potentially increase exposure and prestige in some cases, interviewees either reported never using the tactic or found the results lackluster.[40]

Regan tried to redirect traffic from MiceChat's Facebook groups to the Mice-Chat website to generate advertising revenue. In an ideal online milieu, Regan felt, advertisements on Facebook groups should generate a percentage of money for group administrators (similar to YouTube's payments to channel owners) because the creators developed and posted the content that drove visitors to regularly use Facebook.[41] In addition, Regan was also chagrined at fans who enjoyed the MiceChat website's curated content for "free" while using ad blocker extensions on web browsers that denied the website revenue from advertising impressions.[42] MiceChat's popular Monday morning (California time) Disneyland Update is only available on the website but is promoted with backlinks across all MiceChat social media accounts. Regan faces deadline pressure on Sunday nights to post the Monday update by sunrise; otherwise, visitors check the site, do not see an update, and fail to return assuming no update will be posted at all.[43] Regan works on MiceChat approximately fifty hours per week hoping to break even financially to pay the monthly hosting service bill and other associated costs while also working other professional jobs.[44]

The social media influencers of the 2010s also derived relatively little economic value from the online platforms used to present content, though they did not need to pay the platforms any money to upload, display, and store content unlike the web discussion board owners. The long-term influencer goal has been to use their cultural capital to steadily build the social capital of a large, engaged (measured by views, likes, shares, and comments) audience in order to impress Disney and form a partnership or get a full-time position with the company.[45] Disneyland influencers generally focus on evergreen content, such as videos on how to do the most rides in a day, finding the "secret" bathroom locations, or great photo spots, which can be relevant to fans for years of ever-accumulating views, unlike the weekly park news–style updates of MiceChat, MousePlanet, and Laughing Place that become outdated shortly after being posted. Regan contends a key operational difference between Gen Xers and young social media influencers is that Gen X content creators have focused their lens primarily on the park itself, while the young influencer lens has focused mostly on themselves with the park as a backdrop.[46] Resonating with Soto-Vásquez's finding that the platform affordances of YouTube and TikTok could produce respective outward and inward gazes among fan vloggers at Shanghai Disneyland, a generational divide at Disneyland in California manifested in the outward gaze of Gen X creators with disembodied ride-throughs and informational observations while millennial and Gen Z creators gazed inward to focus on their personal park experiences.[47] The young social media influencers have performed primarily to an under-thirty-year-old audience who want to see more than pretty pictures of the park and rather prefer the story-driven personal posts of coeval influencers.[48] Younger fans valorize personal storytelling more than older generations, particularly through sharing live experiences online.[49] MiceChat has attempted to appeal to the broad range of age groups with a "full buffet" of park news and information[50] but has continued to attract a comparatively older audience as part of the generational divide among Disneyland fans.

Fragmentation of the Fandom Due to Generational Divide

While in this book I find similarly with Bury et al. that older members of fandoms tend to stick with early online social media platforms due to the established, secure nature of the spaces created in those technologies, I further observe a generational divide and antagonism in uses and practices among the different platforms.[51] A new generation of Disneyland fans came of age with social media in the late 2000s and used the revolutionary platforms to connect with each other by spotlighting themselves at the park. By contrast, older fans customarily connected by foregrounding the park rather than themselves. A prominent Disneyland social media influencer recalled joining the MiceChat discussion board as a young teenager new to Disneyland online fandom but feeling out of place with the seemingly older crowd.[52] Instagram and YouTube felt more comfortable because "you can see who you're talking to and relate to them in a different way than you would on kind of an anonymous message board."[53] The influencer also pointed out that Disney prefers to work with influencers through Instagram and YouTube as primarily visual platforms and not through text-laden fan websites and discussion boards. The influencer's public Facebook page was not used as much to connect with fans because Instagram and YouTube were more useful for sharing new content, connecting with new people, and growing an audience primarily composed of young people who hoped to work for Disney someday.[54] This trade-off between young fan influencers and companies with unpaid work for experience, exposure, and potential employment has been termed "hope labor" and "aspirational labor."[55] In addition, young people were more attracted to Instagram and YouTube as primarily visual and youth-oriented platforms as opposed to the text-based posts of the older audience on Facebook. The social media influencer felt older Disneyland fans hold

> . . . a general disdain for a younger, burgeoning group of Disney fans who like things that they don't like. I feel like fewer young fans coming into the fandom are like quote unquote purists like a lot of older fans are and they like things like Paint the Night and they don't like Main Street Electrical Parade and they love Guardians of the Galaxy and they don't like Hollywood Tower of Terror, and all of these kind of hard hitting and closed topics in the Disney fandom. And I found that I feel like a lot of these older fans feel I represent the younger demographic.[56]

Main Street Electrical Parade, which debuted in 1972, was replaced by a new nighttime parade called Paint the Night in 2015, and the Hollywood Tower of Terror, based on *The Twilight Zone* television show that debuted in 1959, was reskinned in 2017 as a Guardians of the Galaxy attraction based on the popular Marvel films. On Twitter, where the younger and older generations cross digital paths, young social media influencers sometimes attracted the opprobrium of older fans for being perceived as self-centered.[57] Dis-Twitter and the #distwitter hashtag were used to signify the intense and opinionated tide of Disney fandom on Twitter that frequently divided along the lines of older traditionalists versus younger Disneyphiles.[58]

Fan blogger Tom Bricker sees a division at opposite ends of the Disney fandom spectrum between Pixiedusters who love everything Disney uncritically versus Doom & Gloomers who question and critique everything Disney has done since 1996.[59] During fieldwork and interviews, Pixiedusters were observed as more likely to comprise younger fans while Doom & Gloomers tended to be older fans. Regan took a cyclical view that Disney fans were uncritically idealistic when young but developed a sharper critical eye after getting older.[60] Some younger fans on discussion boards and during fieldwork appealed to the authority of Disney and Imagineering as the foremost experts at creating great theme park experiences and therefore should be trusted to make changes without vocal fan skepticism and griping. Another popular young influencer, who enjoyed using Twitter to communicate with and about brands and Instagram to pose and have fun, felt that

Figure 4.8. Instagram post of Leo Camacho (@mrleozombie) with, from left, Camacho and Sterling in front of the blue wall at DCA. Screenshot taken on June 17, 2018.

A lot of the older fans think we don't know anything. They're very enti-tled. I mean they have every right to be here, they've loved Disneyland for so long. But I definitely think that there are some people who are very opinionated and put people on Instagram down or definitely put people down who are on YouTube . . . but people forget we're just happy to be here to share all these things. And then all these older generation people are just looking at everything in a negative perspec-tive. And always tying in that Walt wouldn't want this and would never want that. I'm like just enjoy it, you're still going to pay. You're still gonna go to these events. You're still going to do all these things that Disney offers, that complaining about is just going to waste energy.[61]

By turning the camera on themselves with the park as a backdrop, influ-encers built cultural capital by promoting themselves as a new personal brand constructed within the Disneyland milieu. In addition, Instagram posts by influencers could demonstrate flattering and creative poses and frames for young followers to set up their own selfies throughout the park. By simply pointing their camera, influencers could make an obscure Disney-park backdrop become Instagram famous with followers subsequently mim-icking the shot, such as the blue wall at DCA (see Figure 4.8). Amon sees Disneyland visitor social media posts as a performance and expression of park identity to audiences outside the park and free of the participation

Figure 4.9. Instagram post of Francis Dominic (@francisdominiic) in front of the Minnie Mouse wall in Toontown, Disneyland. Screenshot taken on July 9, 2018.

restrictions and canned engagement activities set by Disney at staged shows such as at the Royal Theater in Fantasyland.[62] Each social media like, share, and comment to a post validates the performance "just as the applause of an audience at the end of a show signals approval."[63] Korda lamented the exacting construction undertaken by younger Bats Day participants for stylish self-presentation on social media to the exclusion of the music, art, and history of the goth subculture.[64] On the other hand, older fans are considered by younger fans to not be particularly adept at Disneybounding, which also serves a social function for young park visitors who observe and try to guess bounds by approaching other bounders to ask and start a conversation.[65] To make this fan game even more challenging, Disneybounders often prefer to bound as secondary or tertiary characters from Disney films, such as Hermes from *Hercules* or Twitch from *Toy Story 3*, so accurate recognition reveals an inquirer as a most perceptive and erudite Disney fan.

While Disneyland has always been a remediated environment comprising the company's films, television, and music,[66] the park became mediated again through personal digital technology that obscured the original mediation.[67] At first, Disneyland managers could not understand why a blue wall in an indistinct corner of DCA could become so popular on Instagram but eventually stationed a PhotoPass cast member (official Disney park photographer) at the location to help visitors take their shots and profit from sales of the photos.[68] The Instagram account @bluewallpics had over ten thousand followers by 2019. In July 2018, Disney purposely refashioned a park wall to be Instagram-worthy by repainting the large drab green double doors next to Minnie Mouse's Toontown cottage into bright red with white polka dots. Soon after, influencer Francis Dominic posted a photo to Instagram in front of the new wall (see Figure 4.9). The Disney Parks Blog even published an article titled "9 'Walls' Disney Parks Super Fans Deem Instagram Worthy" to suggest wall locations to fans with ready PhotoPass photographers.[69] Whether Disney's deliberate production of Instagram-worthy walls could ever be as popular as the ones organically chosen by fan influencers is doubtful. Setting up selfies at Disneyland for Instagram enables a fan to curate and make meaning through what Lobo sees as "narratively organizing one's experience of the world" and "performing a narrativized identity."[70] The coconstruction of selfies with fan influencers who seemingly set up shot locations independently fosters a greater impression of authenticity and relatability than taking one's image cue directly from a canned corporate setup. And there are a few wall photo spots at the resort that Disney would presumably never promote or station a PhotoPass photographer such as the bathrooms at Trader Sam's Enchanted Tiki Bar adjacent to the Disneyland Hotel, where some fans enjoy taking mirror selfies against the backdrop of the 1970s abstract tiki wallpaper originally designed by legendary Disney artist Mary Blair.

For MiceChat to remain relevant in the social media era, Regan aimed to appeal to younger fans by not only posting regularly to Instagram and YouTube but also adapting his media persona and presentation. Before 2015, almost all MiceChat photos and videos showcased the park with Regan rarely seen on camera. At the MiceChat Sunday meets, new participants often only knew Regan by his online handle, Dusty Sage, and were unaware of his physical appearance, while young influencers used their real names to become park celebrities that young visitors sought out to approach for selfies.[71] Although critical of the reality show aspect of cattiness and feuding sometimes found within social media influencer circles, Regan began in 2015 to somewhat reluctantly post occasional personal photos on the MiceChat Instagram account interacting with costumed characters, trying new park food and beverages, and posing in front of attractions. Regan also shot personal on-camera intros and outros for YouTube park walkabout videos and recruited younger contributors to handle some of MiceChat's photography and social media duties. Regan admitted trying to put the "millennial lens" on MiceChat content,[72] though attracting millennials and Gen Z into the older-skewing MiceChat fan base would be difficult. If Regan changed MiceChat's style, content, and delivery too drastically, there was a risk of upsetting the older fans who comprise the longtime foundation of the MiceChat audience. The acknowledgment of cultural capital among Disneyland fans became predicated by generational affiliation. A MiceChatter in her early thirties, who was looked upon suspiciously and rebuffed at the first few Sunday meets in the mid-2010s as a young newcomer by older members, contended older Disneyland fans "just don't like change."[73] Understanding the importance of inclusivity with a new, younger member in order to attract other young adults, Regan looked after and encouraged the newcomer to keep attending until receiving eventual acceptance from older members.[74] Another thirty-something fan faced a difficult choice on Sundays choosing between the MiceChat assemblage and groups with younger members. As an older group, MiceChatters sometimes enjoyed alcoholic beverages at the park but usually disbanded in the afternoon after enjoying only a ride or two together. Groups with younger members could not consume alcohol legally but usually spent the entire day and night enjoying the park.[75] There were so many social events, clubs, and meets, especially on Sundays, that anyone could self-select into a specific group but not always one spanning the divide between generations.

Fan Discontent with the Direction of Disneyland

The perspective of octogenarian Disney Legend and retired Imagineer Bob Gurr was echoed by fans unhappy with the direction of the park: "I'm sad to see Disneyland change so it's no longer Walt's park."[76] This frustration was shared by one longtime fan who visited the park almost every day: "I'd love to have lunch with Walt Disney. He's my hero. The way Walt wanted this park to be and the way with his attention to detail and his whole vision for this and how it's just wrong (now) just amazes me."[77]

Gurr heard from fans at events and conventions that the acquisitions made during the tenure of CEO Bob Iger of Pixar, Lucasfilm, and Marvel, and their concomitant expanding roles in the parks, diluted the trademark Disney feel of Disneyland and the Disney company. Walt Disney and the original Imagineers, including Gurr, designed Disneyland to be a "happy place" in the famous words of the park's 1955 dedication speech. However, for the Star Wars land called Galaxy's Edge that opened in 2019, Gurr felt, based on the models and illustrations, "everything is true to *Star Wars*, but it's kind of a morose-looking place."[78] In the mid-1960s, Walt Disney directed Imagineering not to make the exterior of the Haunted Mansion appear ramshackle from the outside but pristine to match the rest of the spotless park. The setting of Galaxy's Edge, a rundown spaceport replete with smugglers, stormtroopers, and rebel spies clashing between weather-beaten, blaster-strafed, rusted buildings, does not recall Disney's trademark architecture of reassurance that made Disneyland a sunny Edenic place of attachment for many Southern Californians. Even the land's trash cans were themed to the ramshackle environments of the *Star Wars* films with prechipped paint and stains of orange rust. In a first for a Disney theme park, Imagineering did not use nondiegetic background music throughout the land in a bid for immersive authenticity that sidelined the famous, emotionally resonant *Star Wars* scores of John Williams. One fan reported on the MiceChat Facebook group of returning to Main Street to enjoy the cheerful Disneyland marching band as a "palette cleanser" after visiting the new Galaxy's Edge land that resembled a "bleak abandoned nuclear facility." Imagineering opted for stark, gritty realism true to the environmental diegesis of the *Star Wars* films over the fantastical hyperrealism of Disneyland. Gurr conceded Galaxy's Edge would probably give ardent fans one more reason to hang out at the park and thus contribute positively to Disney's laser-like focus on the financial bottom line.[79] Indeed, just to enter the Savi's Workshop attraction when the land opened required a US$200 up-front payment to custom build a toy lightsaber.

Fans also worried when the former head of Disney consumer products, Bob Chapek, was named the chief of Disney parks in 2015 (subsequently promoted to CEO in 2020 and ousted in 2022). Fears of a return to the Paul Pressler era only heightened with a 2017 restructuring of Disney corporate that included the merger of the parks and consumer products portfolios into one mega division called Walt Disney Parks, Experiences, and Consumer Products with Chapek at the helm. After reports surfaced within online fan groups and forums of cutbacks to entertainment and attractions at Galaxy's Edge, fans started to dub Chapek as Bob "Paycheck." Even a CNBC host of the "Squawk on the Street" show accidentally referred to Chapek as "Paycheck" on live television in 2022.[80] In 2017, MiceChat's Regan presciently observed the Disney management news through a historical arc of ". . . a very interesting series of booms and busts for Disney. And we're there to write when times are high, we're talking about how fabulous things are. When times are low, we're talking about how bad they are. And right now Disney is riding a sort of high. They're cresting and they're about to head back into potentially some darker waters."[81]

When the magic has been perceived to be wrung out of the parks for ever-increasing profit, fans like Regan have seen themselves as watchdogs ready to begin a new Save Disney campaign, if necessary.[82] In 2012, the *Orange County Register* referred to MiceChat as a Disney watchdog site.[83] Almost every Monday, the Disneyland Update column needles Disneyland managers on some neglected aspect of the park from perpetually peeling murals of Toontown to unsightly plastic hedge dividers at the River Belle Terrace restaurant. Disney executives have told Regan that MiceChat's critical coverage has, at times, been infuriating but also helped the company improve.[84] Company insiders have leaked information to fan columnists such as Lutz, Regan, and Hill since the advent of online platforms in the 1990s. Jim Hill recounted that, as the Disney company has grown immensely in the past few decades, the leaks have only increased:

> Disney is really like 32 little companies, all of which have their own agendas, their own schedules, their own projects that they're working on. And they often butt heads so they come at things from different angles and sometimes just getting them to coordinate it, to push a film like say *Coco*, really is wrangling cats. They're getting better at it, but it's a lot of stumbling and fumbling. But on the other hand, what's great about when people stumble and fumble, they get frustrated and they need to vent. And that's typically when somebody gets on the phone to me and starts sharing stories that I probably really shouldn't hear.[85]

Unless Disney were ever able to achieve perfect coordination, comity, and cooperation between all the company's competing personnel, departments, and agendas, fan columnists will continue to be afforded opportunities to report insider news and gossip later picked up by traditional media outlets.[86] However, in the era of social media platforms, the publication of leaks by website columnists such as Regan and Hill no longer swayed the discourse with fans or Disney as in the previous eras of Usenet and web discussion boards.

FAN RESIGNATION IN THE ERA OF SOCIAL MEDIA PLATFORMS

The peak of fan resistance to Disney was in 2005 with the toppling of CEO Michael Eisner during the online Save Disney campaign. Although Mice-Chat's Regan proclaimed to stand ready to start another Save Disney campaign if management returned to the "dark times" of the Pressler era, it is highly doubtful such a campaign could garner sufficient online support to affect the decisions of Disney in the new internet milieu of the late 2010s. Online Disneyland fans' inability since 2006 to muster opposition potent enough to influence Disney management to change a decision or oust an unpopular executive has been due to two factors. First, the voice of the fandom fragmented into a vast number of groups on social media platforms, particularly Facebook. Second, the Disney strategy of co-opting fan website owners and

Figure 4.10. Bride auction scene in the Pirates of the Caribbean attraction at Disneyland, November 2017. Still from video: Author.

social media influencers by offering access in exchange for positive online coverage quelled resistance from the fan leaders who possessed the necessary cultural and social capital to lead a potential resistance. Even MiceChat's Regan in mid-2018 started attending early-access events at Disneyland in order to obtain the photos and videos necessary to stay on par with all the influencers, groups, and websites that had long been cooperating with Disney. While MiceChat continued to bring cosmetic issues to Disney's attention such as replacing an unsightly plastic hedge or servicing peeling paint, if Regan wished to continue to enjoy early access to park events then sweeping, biting criticism would need to remain mostly muted. Johnson termed the phenomenon of media producers engaged in ongoing struggles with fans as fantagonism with corporations eventually able to reassert dominance by "reframing 'normative' fandom within 'proper' spheres of consumption."[87] Disney, in this case, primarily reasserted dominance over fantagonism through understanding the nature of web discussion boards and social media platforms to induce fan resignation.

A notable failure in fan resistance was the outcry over the truncating of the Walt Disney–designed Rivers of America in 2016 for the creation of the new Galaxy's Edge land. Walt Disney designed the park as thematically coherent lands interspersed with a variety of intellectual properties and original stories, and never a single narrative dominating an entire land. On online discussion boards and Facebook groups, and in conversations with fans in the park during fieldwork, most fans welcomed a Star Wars–themed land but preferred a location in the already thematically confused DCA or in a new purpose-built third gate park that fans sarcastically proposed be named "new-IP-acquisition-land." In 2017, many fans, primarily older, were upset when Disney announced that the bride auction scene from the venerable Pirates of the Caribbean attraction would be replaced (see Figure 4.10).

There was no previous public fan protest calling for the scene to be changed, so the reason for the removal was internal to Disney. Outraged fans lit up web discussion boards and social media platforms to condemn the change to one of the most cherished attractions in the park. However, the era when a few fan leaders with social capital could organize and project a united fan voice from alt.disney.disneyland and DIG in the 1990s or the few popular web discussion boards of the early 2000s was long gone. By the early 2010s, the fan voice had dispersed among hundreds of groups, boards, and accounts strewn across an expansive online social media landscape. In addition, some fans, primarily younger, supported the change as a nod to modern sensibility in a bitter generational break with older fans. In the end, disgruntled fans resigned themselves that Disney was going to do as it wished in the park so there was no point even attempting an organized protest to change the company's mind. The only recourse was to vent online and within one's social circles at the park. Disney replaced the scene and reopened the attraction in June 2018 with Pirates of the Caribbean continuing to be one of the most popular rides in the park.

The resigned perspective was a stark shift from the internet era discussed in the previous chapter, when online fans believed they had real power to compel Disney to make substantial changes such as canceling a lackluster parade, ousting top corporate executives, or balking at patronizing the bland, trite DCA upon opening. If the same DCA of 2001 opened today, the park would most likely be packed to capacity with influencers, groups, clubs, and everyday fans all vying to be first with photos and videos uploaded to the most popular social media platforms of the 2020s, particularly the visually-oriented Instagram, TikTok, Twitch, and YouTube. When Disney released new "limited edition" popcorn buckets for sale in the park in 2019, the purchase line stretched for hours and a torrent of images immediately cascaded onto social media platforms. Unlike 1990s Disneyland fans who eagerly anticipated Al Lutz posts full of gossip and news to critique and challenge Disney on the newsgroup, there was no longer, and probably never again will be, a ringleader or two recognized by popular fan acclaim with the cultural and social capital necessary to lead a unified fan protest against the company. Fans were now diffused among so many groups and platforms that an Al Lutz post today would only reach a fraction of the online Disneyland fandom. In addition, Lutz's cerebral personality and demeanor would be poorly suited to the oral and visual spotlight of Instagram, TikTok, Twitch, and YouTube.

The young photo-savvy influencers who dominate those platforms with tens and hundreds of thousands of followers want to work with, not against, Disney, so resistance is unlikely to arise from their quarter. Similar to fans from the previous generation who thought they could profit financially by working with Disney through their dot-com–era fan websites, social media influencers also hold the belief that career success resides in a close, agreeable relationship with Disney. On the micro level of social media platforms, individual fans could still interact with other fans, but only within smaller slices of fandom under the top-level governance of big technology companies. On the other hand, all those small slices offered a great deal of choice for each fan to find a steady and suitable social group. On a macro level, the fragmentation of Disneyland online fandom by social media platforms led to collective fan resignation that precluded the possibility of any united resistance to Disney. However, a by-product of the fragmentation caused by social media platforms was the rapid increase in the number of fan events, clubs, and meets in the park, as discussed in the next chapter.

CHAPTER 5

Fan Events, Meets, and Clubs at Disneyland

From a Few to a Multitude, 1990–2020

The previous two chapters illustrated the transformation of Disneyland fans online from a stance of unity and resistance to fragmentation and resignation due in large measure to the characteristics of the online social platforms of the last three decades. This chapter examines the role of these online social platforms in transforming the ways local fans have used the park for events, meets, and clubs. The development of fan agency with park practices led to an evolution similar to Parrish's observation of the shift within fan fiction from the "fan within a space" to the "process of making that space."[1] Fan organized activities at Disneyland were few in the 1990s and 2000s but increased exponentially during the 2010s. While early online social platforms fostered a unified fandom capable of mustering resistance to Disney's management of the park, those same platforms also suppressed the creation of new fan-organized park activities. The number of fan-owned websites was limited due to the high transaction costs of owning and running a popular site, and the number of fan leaders with the social capital needed to create and organize events in the park was also limited. However, the low transaction costs for creating new online fan groups on the new social media platforms, particularly Facebook, led on one hand to the fragmentation of Disneyland fandom and on the other hand the enablement of any fan for the first time to organize events, meets, and social clubs in the park. The fans who previously found the few existing in-park fan meets and events socially incongruous suddenly enjoyed an extensive array of choices to find a compatible group, especially with the advent of social clubs. This chapter provides a historical overview of fan-organized events, meets, and clubs at Disneyland from only a few in the 1990s to a multitude during the 2010s, as shaped by the characteristics of the predominant online social platforms over those three decades.

DISNEYLAND AS A SAFE SOCIAL PLACE TO MEET STRANGERS

While internet social platforms provided the opportunity to initially establish contact online and then arrange an in-park meeting, most fans did not avail themselves of this affordance. Only 15 percent of survey respondents reported with a five or higher on the Likert scale as often going on a typical day to Disneyland with someone they met solely through social media or discussion boards, and 61 percent reported never doing so (see Figure 5.1). However, 62 percent of respondents reported having attended a fan-organized event in the park, and 80 percent learned of the event through Facebook. Disneyland fan practice established discovering meets, clubs, and events online and then attending in person to meet new people within a large group rather than using online social platforms to arrange one-to-one get-togethers in the park. A majority of respondents, 55 percent, reported making friends with a stranger at Disneyland. From even the earliest days of online social platforms, MiceChat's Regan saw meeting strangers within a crowd at park events or meets as safer and more desirable:

> In the early days before Facebook, to meet somebody you really needed to show up to a meet-up. So nobody used their real name. Everyone was an avatar. You didn't want to go meet some stranger with Monorail Blue as their name. So MiceChat was a safe place for these people to meet and get to know each other . . . I encourage people to come to our meet-ups and comment on articles and I don't care what their level of interest is, whether they're a true fan, loves Disney, grew up with Disney, wants more information or they're what Disney calls a foamer: somebody who lives and breathes Disney . . . so they're at Disneyland almost every week or some cases everyday . . . I create a space for people of all types to get some information or community. They need that and I try to provide them all with that healthier experience and personally am trying to promote that healthier fan experience.[2]

Meets, events, and social clubs have provided a safe way for fans to meet strangers with the same shared interest contemporaneously in large group social mixers at Disneyland without the potential awkwardness or risk of

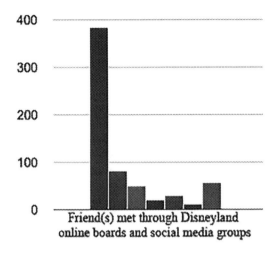

Figure 5.1. Do you typically spend a day at Disneyland with (1 Never—7 Very Often) (n=637).

initial one-to-one personal meetings arranged online. Within large group social mixers at Disneyland, a fan can judiciously self-select into a small, cozy group of like-minded compatriots with comparatively less pressure or fear of judgment. With airport-style security checkpoints at every entrance to the resort district as well as extensive security personnel, Anaheim Police Department officers, bomb-sniffing dogs, surveillance cameras, and other public safety mechanisms throughout the resort, Disneyland provides perhaps the most secure place in Southern California to get to know and hang out with new people after discovering and selecting online among the many fan-organized meets, events, and social clubs.

EARLY FAN EVENTS AND SWING DANCING IN THE PARK

Although Disney first started selling APs in 1984, the program had a low profile and was only lightly promoted until the early 2000s.[3] At the start of the program in 1984, APs were perceived as primarily for locals with a strong reason to visit regularly, such as the swing dancers who had been coming to the park on weekend nights since the late 1950s. However, the popular diffusion of the internet in the 1990s allowed fans not only to interact with each other but also to discover and exchange information about the relatively inexpensive annual pass program, which only cost US$140 up to the late 1990s. As a cast member in the 1990s, Pellman observed over the decade an increasing number of people who were regularly in the park but were not company employees. Annual passes became especially popular among teenagers of the extensive goth, punk, and ska scenes in Southern California at the time. The teens enjoyed hanging out at Disneyland so much that a tacit understanding prevailed not to plan parties in Orange County on Friday nights because everyone would be at the park.[4] Parents were happy to drop their teenagers off for the night at the ostensibly safe place of Disneyland, though a seventeen-year-old once got arrested in front of Sleeping Beauty Castle for selling LSD to goth teens.[5] One teen group in the late 1990s arguably became Disneyland's first social club, calling themselves the Disneyland Arcane Crew while hanging out in Tomorrowland garbed in goth attire.[6] These teenagers, often sporting Mohawks, dog collars, and anarchy patches, were called "wall plants" by cast members because they enjoyed gathering next to specific walls in the park.[7] Disney did not heavily promote the passholder program at the Disneyland ticket booths and website until 2000 when the price increased by 25 percent to US$199, after they realized a large local fan base existed that was willing to pay for year-round access.[8] Since 2002, Southern Californians have been provided exclusive access to regional passes for purchase at a sizeable discount. And in 2008, to entice even more locals to become passholders, a no-interest monthly payment program for passes was instituted only for Southern Californians, thus enabling even more locals to visit Disneyland on a regular basis. As a part of AP culture, some passholders enjoyed flaunting their annual passes in lanyards dangling around their neck while purchasing park merchandise, food, and beverages with an AP discount. Disney derived a consistent revenue stream by selling APs, which led to the park being filled with locals potentially buying food, drinks, and merchandise every day of the year. In addition, without the AP program most fan-organized events, meets, and clubs would never have kicked off due to the prohibitive expense of purchasing single-day tickets on a regular basis.

Although Disney has promoted and staged events for locals since the 1950s, the most enduring, since 1958, has been swing dancing at the dance floor next to Sleeping Beauty Castle where Walt Disney regularly danced with his wife, Lillian. The weekly meet has been cited as the world's longest continuous swing dancing event.[9] Many participants have been regulars with APs to make the weekend night visit, and some have been coming since as far back as the 1980s, and even a few from the 1970s. Of the survey respondents, 16 percent reported going swing dancing at Disneyland. The administrator of the Disneyland swing dancing Facebook group calculated the cost of Disneyland annual passes as more economical than weekly trips to a Los Angeles swing dance club, plus the park's many other attractions could

Figure 5.2. Disneyland swing dancers dressed up for Mouseketeer night, October 2017. Photo: Author.

also be enjoyed.[10] Most dancers discovered the event through word of mouth from friends or stumbled upon the dancing while strolling through the park on a weekend night. Swing bands were hired and paid for by Disneyland, so the regulars made a concerted effort to bring newcomers off the sidelines and onto the dance floor to demonstrate to Disney management the ongoing mass appeal of the event. The regulars understood that Disney management could save money by scrapping the beloved event if attendance ever ebbed too low.[11] Friendships and relationships blossomed from the weekly dances where the Facebook swing dancing group administrator reported, "we've seen them from when they meet, they start dating, they're engaged, they're married, they're having kids."[12] When one of the regulars had a birthday, the band of the night (Disney rotated the schedule with four to five area bands) would summon the person to the fore and play upbeat music while the other regulars gathered around to congratulate the celebrant. The swing dancers created their own theme nights without Disney involvement, such as Mouseketeer night, when regulars donned Mickey Mouse ears and white T-shirts with their names in block lettering (see Figure 5.2). However, while fans have engaged in their own promotions and practices, the swing dancing event has always been entirely organized, operated, and controlled by Disney.

During the mid-1990s, Disneyland allowed a tour company to hold an annual private event called Gay Night after the park had already closed for the day. Most shops and restaurants were closed and there were no fireworks or parades. When Gay Night was canceled for 1998, two fans organized Gay Days as a replacement without the involvement or permission of Disney. The event took place during standard park hours, so participants mixed with daily Disneyland visitors rather than being segregated. As a statement of presence more than protest,[13] gay couples, in full view of all park visitors, could hold hands walking down Main Street USA, a potent symbol of Americana at Disneyland. Cofounder Eddie Shapiro never liked the separate Gay Night event, which felt akin to being given access on the side through a service door after families had gone home.[14] The event attracted over two thousand participants in the first year and grew to become one of the biggest annual fan events at Disneyland, drawing tens of thousands to the resort for the weekend.[15] While other fan events in the park predominantly draw attendance by locals, Gay Days attracts participants across the country and internationally, with some making the event their only visit to a Disney resort for the year. Disney helps facilitate the event by working with the event organizers, but the company provides no input into the activities and programs beyond promotions such as screenings at the Grand Californian resort hotel of select ABC shows such as *Will & Grace*.[16] When asked whether direct involvement from Disney would be welcome, Shapiro replied, "our programming is of our own choosing and I am very happy not to require Disney's sign-off on what we do during Gay Days."[17] The organizers distribute a glossy brochure full of activities for the three-day weekend (see Figure 5.3). Participants are encouraged to wear red T-shirts to signify their large presence in the park and identify each other for socializing. Marketing for the first event in 1998 consisted of word of mouth, passing out fliers in West Hollywood, canvassing at festivals and street fairs, and posting messages in internet chat rooms.[18] With the rise of social media, Facebook became the primary platform for reaching potential participants and keeping in touch with past attendees.

The other long-running fan event founded in 1998 was Bats Day. Noah Korda and his Long Beach goth club recruited approximately ninety event participants in the first year.[19] Unaware that Gay Days as a fan-organized event had taken place earlier that year without interference from Disney, Korda did not know what to expect from park management if caught facilitating Bats Day in the park. In the early years, news of the event spread by fliers in clubs and word of mouth as Korda enjoyed the delicious irony of gloomy goths meeting at the self-proclaimed "Happiest Place on Earth."[20] The number of attendees increased every year, with 170 in the second year, 350 in the third, 500 in the fourth, and 800 in the fifth.[21] Korda saw the launching in 2000 of the Bats Day website, featuring many event photos, as helping popularize the event to draw a wider fan audience. Bats Day eventually grew to thousands of participants for the weekend with activities at the park, and a marketplace and costume ball at a nearby non-Disney-owned hotel.

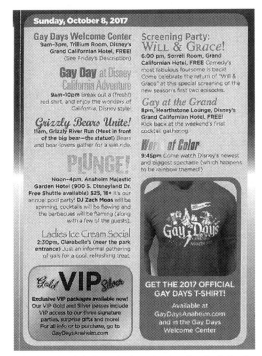

Figure 5.3. Gay Days Disneyland 2017 brochure interior listing the weekend's activities. Photo: Author.

Before social media, Disneyland witnessed few fan-organized meets, clubs, and events. First, many fans in the early years were not only unaware of the few fan events that existed, being primarily marketed by traditional offline means, but also did not know it was even possible to organize an event in the park without Disney's permission. Lack of awareness and precedent inhibited the growth of fan-organized events in the 1990s and 2000s. Second, potential organizers feared Disney would quash any fan-organized events in the park and so did not dare try. Third, the few venues for fans to congregate online in the BBS, Usenet, and web discussion board era correlated with the limited number of events and meets in the park. Due to the high transaction costs of owning and running a website with a discussion board, the number of fan-owned websites was limited. In addition, any fan attempting to garner publicity for a newly created event with a concomitant new website faced a tremendous uphill battle from the bottom of search engine rankings. The small number of fan website leaders meant a limited number of scavenger hunts and/or anniversary parties occurred during a given year. The nature of the online platforms of the time that united the fandom on only a few sites also meant very few fan events in the park. For event organizer Korda, the advent of social media extended the reach of the Bats Day event to new participants through the sharing of news and photos, initially on MySpace and then Facebook, to increase attendance in the late 2000s.[22] Of the very few new fan-organized events in the 2000s, the emergence in the latter half of the decade of Harry Potter Day in 2006 and MiceChat's Gumball Rally in 2008 coincided with the early ripples of social media before the new online platforms triggered a deluge of new fan-organized in-park social formations in the following decade.

POST-2010 SURGE IN NEW FAN EVENTS AND SOCIAL CLUBS AT DISNEYLAND

In the 2010s, the low transaction costs of social media platforms led to tremendous growth in new fan events and the advent of social clubs. Some fans looked to the long-standing Gay Days and Bats Day events as exemplars for starting a day in the park dedicated to their passion. Drawing inspiration from Bats Day as a dress-up event, the cofounders of Lolita Day felt Disneyland could use an outing dedicated to harajuku fashion and style.[23] The cofounders contacted Korda of Bats Day to get advice on organizing and running an event. Establishing online outposts for the event was technologically simple with a website, sans discussion board, using the WYSIWYG builder Wix (http://disneylandlolitaday.wixsite.com/home), a Facebook group, and an Instagram presence. Updating content each year is straightforward and easy with Facebook as the primary platform to reach and communicate with participants, though the organizers deem the website better organized and easier to navigate.[24] No money is made from the event, which attracted approximately 150 participants in the late 2010s, though the organizers have spent a bit of money on Facebook advertising and the creation of annual event buttons for registered participants. Even though Lolita fashion has no direct relation to Disney, cofounder Ruszecki believes almost any fan interest can be connected to Disney in some manner, so Disneyland and one's hobbies or interests can simply be conflated and enjoyed together.

For Galliday, Amy McCain also looked to Bats Day as inspiration for a Dr. Who–themed event in the park. Although McCain started a website, without a discussion board, and also used Wix (https://www.galliday.com/), as well as Tumblr, Twitter, Instagram, and YouTube accounts, the event's Facebook group and Messenger app were considered the most effective for reaching and interacting with participants.[25] The founder of Steam Day, which has a website with no discussion board (http://steamday.com/), concurred with McCain that Facebook and Messenger were the most instrumental in attracting and interacting with participants, as well as the benefit of asking past fan event organizers, especially Korda of Bats Day, for advice.[26] The first Steam Day in 2012 attracted only seven people, but in 2017 approximately thirty-five people participated. The organizer attributed the lower numbers of participants to the relative intricacy and scarcity (not easily available at the mall) of steampunk attire (though dressing up is not required to join the event) compared to the relative simplicity of being able, at a minimum, to wear black on Bats Day or stylish clothing on Dapper Day.

As a former DJ and party coordinator, Mike Marquez benefited from past professional experience to promote and stage many fan events every year at Disneyland, including Nerdy Day, Superhero Day, Haunted Mansion Fashion, GLOW Disneyland & Pajama Jam, Star Wars Day: Light vs. Dark, Awareness 4 Autism, Conga Line Day, Alive in Our Hearts (Awareness for Pregnancy and Infant Loss), Disney vs. Pixar, Pokemon Go 2, Date Nite Under the Starlight, Raver Day, and more, with each having an individual Facebook event profile and no other online platform for promotion. Dapper Day (http://dapperday.com/) started in 2011 as an event dedicated to stylish fashion, both vintage and modern, so participation was accessible to anyone willing to dress up for a day in the park without Disneybounding or wearing a costume. Besides a marketplace at the Disneyland hotel ballroom that charged US$10 for admission to access clothing sales, haircuts, and a few workshops, Dapper Day does not feature in-park activities or group

Figure 5.4. MiceChat Gumball Rally group photo on Big Thunder Trail at Disneyland, February 2018. Front center reclining in sunglasses and blue/white gingham shirt is Todd Regan, MiceChat CEO. Photo: Author.

photos, so intergroup sociability is much more limited compared to other fan-organized events. Dapper Day is simply a day to see and be seen in voguish attire around the resort. Disneyland scavenger hunts have always been popular with event organizers and participants from large groups such as Gay Days to small ones like Steam Day. One annual event that is entirely a scavenger hunt is MiceChat Gumball Rally, which had almost 400 participants in 150 teams for the tenth anniversary rally in February 2018 (see Figure 5.4). Although some fans come for the events from other states and even abroad, locals and annual passholders have generally comprised most participants.[27]

Although fan-organized events occur at Disneyland almost every weekend of the year, the mix of people varies at each specific event. Before social media, fans looking for an organized and consistent weekly group to enjoy the parks together had only a few options with MousePlanet, and then MiceChat, Sunday meets, or by searching the community section of website discussion boards such as Laughing Place. However, for fans who had dissimilar interests or felt socially incongruous with the majority of members of the few web boards, the new online social media platforms afforded a wide-ranging landscape to find park companions due to the low transaction costs of forming online groups. Social clubs started informally as early as the 1990s, but from 2013 began to be identified, known, organized, and defined. A Facebook group, the Social Clubs of Disneyland, has served as a gateway for clubs to post information and recruit members. The group maintains a spreadsheet with the history of all known Disneyland social clubs that as of the last update in November 2021 comprised a total of 741 clubs, although the status of over two-thirds is noted as disbanded, inactive, defunct, unknown, merged, or presumed extinct. Each club usually possesses its own logo, bylaws, and constitution. And no club can be added to the list without a club patch and a couple months of operation to demonstrate earnestness, though probably a hundred more social clubs have existed and never been added to the Facebook group.[28] With so many active clubs on tap, the group coadministrator believes a club exists for everyone, no matter their personality or social preferences.[29] The clubs use social media to notify and get together with other members in the park and are easy to spot with their denim vest jackets and patches identifying affiliation. Though dubbed the "Gangs of Disneyland" in a feature article in *VICE* magazine in 2014,[30] club members in the survey specified a feeling of family and information exchange as the primary motivations for joining a social club. Besides MiceChat and social clubs for meets, the Disneyland Fan Club on meetup.com was established in 2011, comprised over 5,000 members in 2019, and grew to over 7,000 by early 2024. Though the meetup.com group generally meets officially at Disneyland only once per month, in addition to special events such as releases of new Disney films or Dapper Day, members occasionally post messages and receive replies from others in the club to enjoy an impromptu meet-up in the park.

Smartphones provided another way for fans to meet each other while in the park through the fan-developed MouseWait app, released in 2009 as a vehicle for crowdsourcing attraction wait times at Disneyland. Though not devised as a social tool by the app's developers, through the app's lounge fans found a way to interact while in the park and plan meets and ride takeovers.[31] Members identified themselves by printing their app screen names on specially designed buttons rather than using their real names, with even the app owner known and referred to simply as "admin."[32] By wearing the button, one identified as a MouseWait member able to join up with anyone else in the park also wearing a MouseWait button. Ride takeovers would often comprise more than fifty members after receiving a message about the group appointment on the app only a few hours earlier. The MouseWait club became so large that annual events were held in a ballroom at the Disneyland Hotel in the early 2010s.[33] In 2013 and 2014, the large MouseWait community began to splinter due to a rise in cliques, gossip, and personality conflicts that led some members to leave for the new, at the time, social clubs, while others simply closed ranks within a small personal group and no longer associated with other app users.[34]

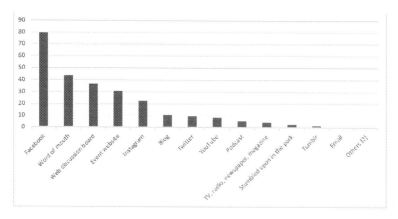

Figure 5.5. All ways attendees discover fan events at Disneyland (n=393).

Fragmented Fandom of Myriad Events, Meets, and Social Clubs

From the survey, 62 percent of respondents attended a fan-organized event or meet at Disneyland. Fan activity animated the park on almost every weekend in the 2010s, with Dapper Day, Gay Days, Bats Day, and the MiceChat Anniversary Weekend ranking as the most popular in participation (see Table 5.1). In the survey, fans recorded participation in thirty-eight different events and meets at Disneyland, although at least a couple dozen more can be found with corresponding Facebook groups. Survey participants learned about events and meets primarily from Facebook, followed well behind by word of mouth, web discussion boards, and event websites, respectively (see Figure 5.5). However, Korda cautioned that even though Facebook afforded anyone the opportunity to create a group for an event, that initial low transaction cost did not mean an easy path for event organizers to attract a critical mass of participants to be successful.[35] Korda estimated that Bats Day attendance peaked in 2013, with stagnation and decline since that time due to the proliferation of fan-organized activities in the park that sapped event loyalty due to: ". . . short attention span theater, it's kind of like I'm getting bored with this event, what can I do now? Which event can I jump to? Because there's such a vast variety of these events out there now with these theme days. It's easy to hop back and forth at different events."[36]

Galliday ran every spring and fall starting in 2014, with the first event attracting 200 people, snowballing to 1,500 by 2015, but dipping back to 350 by fall 2017, which McCain attributed to fatigue with the large and growing number of fan events in the park.[37] With so many events and meets, in

Table 5.1 Fan organized events or meets ever attended at Disneyland (n=393).	
Dapper Day	75%
Gay Days	46%
Bats Day	27%
MiceChat Anniversary Weekend	17%
MiceChat Gumball Rally	13%
MiceChat Sunday hub meet	11%
Harry Potter Day	11%
Steam Day	8%
Galliday	7%
Meetup.com Disneyland Fan Club meet	6%
Lolita Day	5%
Mouse Adventure	4%
Ska World	4%
Tiki Day	4%
Glow	2%
Homeschooling meet	2%
Star Wars: Light vs. Dark	1%
Pin-Up Day	1%
MouseWait meets	1%
Haunted Mansion Fashion	0.6%
Awareness 4 Autism	0.6%
Disney Addicts	0.6%
Seventeen other events or meets	< 0.5%

addition to social clubs, attracting participants became much more challenging for old and new organizers.

Of survey respondents, 22 percent claimed membership in a social club, with most members, 73 percent, joining a club from 2014 onward. A large majority, 69 percent, used Facebook as their primary online platform for social club organization and communication (see Figure 5.6). Regarding the reasons

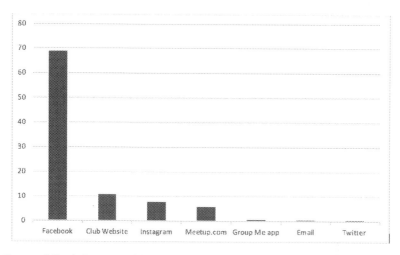

Figure 5.6. Online platform your social club primarily uses to organize and communicate with members (n=142).

social clubs became so popular as to displace older and larger meet groups, the coadministrator of the Social Clubs of Disneyland Facebook group said:

> I think that a lot of little groups, instead of one giant group where you get lost kind of in it, the little ones are better because you get to know the people more one on one. If you have a giant group, you don't get that personal one on one closeness of knowing everyone as much. So, I think that's why it started breaking off into smaller groups. So I know that's why my group, we have to keep it small because we liked the one on one, get to know them, so we meet every Sunday . . . so most of them, about four or five of them, come every Sunday, and then the other ones that work here [at Disneyland], they'll do it before work to come and then go to work afterwards.[38]

The smallest social clubs became as tiny as only two members.[39] The largest social club, Main Street Elite, formed in 2012 and grew to hundreds of members before disbanding due to the complications of managing such a large group of different personalities.[40] Then, after disbanding for a time, Main Street Elite reconstituted with a smaller, more manageable number of members and is still listed as active on the Social Clubs of Disneyland Facebook group spreadsheet. As Shirky observed, in general, memberships in large groups tend to be less tightly connected, and, therefore, fracture more easily.[41] Jones termed this kind of fluid membership process as a "lava lamp effect" while studying

American Civil War reenactors whose units often factionalized and disbanded within a few years of formation, so members regularly needed to find and form new units.[42] Most social clubs have tended to meet on Sunday not only due to weekday work schedules but also to be more socioeconomically inclusive, because lower-tier annual passes have generally not been blocked by Disney on Sundays. New recruits often prospect with different social clubs before settling into one for a tryout over a couple weeks or, according to Williams-Turkowski's autoethnography with the clubs, even several months.[43] Members of the group then take a vote to admit or deny the newcomer.[44] One former social club member compared the process to rushing a university fraternity or sorority.[45] The coadministrator of the Facebook group for social clubs acknowledged the clubs were sometimes stigmatized as gangs by other Disneyland fans but contended members were predominantly composed of "Disney nerds just like everyone else in the park."[46] Nevertheless, some regular park visitors have felt uneasy with the clubs after hearing stories of disruptive initiation rites, theft of attraction elements, line-cutting, disability-assistance abuse, drug use, or altercations between rival clubs over park turf.[47] Williams-Turkowski reported cast members as being conspicuously suspicious of the denim vest–clad club members.[48] On the other hand, I was informed by social club members that many clubs included members who were current and former cast members and maintained good relations with park employees. Seemingly, perspectives on the social clubs have varied widely from benign to malevolent among cast members, annual passholders, day visitors, and club members. In addition, some fans feel Disneyland itself should be the primary show, so club members with their custom attire, as well as black-clad Bats Day goths and Disneybounders, have been perceived as detracting from a magical Disneyland experience. With such a large number and broad range of clubs, generalizing any traits would be dubious, except to say that the huge number of clubs overall made sustaining a big, all-encompassing club a practical impossibility.

Besides the denim vest–clad social clubs, there were social cliques that maintained Facebook groups with exclusive membership, such as Disneyland bride communities consisting primarily of women planning weddings at the park. To gain admittance to the group, a prospective bride needs to show a signed Disney wedding contract, answer a questionnaire to prove a relationship with Disney, and provide the specific venue and date for the nuptials.[49] After admittance, the new member is required to interact with the group to a certain posting threshold or risk being booted. The bride group with the strictest admission protocol had 119 members as of October 2017. The members took the Disney bride identity earnestly, with special group shirts and Mickey ears along with occasional meets in the park and an annual charity event.[50]

Korda believed with so many events and meets in the park all attempting to outdo one another that a shakeout was bound to happen, as well as a possible crackdown by Disney.[51] Regan lamented that the possibility of uniting the Disneyland fan community had passed due to fragmentation from the constant proliferation of groups and events.[52] Since most social clubs and meets, as well as events, were scheduled on Sundays, local fans reported feeling somewhat compelled to choose one group for consistent weekly participation to avoid the perception of being seen as a social dilettante, which subsequently narrows the opportunity to explore other new social groups. On the other hand, the much greater choice in fan-organized events, clubs, and meets afforded by social media platforms, particularly Facebook as cited by fan event organizers and participants, meant greater opportunity for each fan to find the group(s) that suited one's social needs and desires.

Market Pressures on Fan Labor

Fans trying to monetize labors of love have usually found lucrative financial outcomes notoriously difficult to achieve.[53] Although the creation of a Facebook group for an event is free, putting together a successful event in Disneyland requires a major time investment and even a bit of money. McCain said Galliday required a huge amount of effort to pull off successfully but felt fortunate to have forged friendships with fellow fans and worked with volunteer assistants creating event buttons, answering questions, and directing crowds.[54] As for monetary compensation from the event, McCain said there was "nothing out of it other than saying, 'hey, I did this.'"[55] The Steam Day event organizer saw the trade-off as losing money but gaining friends and building a community.[56] While fan organizers possess cultural capital as leaders within the fandom and social capital from growing a network of fans year after year, most have obtained no economic value. Only fan events that draw large crowds in the thousands to Disneyland can attract major sponsors, such as the famed clothier Brooks Brothers for Dapper Day and Delta Airlines for Gay Days. These corporate sponsors, as well as ticketed evening parties in non-Disney venues, financially enable these large event organizers to rent ballrooms at the Disneyland resort hotels for marketplaces, seminars, and information centers. In 2017, when Dapper Day started to charge a US$10 entrance fee to its previously open marketplace, some fans complained about overt monetization.[57] This kind of criticism is a common sentiment throughout media fandoms when fannish activities are commodified by fan leaders and profit-making is perceived as a sign of inauthenticity.[58] Korda attributed fan accusations of using Bats Day as a personal financial windfall to unawareness of the costs to run an event, such as the need to pay Disney to be allowed to take group photos of over fifty people in front of Sleeping Beauty Castle and the Haunted Mansion.[59] Korda recalled even being chastised on web discussion boards in 2006 for "splurging" on a "BATSDAY" vanity license plate.[60] The Bats Day marketplace, called the Black Market, charged US$5 for early entry, but Korda was surprised some fans chose to wait outside until the minute after the paid entrance window closed in order to avoid the small fee that helped pay for the venue. Regan thought most fans understood no profit derived from the MiceChat website or events where authors of Disney-related books are not charged to set up a sales table even though MiceChat pays for the venue.[61] Events with narrower and less commercially viable themes, such as Dr. Who, steampunk, or harajuku fashion, are not able to attract sponsors or vendors to rent a ballroom or set up a marketplace at a hotel in or near the resort. However, almost all event organizers commented that Disney must enjoy the money that participants spend in the park as the social capital of fan event organizers gets transformed into economic capital for the company.

As an organizer of many events, Marquez believes Disney could do a better job of embracing fan organizers because the events brought additional people and revenue into Disneyland.[62] In particular, Marquez cited Glow Days, which encourages fans to buy Disney glow sticks for a night of luminous play at the park as a popular annual fan event that presumably earns Disney extra revenue from increased glow stick sales. However, Disney heeded fan concerns for one longstanding event. In 2012, Disney shut down the Carnation Plaza Gardens area, where weekly swing dancing had been staged since 1958, in order to construct a new princess meet-and-greet area called Fantasy Faire. The administrator of the swing dancing Facebook group created and submitted a petition of fan signatures to lobby then Disneyland President Michael Colgazier to retain the area as a swing dance location after the conclusion of construction.[63] In June 2013, swing dancing returned to the same spot, renamed the Royal Theatre, with the original intact dance floor where Walt and Lillian Disney had danced decades earlier. On reopening night, the Facebook group administrator approached Colgazier, who immediately recognized and thanked the fan event organizer for the petition to let park management know the importance of Disneyland's weekly swing dancing to so many fans.[64] Disney was perhaps more amenable to an event such as swing dancing that the park maintains complete authority over with a fixed time and location than fan-organized events such as Glow Days over which Disney possesses no direct control. However, tension between fan activity organizers and park operations gradually grew over the decades due to the proliferation of events, meets, and clubs, as I discuss in the next chapter.

FROM A FEW TO A MULTITUDE VIA ONLINE SOCIAL PLATFORMS

Whereas early online social platforms afforded the creation of only a limited number of events and meets at Disneyland, the nature of social media platforms enabled a tremendous increase in events, meets, and clubs in the park. Facebook and Messenger were key for new fan organizers to start, develop, and facilitate their event dreams into reality at the park. Social club members, in particular, reported feeling not well matched socially within the limited number of meets and events of earlier online social platform eras and appreciated the extensive choice of Disneyland social groups afforded in the new era on Facebook. For many fans, Facebook was the first platform used to connect online with other Disneyland fans, as reported by 57 percent of survey respondents, while web discussion boards were 21 percent, and Usenet newsgroups were only 3 percent. Overall, 70 percent of respondents felt that online social platforms had a positive effect on their park experience. The standardized presentation of profiles, content, and discussions on Facebook meant longtime prolific posters on older platforms could no longer showcase a plumage of distinctive avatars, signature files, and status badges that could intimidate newcomers. Likewise, Facebook group administrators possessed limited digital plumage to reward regulars, so loyalty to a specific group became less important as fans could simply shuttle among a multitude of groups for any reason. Facebook democratized shared interest group creation by establishing a simple, fast, free, and standardized process with access to the largest potential audience of any online platform, which then precipitated the rapid proliferation of new fan events, meets, and clubs in the park. Every fan could discover a multitude of groups online, go to the park to meet and hang out with the different groups, and eventually settle on the most suitable one(s) to meet up with regularly.

On a micro level, individuals went from a scarcity of choice in online social groups and events, meets, and clubs in the park during the 1990s and 2000s to a panoply in the 2010s. On a macro level, the number of fan organizers of events and meets during the first two decades of online platforms enjoyed cultural capital as an elite few and thus were able to achieve stature and sway as exceptional fans by accruing social capital from connecting so many people in the park. Their cultural and social capital was subsequently diluted by the entrance of many new fan event, meet, and club organizers, who were often younger, more technologically nimble, and empowered by the low transaction costs of social media platforms (see Table 5.2). Influencers were a new kind of exceptional fan but unable to connect people socially in the park due to restrictions by Disney-park operations (as I discuss in the next chapter).

Table 5.2

Proliferation of events, meets, clubs, and fan social organizers at Disneyland, and the transaction cost of establishing new newsgroups, web discussion boards, and Facebook groups on the three major online social platforms from the 1990s to 2010s.

	Usenet Newsgroups	Web Discussion Boards	Facebook (Social Media Platforms)
Events and Meets	Very Few (less than six)	Few (less than twelve)	Many (50+)
Clubs	None	None	Many (200+)
Fan Social Organizers	Few	Few	Many
New Group Transaction Cost	High	High	Low

Disneyland was not originally designed and shaped with fan production in mind, and only recently has Disney instituted such additions with Instagram-worthy walls, merchandise, food, and beverages. Productive activities undertaken by fans in the park have sometimes caught Disney by surprise and have not always profited the company. Jenkins (2013) observes media corporations as preferring to set the terms of participation for fans and even perceiving fan production as a threat to their creative and economic control.[65] The fan organizers of events, meets, and clubs provided in-park play and social experiences that Disney has seemingly been unwilling to offer. However, fan-organized activities in the park did not displace the economic value that would have normally accrued to Disney and instead actually benefited the company with increased attendance and concomitant food, beverage, and merchandise sales. In the next chapter I look at the evolution of Disney's strategies to control and regularize fans, including the 2010s proliferation of fan-organized social formations and activities in the park.

CHAPTER 6

Contestation of Disney and Fan Power Online and at Disneyland, 1990–2020

Efficiency, predictability, calculability, and control have often been cited as hallmarks of Disney theme park operations.[1] Disneyland was designed and constructed in the 1950s under the assumption that locals would only visit occasionally, without any conception that fans would one day organize their own events, clubs, and meets in the park. However, the last three chapters showed the different roles that online social platforms from the 1990s to 2010s played in transforming the relationship between fans with each other and the Disney company online and in the park. While Disney owns the Disneyland and DCA theme parks, the 78,000 unique visitors who pass through the gates on an average day often engage their own ideas, motivations, and practices once inside. As I discussed in chapter 3, Usenet and web discussion boards allowed fans to organize and protest Disney policies with a united voice online, but only a few fan-organized activities emerged in the park during that early internet era. In chapters 4 and 5, I discussed the rise of social media platforms leading to the fragmentation of fan groups online, which concomitantly facilitated the creation of a multitude of social formations in the park, as well as the fracturing of online fan discourse into ever-thinner slices often divided by generation. By examining the relationship between the three decades of online social platforms and the contestation of Disney and fan power online and in Disneyland, this chapter demonstrates that Disney has rarely used coercive power over park fans and, when employed, it has frequently been unproductive. Instead, Disney gradually devised a strategy to shape online discourse by using the nature of online social platforms and co-option of fan practices, media, and activities to eventually construct a knowledge environment inducing fan internalization of corporate authority in all regards except fan-organized in-park social formations.

THE 1990S: DISNEY POWER IN THE PARK AND FAN POWER ONLINE

Similar to other media companies in the 1990s, Disney initially used coercive power online by sending fans cease-and-desist letters to combat copyright infringement. However, targeting fans for intellectual property violations online not only was ineffective in abating online fan criticism of the company's handling of Disneyland but actually exacerbated the increasingly tense relationship between fans and Disney. The media conglomerate was caught flat-footed by the 1990s online social landscape establishing a unified fan voice to challenge the company's actions and plans. There was no way to buy a Usenet newsgroup or its governance structure (since there were no owners or moderators) to control and silence a fan community, and there were so many posters, often using anonymous handles, that attempting to co-opt the burgeoning number of online critics was impractical. Disney tried to counteract the negative online discourse about Light Magic by utilizing the legacy media strategy of running television and radio ads with purportedly real park visitors singing the praises of the new parade.[2] However, this old-fashioned media spin campaign failed to stem the negative chatter online. In response as a preventive measure, Disney ceased AP preview events after the Light Magic debacle due to fears of instant postevent backlashes on the internet.[3] "Light Tragic" became a galvanizing force for online Disneyland fans to develop a new discourse on Usenet as a platform outside Disney's control to challenge the company. In the 1990s, Disney faced organized dissent online from newly empowered fans able to disrupt and offset Disney's long-established media campaign strategies.

Disney had to deal with two new issues in the 1990s within the park. First, the company had to devise a policy to govern cast members who criticized or commented online about their employer. Pellman wrote regularly on BBSes under his real name while working in Disneyland as an eighteen-year-old cast member. After someone printed out and submitted his online posts to park security, Pellman was called to an office with upper-level managers and given a stern lecture even though nothing confidential or damaging to the company had been written on the boards.[4] Disney employed coercive power to impose strict rules forbidding cast members from identifying as company employees when posting online or ever writing anything negative about Disney or Disneyland. However, cast members such as Pellman could only get caught if they attached a real name to their posts. Since deindividuation was an accepted practice of early online social platforms, cast members could easily work around the restrictive company posting policy by using a handle for pseudo-anonymity. Participants in The Castle BBS often reminded each other not to post using any personally identifying information because Disney was presumed to monitor the board closely for transgressive posts by cast members.[5] In addition, Disney could not prevent annual passholders from writing criticism of the company online. Since many Usenet posters used handles, linking posts to the real names of AP holders was impractical. In addition, revoking APs and banning local fans from the park for voicing criticism online of the company would have resulted in a public relations debacle. Since coercive power proved ineffectual in quelling early fan protests online, Disney in succeeding decades learned to adopt subtler techniques of disciplinary power to shape online discourse in its favor.

Of the first two fan-organized events at Disneyland, only Gay Days had such a large number of participants as to be noticed by park operations. Though Disney adopted an approach of benign neglect to Gay Days by calling the event unofficial with no listing on the park calendar (all fan-organized park activities have consistently been deemed unofficial by the company), park management offered refunds in the early years to any visitor who complained about sharing the park with LGBTQ+ fans. For Bats Day, Korda recalled that Disney was unaware the event was taking place in the park for the first five years, even when scores of participants wearing all black posed for photos in front of the Haunted Mansion. Since fan-organized events were novel at the time, the discourse of whom to contact among local fans for guidance on whether and how to work with Disney had not yet been established. In the early years, Korda worried the event could be terminated by security if discovered by park managers. Outside of Gay Days and Bats Day, there were no other themed fan-organized events in the 1990s because nobody knew whether Disney would grant permission, there were no precedents to abide and a general lack of awareness of the few existing fan events, and the time, effort, and expense of marketing and staging a successful event were daunting. In the 1990s, Gay Days and Bats Day were mainly marketed through traditional offline means such as word of mouth, posting fliers in clubs, and ads in print periodicals. Even further under Disney's radar, a few small groups of fans started to use the early online social platforms to organize occasional scavenger hunts and meets in the park that could be seen as a portent of the surge in small-scale events, meets, and clubs to come in later decades.

Apart from Gay Days, fan events and meets in the 1990s were so few in number and small in size that Disney hardly noticed them, if at all.

THE 2000S: DISNEY POWER IN THE PARK AND ONLINE

Following the prolonged acrimony between Disney and fans during the Eisner/Pressler era, Bob Iger's ascension as CEO enabled a reboot of the company's relationship with online fans weary of the decade-long opposition to Disney management. The early 2000s also saw the migration of fans to web discussion boards as Usenet activity rapidly and sharply declined. Disney no longer needed to deal with the vocal denizens of an ungoverned, unowned, and contentious alt.disney.disneyland newsgroup, and instead could focus on a few web discussion boards that were owned and governed by a small number of fan leaders. In the 1990s and early 2000s, Disney viewed online fans warily. At press events, Disney invited print and broadcast journalists but no representatives from internet-only sites, which essentially meant abandoning online discourse about the park to the fans. However, Disney eventually realized that working with fan websites could lead to a mutually beneficial, and even profitable, relationship. When a print journalist was unable to attend a Disney press event in the early 2000s, the reporter asked Laughing Place's Moseley to cover the function instead. At the event, Moseley met Disney public relations managers who knew little of online fan media but started to invite Laughing Place to future park events as probably the first internet-only outlet on Disney's press list.[6] Disney had unknowingly taken its first step toward reshaping online discourse about the park. Thereafter, Moseley felt Laughing Place was treated the same as any other traditional news outlet with Disney paying attention that the fan website owner got the right camera shots and interviews. Moseley already possessed a great deal of social capital with online fans through the Laughing Place website, discussion board, and annual event, but invitations to Disney events provided Moseley with additional social value by meeting and making connections with Legends and Imagineers and developing many long-lasting friendships.[7]

Disney soon thereafter started to offer access to special events, such as press screeners of new Disney films or park attractions, to proprietors of popular Disneyland fan websites in implicit exchange for positive reviews online. In addition, bloggers, who were not Disney or Disneyland-focused and instead appealed to more general audiences by covering mothers and young families, themed entertainment, travel and tourism, and youth and teen culture, were given access to Disney press events. The bloggers were excited to receive perks from working with Disney and gladly provided positive coverage online in return. Disney also sometimes supplied exclusive cultural capital–building opportunities for fan bloggers invited to preview events by providing special souvenirs or character meet and greets not available to regular guests, which could then be displayed on their blogs and websites. Fan sites generally obliged Disney's wishes for fear of losing a lucrative relationship that provided early access to coveted content for their growing audiences, while Disney benefited from online discourse reshaped as positive about the company and park. The negativity of Usenet users changed to the positivity of website owners and bloggers. Disney enjoyed distributing information through fan-owned sites and blogs with seemingly authentic fan voices because the company had not figured out how to communicate directly and effectively with fans online and social media platforms had not yet become popular.[8] MiceChat declined Disney's access media model to remain a critical voice of Disneyland's shortcomings, and hence Regan was often not invited to Disneyland press events.[9] In addition, Disney attempted to use astroturfing on the MiceChat boards to fabricate a more positive discourse, but site moderators publicly exposed the corporate poser posters after tracing their internet protocol addresses to the Team Disney Anaheim building behind Disneyland's Toontown land.[10] MiceChat's critical perspective became so notorious that when a site column proclaimed genuine affection for a new Disneyland attraction, some fans accused Regan of being a Disney sellout.[11] Nevertheless, the fan migration away from Usenet to websites enabled Disney to establish a quid pro quo providing access to company events for positive coverage by the limited number of Disneyland fan site and blog owners. Disney was therefore able, for the most part, to establish control of online discourse about the company and park.

By the fifth year of Bats Day in 2003, as hundreds of black-clad goths squeezed in front of the Haunted Mansion for a group photo, Korda realized a new plan was needed to manage the burgeoning event crowd. An assembly line approach was tried in which event participants queued en masse for the attraction and passed as small groups in front of the mansion doors while Korda had each group briefly pause for snapshot after snapshot. However, after about a dozen photos, Korda knew the snapshotting was disrupting the park and the group could soon get into trouble with park operations. A cast member approached Korda to suggest contacting park management to help with coordination. Though previously anxious about approaching Disney for fear the event could be completely shut down, Korda was pleasantly surprised when management offered assistance in getting set up for the desired photos. Disney also provided Korda with liberal guidelines for acceptable goth fashion in the park that only prohibited participants from cosplaying Disney characters, carrying real or fake weapons, or wearing costume accoutrements that could snag, injure, or interfere with the mobility of other visitors. Korda credited Bats Day for paving the way for Disneyland to adopt an agreeable approach in regard to fashion affordances and constraints for future events (Steam Day, Lolita Day, and so on) and Disneybounding.[12] Korda originally feared Disney would abruptly cancel the event, but instead, Disney used the opportunity to set the rules of practices and procedures for fan event organizers to follow in order to regularize the few fan activities in the park at the time. The number of fan-organized events remained limited due to the high transaction costs of establishing fan event websites and the difficulty of in-park organizing in the era before widespread use of social media platforms and smartphones.

By luring most website and blog owners with forms of cultural and social capital, Disney was able to reshape, in large measure, online discourse to establish control of a fandom that Disney had observed at the beginning of the 2000s as a nuisance and threat. The few event organizers of the time internalized Disney's rules of engagement with the park. However, this brief period of Disney power online and in the park would dramatically change with the diffusion of social media platforms and smartphones in the following decade.

THE 2010S: DISNEY POWER ONLINE BY CO-OPTING SOCIAL MEDIA INFLUENCERS

Laughing Place's Moseley marveled at Disney's swift turnaround from originally issuing press event invites exclusively to print and broadcast journalists to an outright embracing of fan website reporters and social media influencers.[13] MiceChat's Regan estimated that nearly 90 percent of invited guests at Disneyland and Universal Studios theme park press events that he attended in 2017 were internet-only outlets and, of those, mostly social media influencers. Some influencers had less than five thousand followers or subscribers to their accounts, but the theme parks saw these nano-influencers as an effective way to reach a large aggregate young audience. Although the ad-sponsored YouTube videos of influencers and vloggers in Disneyland violated Disney's rule against commercial filming in the park, Disney did not curtail the practice, presumably because the videos provided free advertising of the park's food, beverages, shows, and attractions. However, Disney has often prohibited influencers and bloggers invited to new attraction press previews from filming on-ride videos with their own cameras and instead have provided Disney-produced canned footage of the invitees on the ride to be posted on their social media accounts. Unlike early fan website owners, such as Lutz, Regan, and Moseley, many young influencers viewed a growing social media presence as a stepping-stone to getting noticed by Disney for a full-time position within the company. And since the goal was a job with Disney, the influencers shied away from any negative criticism and accentuated the positive of the company on their social media accounts: "I'm not down to fight about things like the Tower of Terror getting rethemed [to *Guardians of the Galaxy*] because at the end of the day it's going to happen anyway. It's not worth having bad blood with Disney if I'm hoping to become employed by them someday."[14]

The young influencers deferred to Disney's brand authority to make changes in the park, thus shaping the online discourse by setting norms, especially for their young followers, on the company's terms. The content created by influencers was not limited to Disneyland but included other Disney departments, including the studios, animation, interactive, and consumer products, as a leveraging of the conglomerate's synergistic media assets.[15] Rather than using established YouTube channels with millions of subscribers, Disney recruited young social media influencers with only tens of thousands of subscribers but an "authentic" fan voice showcasing Disney-centric content.[16] Many brands, including Disney, learned to focus on micro-influencers with 50,000 to 250,000 followers, or even nanoinfluencers with only thousands of followers, in order to tailor messages to niche groups.[17] Disney became willing to recruit influencers with sizable young audiences even if they previously violated company copyrights on YouTube. Todrick Hall, a former cast member, had posted provocative parodies of famous Disney songs but the company hired Hall anyway to be the mentor of the new Mickey Mouse Club.[18] To cultivate and profit from social media influencers, Disney in 2014 purchased Southern California–based Maker Studios, one of the biggest multichannel YouTube networks at the time, for US$500 million. At the time of purchase, Maker Studios represented approximately 55,000 YouTube creators (including stars such as PewDiePie) with an aggregated content of over 5.5 billion views from 380 million subscribers.[19] However, lower-than-expected revenue growth and persistent unprofitability prompted Disney in 2017 to cut jobs at Maker Studios, scale the roster back to only 300 content creators, and absorb the remnants into the Disney Digital Network, which worked with influencers across Disney's various business units.[20]

At first, Disney had strict rules prohibiting identifiable cast members from discussing Disneyland on online platforms, even in a positive manner, until the policy changed in the early 2010s with the rise of social media platforms.[21] According to Disney's Employee Policy Manual, posting on social media about the park was permitted except for speaking on behalf of the company, disclosing confidential information, taking photos of any backstage area privy only to cast members, or revealing the personal identity of costumed characters such as Mickey Mouse, Woody, Maleficent, and the rest.[22] Disney recognized that young, social media–savvy cast members could actually be an asset in promoting the company's products online. Some of the most popular Disney-centric influencers have also worked in the park as cast members. Sarah Sterling posted YouTube videos about working for two years as a cast member and Francis Dominic was a cast member until late 2017. Influencers such as Sterling and Dominic were transparent about their Disney employment, past or current, but others have not been candid about their relationship with the company, thus leading to concerns of ethical disclosure and conflict of interest. A cohost of the Magic Journeys YouTube channel (75,600 subscribers in 2019), dedicated to the enjoyment of Disneyland dining, worked in Disneyland as a server in the exclusive members-only Club 33 restaurant but the Disney employment was not disclosed on the channel. Disneyland food and beverages showcased on the Magic Journeys channel are customarily proclaimed delicious. According to one popular influencer and former cast member, Disney was fine with cast members having an active social media presence focused on Disneyland as long as everything was "professional and very civil."[23] However, cast member influencers could not allow followers and subscribers to disrupt their job duties at the park by, for example, taking selfies together if approached.[24] Employing influencer cast members gives Disney significant leverage, implicit or otherwise, over their content since the cast members are dependent on the company for their everyday jobs, which frequently do not even pay enough for basic living expenses in Southern California.[25] For the influencers who were not current cast members, their aspiration to work for Disney also provided the company with significant implicit leverage in ensuring positive coverage. Therefore, influencer posts to social media platforms were not genuine brand cocreation because the relationship between Disney and influencers was decisively unequal in favor of the company. Since influencers of their own accord already uploaded plenty of positive Disneyland content, Disney also provided access to other sections of the company beyond the theme park so influencers could create positive content about all divisions of brand Disney (see Figure 6.1). This access by Disney allowed influencers to steadily accrue the cultural capital necessary to increase subscriber and follower numbers to their social media accounts. As similarly observed by Kiriakou, Disney put influencers in a privileged position with access to

Figure 6.1. Instagram post of Leo Camacho (@mrleozombie) at Pixar Studios promoting the release of the *Incredibles 2* film in partnership with Disney Digital Network, May 2018. Screenshot taken on June 25, 2018.

experiences unavailable to most park visitors or fans.[26] Influencer social capital became economic value for Disney in the form of ticket, food, beverage, and merchandise sales across all the company's divisions due to the glowing positive coverage on influencer accounts.

Influencers could also, knowingly or not, start a sensation around a Disney consumer product. An Instagram post of a popular influencer wearing a rose gold Disneyland spirit jersey helped the park sell out the shirt the following weekend, and after it got restocked the following week, it sold out again.[27] Rose gold became such a hit that Disney marketed products from Minnie Mouse ears to churros in the suddenly in-vogue color. Regan observed new attractions, food, beverages, and park designs becoming increasingly crafted by Imagineers with careful consideration paid to Instagram worthiness.[28] Martens, who covers Disneyland for the *Los Angeles Times*, reported that the new Galaxy's Edge land was designed to be an "Instagrammer's paradise" with the famous lounge area of the walk-through Millenium Falcon showcasing details such as the Dejarik chess-like game table.[29] Themed entertainment industry observer Niles reported, "Disney (and other theme parks) design their food as much for Instagram as for customer's taste buds these days."[30] Soto-Vásquez found the Instagram posts of Disneyland fans full of park food presented in bright and vibrant colors,[31] but a MiceChat reviewer revealed a potential problem with

Disney's Instagram-worthy food: "Captain Marvel also has some of her own special food offerings. The items are colorful. Lots of red and blue food coloring. Unfortunately, sometimes food meant for Instagram isn't always the best tasting. Now that we have photos of these items, we likely won't buy them again."[32]

In April 2019, Disney even opened a pop-up Mickey Mouse museum optimized for Instagram photo-taking as a separate ticketed attraction in the Downtown Disney district. The power and influence of the Instagram platform necessitates the regular updating of Disneyland's optics by Imagineering since influencers and everyday visitors relentlessly wish to upload images of something new, interesting, or cool in the park. Disney has obliged with frequent menu changes at park eateries, seasonal food and beverage festivals, holiday decorations, film studio promotions, redesigned walls, and temporary attraction overlays for Halloween and Christmas in order to maximize exposure via the posts of influencers and regular visitors on Instagram and other social media platforms all year round. Consequently, any new offerings by Disney can cause long lines on their first day of availability as streams of vloggers, bloggers, and influencers vie to be among the first to post photos and videos about park novelties to their social media platforms.

The relationship between the influencers and Disney became a quid pro quo where influencers gained access, prestige, and content by attending special events and trips to Disney parks and properties around the world, while the company received enthusiastic, positive coverage from youthful influencer voices establishing Disney's norms of preferred discourse to their young followers and subscribers on social media platforms. However, there are two provisos to note in this relationship of unequals. First, influencers need Disney much more than Disney needs any particular influencer. Without access to Disney's cultural capital, most influencers would be unable to create enough compelling content on their own to attract and hold so many subscribers and followers. Any individual can be replaced by Disney with a bevy of young budding influencers eager for opportunities with the company. This tacit internalization of disciplinary power by influencers ensures an online discourse normalized to praise all things Disney. Second, the relationship between influencers and their followers is also one-way; the cultivation of cultural capital on platforms such as Instagram and Twitter necessitates scaling a large audience without reciprocation. Influencers accrue social capital, but their followers do not. While fans, in a general sense, provide direct economic value to a media company by watching, listening, or attending, and purchasing primary or secondary products, the influencers provide the coveted indirect economic value of endorsing, sharing, and recommending that helps recruit and retain audiences that sustain and proselytize a media property and corporation.[33]

For fans who enjoyed the social aspect of park events and meets, there was a growing sense of disappointment in the preoccupation of some fans with influencers: "Where everything's heading right now instead of people coming together as a community, there's the outliers that are making money off of this stuff moving away from, 'hey, let's hang out, let's do fun things,' to look at what this guy was able to do because he has who knows how many followers and social media stuff."[34]

Social capital was, therefore, being perceived as cultivated for economic value, not for organizing fan social activities in the park. As van Dijck warned, corporate values often trump public social values due to the characteristics of social media platforms. Regan believed that a cult of personality had developed around some influencers but that this beguiling grip would ultimately dissipate as the young audience discovered that influencers essentially parroted the same unremittingly positive coverage as found on Disney's official social media accounts.[35] Regan's assertion is laterally supported by fan studies research that points to transparency and authenticity as important fan values favoring social motivations over commercial ones.[36] However, this contention assumes young fans will eventually seek the sort of Disney critique that MiceChat has traditionally offered. As influencers set the conventions and norms of the discourse, young fans might wish to continue throughout their lives basking in the positivity and reassurance of Disneyland as a special local place of palliative escape from real-life issues outside the park gates. Indeed, "Disneyland and Positivity," one of the many Facebook groups devoted to the park, had over 5,600 followers in 2019. When asked about implicit pressure to post only positive coverage, influencers said none existed because their love and passion for the park and company displayed on their social media accounts was entirely real and heartfelt.[37] Not all theme park fans consider their participatory activities on behalf of Universal or Disney in the park or online as work or exploitation.[38] A regime of truth that posits Disney can do no wrong allows the company to control the influencers, who in turn influence their young fans.

As for Disney's approach to a longtime fan website such as MiceChat in the social media era, some company departments would reach out to procure news coverage, but others still balked due to a need for control and a fear of negative stories.[39] MiceChat found itself caught in a catch-22 with a reputation as a Disney watchdog that caused the company to distrust the site to do positive stories if provided advance access, while fans complained about selling out to Disney if the site posted news derived from press releases or reviews without critical commentary. In addition, when taking a heartfelt stand at odds with many traditionalist fans, such as supporting Disney's 2017 decision to replace the bride auction scene in the Pirates of the Caribbean attraction, Regan reported receiving vituperation up to and including death threats.[40] However, by mid-2018, Regan relented by attending and posting videos on MiceChat from early-access press events for new park offerings. Regan's reviews from the events were positive, prompting some MiceChat members to grumble about the site selling out to Disney. In fairness to Regan, standing alone as a Disney watchdog is quite a daunting, lonely, and unprofit-able stance. Even the *Los Angeles Times*, the fourth-largest circulation daily newspaper in the United States and largest outside the East Coast, was the target of a short-term Disney news and advertising blackout after Disney said an investigative news article on the company's allegedly shady political and business ties with the city of Anaheim "showed a complete disregard for basic journalistic standards."[41] The *Orange County Register* came to Disney's defense against its cross-county rival by calling the *Times* news story a "hit piece" with a "seemingly pre-determined narrative."[42] Disney was sending a clear message to press outlets, fan or legacy, that unflattering coverage of the company would result in not being invited to early-access park events that generate a lot of website and social media traffic. According to a *New York Times* article on the Disney blackout: "Disney has a history of taking punitive action against news organizations and analysts when they publish articles or analysis that it deems unfair. Company representatives consistently tell journalists that the media's access to its films and executives is 'a privilege and not a right.'"[43]

While the *Los Angeles Times* and MiceChat straddled a precarious fence between coverage and criticism, influencers only needed to post flattering coverage that pleased Disney and met the expectations of young fans while not being obliged to pay heed to criticism leveled by older traditionalist fans and newspaper readers. Disney constructed an approving online discourse about the park, brand, and company by producing an internalized discipline among social media influencers and fan website owners to "authentically" tout what-ever the company needed to promote or risk losing access and perks. However, at the same time, Disney faced a new problem in the park with the burgeoning number of social clubs and events that Facebook groups had enabled.

The 2010s: Fandom Fragmentation Online and in the Park

During the 2010s, the fan voice fragmented into the vast sea of Disneyland fan groups on Facebook and other social media platforms. The low transac-tion costs of starting a group on Facebook also facilitated the creation of a multitude of new fan-organized events, meets, and clubs that resisted Disney's attempts at normalization by operating independently, to different degrees, of

Disneyland park operations. Organizers for Lolita Day, MiceChat Gumball Rally, and the numerous events by Marquez did not inform Disney in advance of holding their events. Advance notice could provide Disney an opportunity to cancel or set onerous preconditions, so the events were run under the assumption that park managers would be reluctant to anger so many fans by shutting down an in-progress event. On the Sunday morning of the Lolita Day event in 2017, the organizers set up a registration area using the wrought iron tables and chairs under the canopy of the former Motor Boat Cruise area in Fantasyland. As a couple dozen participants were queueing to register for the event and take photos, a Disneyland manager approached to ask what the organizers were doing. "It's Lolita Day," one organizer replied, at which the Disney manager's face immediately turned five different shades of panic while presumably making an immediate mental association with the Nabokov novel. As the manager struggled a couple seconds to vocalize a response, the coorganizers clarified Lolita as harajuku fashion and handed over a business card with an explainer. The manager then regained his bearings, wished them a successful event, and walked away. When asked whether Disney would ever be willing to work with Lolita Day in a manner similar to Dapper Day and Gay Days by marketing accompanying merchandise and food, a coorganizer considered the possibility unlikely due to the name "Lolita," the event's narrow niche interest, and harajuku fashion not being broadly saleable by Disney.[44] While Disney may be apprehensive about the event's name, the three organizers, who each comes from a different religious background as Jewish, Christian, and Muslim, exemplifying the spirit of goodwill prevailing in the park, said they plan to continue to hold Lolita Days in the park for many years to come.

For the over 400 participants in the 2018 MiceChat Gumball Rally scavenger hunt, Regan avoided the potential complication of setting up a registration desk within Disneyland by decamping only a few hundred feet away from the park gates at the outdoor patio tables of La Brea Bakery, a non-Disney-owned business that operated until 2023 in the Downtown Disney District. The arrangement benefited both the bakery manager, who welcomed hundreds of Gumball Rally contestants as customers throughout the day, and Regan, who secured a staging area for the event outside Disney's control but still proximate to the park. With so many Facebook groups, social media platforms, apps, discussion boards, and websites for organizing events, clubs, and meets, the lack of awareness among Disney management of everything that happens within two theme parks averaging 78,000 visitors a day is not surprising. New fan-organized events pop up every year on Facebook groups and in the park, with recent newcomers including Adventureland Day in 2018 and Pirate for a Day in 2019. As mentioned in chapter 2, almost half of local fans on a typical visit just enjoy walking around the park while going on few, if any, rides. The continually growing number of events, meets, and clubs constitutes a manifestation of fan resistance to the notion that Disney provides a comprehensive and fulfilling park experience because these activities offer social and creative elements that fans desire but have not otherwise found available in the park. Fans have organized their own activities because they want to play in the park their own way. Considering all the disparate fan activities occurring in the park every weekend, Korda was "amazed that Disney allows us to do the stuff that we do."[45] However, by the mid-2010s, Disney became stricter on dress that veered too close to Disney cosplay and attempted to discourage large group photos of fifty or more people in front of the castle by charging event organizers for crowd control and setup.[46] Some organizers mentioned that Disney by the mid-2010s had definitely started to monitor the social media accounts of their events.[47] When a popular influencer posted to Instagram on Dapper Day offering to take photos of Disneybounds at a certain time in the World of Color viewing area in DCA, Disney security was waiting at the location to scuttle the photo session.[48] Disney can apply coercive power more decisively and effectively with influencers than fan event organizers because the former are beholden to the company for status and perks, unlike the latter.

For popular social media influencers, staging a Disneyland meet is impossible. When Thingamavlogs arranged a park meet in 2015, fans of the influencers lined up to get autographs and take selfies. Disneyland management quickly shut down the meet because the fan queues were snarling park traffic and the influencers were being confused by visitors for bona fide Disney celebrities or characters.[49] As a rule, influencers can post to Instagram while enjoying a day in the park but cannot provide location-specific information for their followers to meet up, so unlike fan organizers of events, clubs, and meets, influencers cannot create in-park social events.[50] Alternatively, influencers have occasionally arranged to meet followers outside the park, such as reserving a table at the Dapper Day marketplace in the Disneyland Hotel or the biennial Disney D23 Expo at the Anaheim Convention Center. Since the mid-2010s, Disney park rules no longer permitted fifty or more people to congregate together without official permission, as Marquez learned when the Awareness 4 Autism event was dispersed by Disney security even though the cause was for charity and children in wheelchairs were present.[51] However, occasionally, Disney needs help from fans for park operations. When swing dancing returned to Disneyland in 2013 after a yearlong absence, cast members were initially unaware of the obvious safety hazard of allowing spectators to stand on the dance floor while dancers twirled, shuffled, and jumped around them. Due to the constant churn of cast member employment, the park that evening did not have staff experienced with running the swing dancing event after a yearlong absence, so the swing dance regulars had to pitch in by reeducating Disney on its own forgotten safety rules and procedures.[52]

Existing outside the Disney intellectual property multiverse can sometimes be an advantage for events, as Galliday participants are allowed to cosplay as their favorite doctor without running afoul of Disney's in-park adult costume ban that applies only to Disney characters.[53] On the other hand, in the first year of Galliday, participants preplanned a ride takeover of the Jungle Cruise with a Whovian captain cracking Dr. Who jokes for the entire boat trip. After Disney management found out about the Whovian-themed cruise, the captain was ordered to never veer again from Disney's approved ride script.[54] Some organizers, such as for Gay Days, Bats Day, Steam Day, and Galliday, have contacted and notified the park in advance of their event. In return, Disney has tried to regularize the fan events by reminding organizers to label the event as unofficial, distributing costume guidelines, and providing discount codes for participants at the resort hotels and ticket booths.[55]

With an 11 percent participation rate for event-going survey respondents (n=393), Harry Potter Day was one of the most widely attended fan events at Disneyland, even though the J. K. Rowling stories have never been part of the Disney multiverse. Started in 2006 as a modest scavenger hunt, the event gradually grew by 2014 into an intricate interactive fan experience produced for free by the organizers, who notified Disneyland's operations and marketing departments about the event in advance.[56] On event mornings, participants would be sorted into four teams within Yensid's (the sorcerer's name from the 1940 film *Fantasia* and "Disney" spelled backwards) Schools of Sorcery (named Dashwood, Rickett, Grizcom, and Willowdell), provided with printed game materials, and then tasked with tracking down faculty scattered about the park, answering trivia questions, gathering clues, and solving a mystery. In the evening, organizers and participants gathered on the Small World Promenade in Fantasyland to hear the results and distribute awards. However, on the 2014 Harry Potter Day, Disney security abruptly shut down the event. The prevailing reason for the sudden termination was unclear, but participants were told walkways were becoming too clogged and faculty were accused of signing autographs when they were actually checking off list items in player booklets.[57] Security rounded up the faculty and threatened park expulsion for anyone who did not immediately cease event activities. Although Harry Potter Day would never again be welcome at Disneyland, the coorganizer shared final thoughts on a blog about the event: "I know that life can provide fantastic, magical and rare moments when a convening of people in a particular place at a particular time can light up one's timeline like a fabulous roman candle exploding across the stars. . . . In conclusion: I formally apologize to Disneyland's current proprietors for inviting a thousand of my friends through your turnstiles. I won't do it again."[58]

As the shutdown of Harry Potter Day demonstrated, Disney owns the place and can assertively use coercive power to stop any event at any time, even though fans consider Disneyland their safe, happy, local place of escape. As John Hench points out in his book *Designing Disney*, "guests feel that they own the park" because Disneyland was deliberately designed to convey that impression by Walt Disney and his Imagineers.[59] Fan event organizers I spoke with reported being unaware that Disney had forcibly shut down the Harry Potter event. The commonly held assumption among park fans was the Harry Potter event organizers had simply ceased running the event for personal reasons. The lack of awareness as to the fate of Harry Potter Day was unsurprising in the 2010s due to the fragmented state of online fan news and the blur of numerous in-park fan activities every weekend. Furthermore, some fans felt that with the increasingly high cost of an AP, Disney was obligated to grant them entry to the park to play with other fans in any manner desired as long as park operations and procedures were not disrupted. Shopping malls are free to enter, so restrictions are expected and accepted by entrants, but the large sum of money for an AP to Disneyland was understood within the fan discourse as an entitlement guaranteeing park access and freedom of social formation. As the "jewels in the crown of this participatory fandom construct"[60] at the theme parks, fan activities are permitted by Disney as long as the company can continue to make money unfettered and legal ownership of the fandom object remains recognized.[61] In a pinpoint application of coercive power, Disney in November 2023 cracked down on a small coterie of pin traders who had taken over benches all day next to the Westward Ho Trading Company shop in Frontierland with large boards displaying pins for sale. Disney instituted a new policy that restricted displays to lanyards and small bags, limited trading to official Disney pins, banned sales between visitors, and allowed trading only from parking opening to 3:00 p.m. With the termination of the Harry Potter event at Disneyland, fans of the J. K. Rowling oeuvre in Southern California could instead visit Universal Studios Hollywood and the ornately themed Wizarding World of Harry Potter land that opened in 2016. Ironically, Universal Studios Hollywood has yet to witness a large fan-organized Harry Potter event.

Fan-organized events generally run only once or twice per year, though participants often attend many different events over the course of a year. Many social clubs, however, have meets in the park almost every weekend, particularly on Sundays. Though some park regulars saw the social clubs as gangs, members perceived their group as a Disneyland family. Disney has implicitly allowed members to wear denim vests with patches identifying club associations and to enjoy the park just as any other visitors. However, a rancorous dispute between two social clubs in 2016 that led to a 2017 lawsuit filed in Orange County could cause Disney to eventually reconsider park policies. The leader of one club accused members of another social club of demanding protection money to run a charity event in Disneyland, issuing threats of violence, defacing club property, filing false police reports, and making defamatory comments about the plaintiff being a pedophile on social media, podcasts, and neighborhood posters.[62] And to get Disney's attention, the plaintiff named Disneyland as a defendant in the lawsuit for failing to take steps in the park to stop the other club's "malicious conduct."[63] Although this was only one of over 100 lawsuits pending against Disneyland in the courts at the time, most suits usually deal with minor injuries caused by the park's physical structure, such as a bumpy ride mechanism or uneven sidewalk curb, and not Disney's failure to protect park visitors from each other. Although by 2023 the case seems to have been settled out of court, a judgment affirming Disneyland's liability in such a case could lead Disney in the future to use greater coercive power over fan activities in the park.

Unlike the 1990s and early 2000s, fans in the 2010s did not succeed in organizing on online social platforms to urge Disney to fire a corporate executive or halt a change in the park. Disney's control of the discourse by co-opting fan site owners and influencers produced an internalized resignation among fans that Disney not only had the authority but also knew better than fans concerning future plans for the park. In the 2010s, this sentiment often became vocally shared by fans online whenever Disney proposed changes. However, fans resisted the company in a new way by creating social and creative experiences with events, clubs, and meets that Disney did not offer in the park. The low transaction costs of social media platforms, particularly Facebook groups, enabled fans who previously felt socially excluded from the few existing in-park fan activities to shape a new online discourse supportive of the creation of many new fan events and clubs. Disneyland became perceived and embraced as a place to serve fan social and creative purposes often without the permission of Disney. A concerted attempt by Disney in the future to use coercive power to dominate the many in-park fan activities is unlikely because it would lead to direct confrontation with potentially tens of thousands of local passholders. Disney prefers park rules be normalized and internalized through disciplinary power as few fans test and occasionally exceed limits with the dress code and activities. Therefore, as an alternative to coercive power, Disney in the late 2010s started to launch official separate ticketed night events similar in theme to long-standing fan-organized events as potential co-opted replacements.

The 2010s: Disney Power by Co-Opting
Fan-Created Media, Practices, and Events

Over the last three decades, Disneyland fans have created a wide variety of media, practices, and events focused on the park. In turn, Disney has not been bashful appropriating the creations for repackaging as new Disney incarnations attempting to supplant the original fan source. While this book phrases Disney's behavior as co-opting, Kiriakou has used the more vivid term "vampiric appropriation" in this regard.[64] The Usenet newsgroups and web discussion boards of the 1990s and early 2000s caught Disney off-guard by allowing fans to develop a new discourse online detached and distinct from the legacy media marketing campaigns of the company. In response, the company produced three instruments comparable to previous fan creations to build its own cultural and social capital within the Disney media ecosystem to connect and influence fans directly and also bypass fan created media, such as websites and apps, and the legacy media of print and broadcast news. Disney also moved to co-opt the fan practices of Disneybounding and in-park themed events.

The introduction of "D23: The Official Disney Fan Club" in 2009 offered fans a quarterly publication, special events, exclusive online content and merchandise, and early access to the biennial D23 convention for a US$74.95 annual membership fee. As the new official Disney club, the company could try to leverage its status and authority to set the parameters of approved fan discourse. Media companies often use official fan organizations and approved convention speakers to regularize audiences,[65] which Disney has employed since the original Mickey Mouse Clubs in the 1930s to codify fan behavior and leverage the economic capital of fan communities.[66] Regan saw D23 as an attempt by Disney to compete with the services previously provided solely by online fan communities, such as MiceChat, by hosting events and conveying Disney history, but

> They will never be able to do what I do because they'll never be able to talk truthfully about themselves in a way I can, nor are they willing to let their individual people rise to stir it up. So at Disney, an attraction just happens, and it opens, and it's magical, and Disney did it, but on the MiceChat site, we'll tell you who built it, what company it was, it's

not Disney that built that ride and that's something Disney, you know, isn't willing to do. So that's where we stay relevant.[67]

The findings of Lee et al. echo Regan's reasoning that marketer-created groups are less likely to attract engagement than consumer-created ones due to the perceived motivation of the corporation to mainly pursue profit when building a community.[68] The club fee was steep, especially for fans not living in Southern California and Central Florida where most D23 events were staged. Disney also used D23 clumsily as a blunt marketing tool to promote the latest studio releases.[69] In response to fan complaints and declining membership, D23 relaunched in 2013 with a revamped website offering ample resources and content, including seven thousand articles from the Disney Archive, and a three-tier membership system with the lowest level being free. Nevertheless, only 33 percent of survey respondents reported being a D23 member, and online discussion of the club has mostly centered on the biennial expo. For fans, Disneyland itself is essentially a never-ending convention party open year round. However, the D23 social media accounts have been successful in attracting large numbers of subscribers and followers.

Disney launched the Disney Parks Blog also in 2009 with numerous categories covering all Disney parks in the world, including Disneyland, and park services such as weddings, honeymoons, special events, dining, vacation planning, art, cast member profiles, and more. Fans could find all the latest news about Disneyland directly from Disney, so the need for fan sites simply echoing Disney's press releases diminished. Regan saw reporting with a strong voice and point of view, such as MiceChat's commentaries, as crucial in retaining relevance with fans, whereas the Parks Blog mostly provided straightforward and up-to-date news.[70] In addition, while the Parks Blog allowed commenting, Disney moderators barred most negative fan comments. To have a vigorous debate about an aspect of Disneyland, fans still needed to go to discussion boards or social media groups not owned, governed, or influenced by Disney.

In 2015, Disney released the official Disneyland app. Some fans had already created their own Disneyland apps, including MouseWait in 2009 and Mouseaddict (affiliated with MiceChat) in 2010, that provided crowd-sourced wait times, show schedules, attraction closures, and dining menus. However, Disney infused the Disneyland app with all the functions of the fan apps, plus official wait times, Disney character locations, dining reservations, ticket sales, and PhotoPass records. In 2017, Disney added digital Fastpass to the app, while Mouseaddict, with a dwindling user base, shut down. In 2018, Disney allowed users to order counter service restaurant food and drinks in the app with a scheduled pickup time and thus avoid, in theory, in-person queues. Also in

2018, Disney released a new entertainment app called Play Disney Parks with trivia, music, and games, including an in-park scavenger hunt, which has long been a popular type of fan-organized activity. The Play app also features a game element for visitors entering Galaxy's Edge to choose to belong to the Resistance, First Order, Citizen, or Scoundrel faction in a setup similar to the wizarding schools from the shutdown fan-organized Harry Potter Day. Although available since 2013 at Walt Disney World, the 2022 introduction at Disneyland of MagicBands (plastic bracelets as wearable technology containing RFID chips to activate at touch points for ticketing, payments, and PhotoPass) included a new interactive game for Galaxy's Edge to join a bounty hunter guild and find virtual bounties throughout the land. Although Walt Disney World has featured several in-park quest-type mobile and MagicBand games since the 2012 release of Sorcerers of the Magic Kingdom,[71] Disney has been slower to introduce digital games at Disneyland that create "individualized interactive spatial narratives."[72] The MagicBand games hold the potential to transform the traditional mode of visitation to an engagement with the fandom object as a process of convergence allowing "for the establishing of identity, personal narratives, individuality, and self-positioning within the space."[73] The MiceChat review of the new bounty hunter game opined that children might want to play every visit, but it was likely a "once and done" for most adults.[74] While this judgment seemingly supports the traditional mode of visitation, local fans have already been establishing their identities, narratives, individualities, and self-positionings within Disneyland for over two decades through clubs, meets, and events. However, Baker perceptively pointed out that Disney has several tangible and intangible reasons for introducing more digital mobile games to the park: ". . . distribution of crowds at the Magic Kingdom . . . , repeat visitation (the holy grail of theme parks), enhancement of brand loyalty (through engagement with multiple film properties), unit synergy (between Studio Entertainment and Parks & Resorts), and related item profit (pins, power-up shirts, spell card binders, rare cards, the paper version of the game, and perhaps food and beverage during extra visits)."[75]

MouseWait's popularity was already diminishing before 2015, but the release of the Disneyland app accelerated its decline because the official app offered features and functions that only Disney could furnish for Disneyland fans.[76] Disneyland officials reported that 86 percent of park visitors in 2019 used the official app during visits.[77] One fan app and site that Disney has not tried to co-opt is MouseMingle, which was founded in 2015 as a dating service to connect fans of Disney, Star Wars, Marvel, and Pixar. Thus far, Disney has not provided any functionality in its official apps for fans to connect socially while in the park.

Although fan events are considered unofficial, Disney has often taken the opportunity to derive economic value by selling niche food and merchandise themed to events and marketing the company's products and services. For Gay Days, there are rainbow cakes and Mickey cookies in the bakeries, prominent store displays of rainbow Mickey ears and tumblers, as well as red T-shirts that event participants are encouraged to wear in the park for the event. At the Gay Days welcome center in the Grand Californian hotel, Disney markets the Aulani Hawaii resort, Adventures by Disney vacation club, the D23 fan club, and Disney Fairy Tale Weddings & Honeymoons. For Dapper Day, Disney stocks additional pin-up style dresses for sale in the park stores. Unwilling to leave any money on the table for outside businesses, Disney in 2019 entered the customized T-shirt business with official graphics and typefaces that visitors with family reunions, anniversaries, or other special occasions can order bespoke from the company's retail website. After the popular success of Disneybounding and Dapper Day as fan creations, Disney has placed a much greater emphasis on fashion merchandising beyond bland resort T-shirts. Disneybounding became a way for fans to embody Disney figuratively and literally into their everyday lives, thus creating a huge new market. Lookbooks and articles by Leslie Kay on the Disney website promote company-approved bounding. Disney also sells Disneybound-inspired merchandise directly to fans, though with a markup in price.[78] In 2012, Disney partnered with Versace, Missoni, Oscar de la Renta, and other designers for a Harrod's window display featuring the iconic princesses dressed in haute couture.[79] Kate Spade, Gucci, Coach, Asics, Vans, Swarovski, and many more have followed with Disney partnerships. Stefano Gabbana declared that the fall 2016 Dolce & Gabbana collection was inspired by the Disney princesses.[80] Disney also partnered with young designers such as Danielle DiFerdinando on a cobranded handbag collection line known as Disney x DN featuring the princesses and Tinker Bell.[81] MAC Cosmetics partnered with Disney to create a line inspired by the character Jasmine from the 2019 live-action film *Aladdin*. Also in 2019, Disney launched a new collection of Mickey and Minnie Mouse ears designed by celebrities, fashion houses, local artists, and Imagineers. Disneyland even hosted a fashion show for the first time in 2018 with an evening event in Toontown featuring a Mickey Mouse theme and the rapper Chance.

While Disney would probably shy away from ever running an official version of Lolita Day, the company has appropriated themes from existing fan-organized events to create official new versions. Since 2006, Disney's hard-ticket nighttime Halloween parties have allowed the company to double dip on daily admission revenue as day visitors are corralled out of the park by early evening to make way for separate-ticket nighttime visitors. In 2018, Disney started new hard-ticket night events as a series called Disneyland After Dark. The first, Throwback Nite, was very similar in theme to Dapper Day with visitors encouraged to wear flashback fashion of the 1950s and '60s while the park provided period music, posters, food, and the original 1950s Disneyland fireworks show "Fantasy in the Sky." For years, fan event organizer Marquez held a small Star Wars event with just a few dozen participants called Light vs. Dark. But after Disney announced its second After Dark event would be themed entirely to Star Wars, tickets sold out so quickly that an additional night had to be added. Disney offered new night events in 2019 themed to the 1990s, Villains, and Valentine's Day, and in early 2020 for an 80s Nite and Pixar Nite. New night events debuting in 2023 included Grad Nite Reunion, Princess Nite with a concert featuring Disney heroines, jazz with Tiana in New Orleans Square, and a candy-themed dance party in Tomorrowland. After Dark events in the future could be themed by decades, popular Disney categories (pirates, Marvel, *Avatar*, and so on), holidays, or adapted from existing fan events. In 2019, for the first time ever, Disneyland Paris took over the park's unofficial Gay Days event to launch an official version with a special parade called Magical Pride and a musical performance by Boy George as the *Los Angeles Times* wondered aloud whether the long-standing fan-organized Gay Days event in Anaheim would be supplanted next.[82] The D23 biennial conventions are, in essence, massive iterations of the annual MiceChat and Laughing Place anniversary events showcasing Disney animators, voice actors, authors, and historians. MiceChat sets up a booth at every D23 Expo at the Anaheim Convention Center, where Regan is constantly surprised to meet fans completely unaware of online Disneyland fandom.[83] Disney's co-option of fan created media, practices, and events has seemingly served to obscure their online fan progenitors. Disney is likely to continue appropriating and commodifying fan originated activities. In the future, Disney could use coercive power, as seen with Harry Potter Day, to shut down a popular fan-organized event such as Dapper Day to launch their own hard-ticket version, but that scenario is unlikely due to poor public relations optics. Instead, over time, Disney's official themed events could eventually supplant the original fan-organized ones just as the official club, convention, blog, and app have done to their fan progenitors. Fans have used their social capital to establish an array of unofficial Disneyland media, practices, and events that, in most cases, have not only produced more economic value for Disney than for the fan progenitors but have also been gradually co-opted by the company.

FLUCTUATION OF POWER AT THE CONTESTED KINGDOM

During the past three decades, the power of Disney and fans online and in the park fluctuated in large part due to the nature of the online social platforms of each time period (see Table 6.1). Since opening in 1955, a hallmark feature of Disneyland has been its highly efficient and regulated park operations that persisted into the first two decades of online social platforms. The few fan events that emerged in the 1990s Usenet era were primarily marketed through print media and word of mouth. Many fans had not yet logged onto social platforms such as Usenet or even gone online at all. Disney maintained control in the park in the 2000s as the high transaction costs of starting and running a website to market an event kept the number of fan-organized activities in Disneyland to a rarefied few. Only in the 2010s did Disney begin to face hundreds of new fan-organized social formations in the park enabled by the low transaction costs of online social media platforms, particularly Facebook. Fans organized in-park activities with an internalized collective belief that Disney would accede to an ever-increasing number of fan events, meets, and clubs because the company had established few direct restrictions on fan activities in the past and, as annual passholders, fans were paying customers who felt a right to use the park for their own social activities and formations. However, since the late 2010s, Disney has become more proactive by creating official themed events to potentially supplant the original fan-organized versions.

Control online has often contrasted sharply with circumstances in the park. The nature of Usenet as an independent many-to-many social platform resilient to structural undermining enabled fans to set the discourse online with a unified voice to challenge Disney. On the other hand, website owners were structurally susceptible to influence by Disney because their number was few and entailed high transaction costs to start up and keep running smoothly and securely. As a mutually beneficial arrangement, Disney provided fan website owners and bloggers with access to Disney press events in implicit exchange for positive news stories about the park that generated revenue through increased traffic and advertising impressions for fan owners, while enabling Disney to establish discourse online through the one-to-many nature of the sites. Since Regan held other professional jobs, the MiceChat site comprised a secondary income, which allowed resistance to a financially beneficial quid pro quo arrangement with Disney. However, in 2018, Regan had to somewhat yield so MiceChat could have access and be up to date with official park previews and events in the same manner as all other competitors including fan websites, influencers, and legacy media outlets. Acceding to Disney in the production of an approved discourse online became a fait accompli where park food and

Table 6.1
Fluctuation of Disney and fan power online and in-park from 1990 to 2020.

	1990–2005 Usenet Web Discussion Boards	2006–2009 Web Discussion Boards Blogs	2010–2020 Social Media	
Online Discourse	Fan Power	Disney Power	Disney Power	Fan Power
	Light Tragic Promote Pressler! Save Disney	*Co-opt Fan Site Owners Disney Parks Blog D23*	*Co-opt Influencers Cast Member Influencers Disneyland app Fragmented Fan Voice*	*Facebook Groups*
In-Park Social Formations	Disney Power	Disney Power	Fan Power	
	Few events and meets	*Few events and meets*	*Hundreds of events, meets, and clubs*	

beverages were invariably delightful, any changes to the park were necessary and expertly determined, positivity abounded at all times, and regular price increases were necessary to maintain a quality park experience.

Social media platforms enabled Disney to control online discourse about the company, brand, and park by co-opting influencers to post only positive coverage in a one-to-many practice of allocution to their numerous followers and subscribers.[84] Resistant viewpoints from fans lacking the prodigious social capital of influencers were overwhelmed and dissipated within the fragmented din of a deluge of many-to-many daily posts to a multitude of social media fan groups. However, the same fragmentation caused by social media platforms enabled fans to produce a new online discourse facilitating the creation of events, meets, and clubs that proliferated and challenged Disney-park operations. Therefore, in the social media platform era, Disney's control of the discourse online about the company and park led to an internalized trust that Disney always knew what was best for Disneyland, but fan control of the discourse on Facebook groups concerning in-park activities led to a fan belief of the right to create social activities and formations at Disneyland that the company failed to offer.

CHAPTER 7

The Evolving Intersection of Fans and Disney on Online Social Platforms and at Disneyland

When the place attachment to Disneyland by Southern California fans combined with the concomitant emergence of the internet and annual passes over three decades ago, a new relationship formed between local fans with each other and Disney as a contest online and in the park predicated in large measure on the characteristics of the prevailing online social platforms of three internet eras. For a summative examination decade by decade, in this chapter I employ the model framework introduced in chapter 1 to illustrate the intersection of the three domains of fans, corporation, and online social platforms over the last three decades at Disneyland, followed by discussions and analyses using van Dijck's platforms as microsystems framework and Bourdieu's forms of capital. Afterward, I discuss potential challenges to place attachment at Disneyland and new developments in the early years of the 2020s decade, including the park's one-year pandemic closure.

Usenet Newsgroups Era

The advent of online social platforms in the 1990s afforded fans a way to interact more efficiently and economically than the print newsletters and zines distributed through postal mail before the mass diffusion of the internet. Figure 7.1 illustrates the 1990s era before smartphones, when fan interaction online occurred primarily from desktops within homes and offices on personal computers and not during visits to Disneyland. The 1990s also saw AP culture take firm root at Disneyland, with local fans

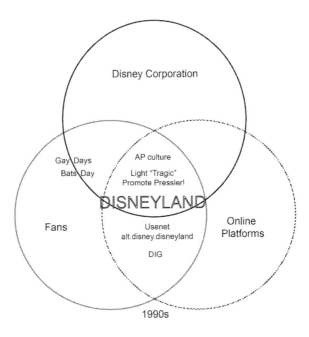

Figure 7.1. Intersection of the three domains during the Usenet era of the 1990s.

undertaking regular visits on a daily, weekly, or monthly basis. Passholders used the new online social platforms to build social capital with other passholders for knowledge and information and to protest Disney's management of the park. However, fan social capital on early online platforms was rarely used for organizing fan-organized park activities that operated outside of Disney's purview. The Usenet newsgroup alt.disney.disneyland provided a common meeting ground for fan discussion, while the Disney Information Guide (DIG) website of Al Lutz served as a persistent, structured, and curated focal point for information and campaigns. Early online social platforms enabled formerly anonymous fans in the park, such as Lutz, to accrue cultural capital online within Disneyland fandom as a prominent newsgroup poster, FAQ caretaker, and owner of a website (DIG). Fan leadership emerged among posters who steadily built cultural capital through frequent postings that shared information and knowledge valuable to fans. However, popularly acclaimed leaders could not exercise control over other fans on Usenet because the only prerequisite for access and participation was an internet connection; the platform was freely available for any user. The newsgroup was a venue where all online fans could gather, unlike the siloed ISP member-only forums on AOL, Prodigy, or CompuServe. Usenet's underlying technology was built into the structure

Table 7.1

Application of Van Dijck's framework to:

Usenet: alt.disney.disneyland

Ownership	Unowned
Governance	Unmoderated
Business models	None
Content	Distinct posts with text only as uniform ASCII formatting
Users/usage	Open with no registration requirement Can lurk undetected Can self-represent by real name or handle, and signature files Can start new threads or reply to existing ones User agency is unrestricted Users are coequal (no central authority or hierarchy)
Technology	Data is public, no metadata collection No processing algorithms Limited protocols (post, reply, killfile, group cross-post) Transparent interface Minimal defaults

of the early internet without a need for updates or ongoing funding for upkeep. User agency was unrestricted by moderation or ownership, and no metadata or processing algorithms undergirded Usenet technology to push advertising or marketing at users. Lutz and other early prolific online posters parlayed their newfound status with Disneyland fans into social capital to campaign online against Disney management and establish norms for fan discourse. Usenet was an ideal venue to attract and organize resistance against Disney because the alt.disney.disneyland group was unowned and unmoderated, and thus impervious to commercial concerns and financial or legal pressure by the corporation. Fans who accrued cultural and social capital on Usenet often did not look to benefit financially since participation on Usenet was free (and web space provided to AOL customers, such as for Lutz's DIG, was also gratis), and the established norms of Usenet discouraged blatant monetization. Table 7.1 summarizes the characteristics of alt.disney.disneyland using van Dijck's platforms as microsystems framework to demonstrate the characteristics of Usenet as a democratic and exceptional online platform for fan leaders to build cultural and social capital unfettered by Disney and organize resistance against the company with the "Light Tragic" and Promote Pressler! campaigns.

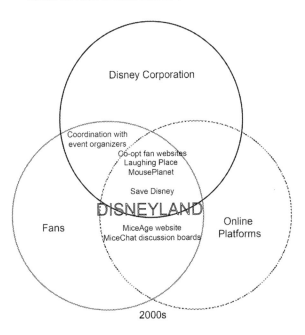

Figure 7.2. Intersection of the three domains during the website discussion board era of the 2000s.

Website Discussion Boards Era

Figure 7.2 illustrates the 2000s era of web discussion boards before the mass diffusion of smartphones when fan interaction online still primarily occurred within homes and offices on personal computers, and not during visits within Disneyland. In the early 2000s, web boards replaced newsgroups as hubs of fan interaction and discussion. Unlike Usenet, the web boards were owned by an individual fan or small coterie, and susceptible to financial pressure due to the need to generate sufficient revenue to cover domain and hosting fees, in addition to the considerable time spent presiding over site administration. Site owners without a web programming background had to hire technology specialists to do site coding and/or pay for third-party WYSIWYG design software such as Microsoft FrontPage or Macromedia (later Adobe) Dreamweaver. Needing to derive economic value from their websites to cover the high transaction costs, fan owners enlisted third-party marketing firms to generate site advertising and opened affiliate accounts with Amazon to earn a small percentage of site-related product sales. Cross-site technology allowed multiple third-party firms to gather and collate metadata on site users across the internet to establish profiles for targeted marketing. While

Usenet allowed for the popular emergence of fan leaders with cultural capital earned by posting useful knowledge and information, website owners could differentiate themselves from everyday fans by accruing cultural capital through the expenditure of economic capital to build, market, and manage a website with a discussion board. Fan owners of web boards could act as autocrats with a handpicked inner circle of moderators to enforce group norms and boot anyone for perceived transgressions. Unlike the ungoverned coequal denizens of Usenet newsgroups, some members could become more equal than others on web boards governed by the personalities and predilections of owners and moderators. The small handful of site owners with popular web discussion boards could accrue cultural and social capital from their position at the top of the fan hierarchy, and became powerful gatekeepers not only of information and knowledge for fans but also the means to participate within online fan discussions itself.

After the conclusion of the Save Disney campaign, Disney's new CEO Bob Iger rebooted the company's relationship with fans. Due to economic pressure from website overhead costs, fan site owners needed to amass a large audience to serve to advertisers and affiliate marketers. The financial constraints of the website discussion board platform compelled fan owners to turn to site monetization and consequently to become open to entreaties by Disney for mutually beneficial cooperation. Disney could leverage the financial privation of fan website owners who needed to accrue economic capital via a regular stream of new content that would attract recurring clicks and concomitant advertising revenue. Disney's co-option strategy benefited fan website owners by cementing their cultural capital at the top of the fan hierarchy with exclusive access and perks that ordinary fans could only view through their screens in awe and envy. Disney, in turn, benefited from the established social capital of fan website owners who reported favorably and enthusiastically with an "authentic" fan voice on the corporate brand and Disneyland. The company could sustain power over online discourse by using early-access press events as a reward—or punishment, since a negative review by a fan website owner often resulted in not getting invited back by Disney the next time. This symbiotic relationship between Disney and fan website owners at park press events also generated economic value for the company in terms of increased ticket, food, beverage, and merchandise sales. Disney also started to coordinate with the few event organizers of the time to ensure park operations would be informed and prepared in advance of fan activities at the park. Table 7.2 summarizes the nature of fan website discussion boards using van Dijck's platforms as microsystems framework to demonstrate their characteristics as undemocratic, restrictive of fan agency,

Table 7.2 Application of Van Dijck's framework to: Fan websites with discussion boards	
Ownership	Individual or small group of fans
Governance	Moderated by owner(s) and select moderators
Business models	Advertising and affiliate marketing (Amazon, etc.) coordinated by site owner(s)
Content	Distinct posts with text and images within the structure of a web forum software package (e.g., phpBB, vBulletin, etc.) implemented by the site owner(s) or externally hired developers
Users/usage	Registration required to post Can lurk but IP address recorded and cookie stashed Can self-represent by real name, handle, avatar, and/or signature file Can start new threads or reply to existing ones User agency is restricted User is peripheral to network center (site ownership)
Technology	Data is public, metadata is collected Processing algorithms used for third-party marketing Limited protocols (post, reply, and message) Interface is opaque, obscured by third-party software package Minimal defaults

vulnerable to financial pressure, and susceptible to co-option by Disney for favorable coverage. In this era, fan cultural and social capital primarily came to serve and benefit the Disney company.

Facebook and Social Media Era

Figure 7.3 illustrates the 2010s era, when the mass diffusion of social media platforms and smartphones meant fan interaction online no longer needed to occur primarily within homes and offices on personal computers but could move physically into Disneyland itself via popular mobile social media apps such as Facebook and Messenger containing fan personal contacts and groups. Disney assertively moved into the space of fan smartphones with two Disneyland apps, the Disney Parks blog, the co-opting of social media influencers, and official Disneyland social media accounts that all helped the company further establish and consolidate positive discourse online about

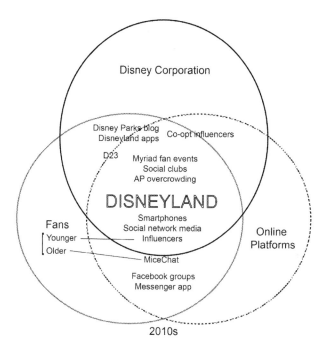

Figure 7.3. Intersection of the three domains during the Facebook and social media platforms era of the 2010s.

the park. Facebook groups and Messenger fragmented the fandom online and in-park into a multitude of events, meets, and clubs, but the segmentation also prevented the formation of a fan focal point to gather and rally resistance to any plans Disney proposed to change the park. Disneyland continued to increase in popularity, with concomitant overcrowding, as the AP population, primarily comprised of locals, topped one million members who often used the park as a backdrop for photos and videos posted to Facebook, Instagram, YouTube, and other social media platforms.

The 2010s saw the rapid decline of fan website discussion boards in favor of interaction on social media platforms. The low transaction costs of social media platforms enabled anyone, especially younger fans, to try their hand at cultivating cultural capital by creating groups devoted to any aspect of Disneyland and thus compete on a new level playing field with the social media outposts of longstanding fan websites. The shift of the audience away from web discussion boards to social media platforms also greatly diminished the economic value of fan websites by steadily reducing their site traffic and attendant revenue from affiliate marketing and advertising impressions and clickthroughs. Fan website owners had no choice but to follow their audience to the newly popular social media platforms, thereby surrendering the economic value and well-established cultural and social capital previously derived from their websites. As the beneficiary of free content created and posted by both displaced fan websites and newly established fan groups, Facebook became the hub that attracted and bound fans to a platform seen as the easiest one to use and where everyone seemed to have an account. By requiring real names, Facebook collected extensive user metadata to establish detailed profiles for sale to advertisers and marketers that generated enormous revenue for the giant social media corporation. The popularity and financial success of Facebook came at the cost of withering audiences and revenue streams for venerable fan websites.

Disney attempted to adapt to the social media era by purchasing Maker Studios, later rebranded the Disney Digital Network, to coach young social media influencers. In addition to appropriating the social capital of influencers, Disney also began to generate its own cultural and social capital by co-opting fan-created practices, such as starting an official blog, club, convention, and two park apps, partnering with fashion brands for Disneybounding-style merchandise, and launching themed night events at Disneyland. Whereas early online social platforms such as Usenet enabled fans to produce their own cultural and social capital with little attendant commercial benefit, the nature of online social media platforms enabled Disney to co-opt well-established fan social and cultural capital for its own corporate economic value.

Table 7.3 summarizes the characteristics of Facebook groups using van Dijck's platforms as microsystems framework to demonstrate the characteristics of the most popular social media platform of the 2010s as motivated by the corporation's need to commodify users as data, its undemocratic nature due to opaque management, the lack of user privacy, and a predisposition toward generating an unlimited number of groups, leading to fragmented fandom.

Fan resistance to Disney was strongest from 1995 to 2005, during the peak popularity of Usenet and beginning of fan-owned web discussion boards. Usenet's ungoverned, unowned, and noncommercial structure facilitated a popular democratic movement among fans to push back against senior Disney executives and unpopular new offerings such as the Light Magic parade and DCA. Would a similar intensity and resolve of fan dissent have manifested if the social media platforms of the 2010s existed and were predominant in that earlier era? With only one newsgroup, alt.disney.disneyland, exclusively devoted to Disneyland in Southern California, and few websites like Lutz's Disneyland Information Guide dedicated to general news, information, and gossip about the park, fans had exceptionally conspicuous online focal points for both interaction and knowledge during that time.

Table 7.3 Application of Van Dijck's framework to: Fan Facebook Groups	
Ownership	Owned by Facebook (parent company Meta)
Governance	Facebook retains ultimate authority in an opaque manner, though user administrators have power within their groups to approve and restrict members and delete posts
Business models	Advertising and sale of user data to third parties
Content	Text, images, audio, video, live streaming, and likes in a reverse chronological timeline within Facebook API structure
Users/usage	Registration required Limited lurking Must self-represent by real name Encouraged to post personal information, photos, and friend network Can start and reply to posts User agency is restricted User is center of friend network, but peripheral within groups
Technology	Data is semipublic Extensive metadata collection by Facebook Extensive processing algorithms Numerous protocols (post, reply, start groups, like, share, friend, message) Transparent interface Defaults favor personal disclosure Unique user ID enables personal information and preferences to appear on connected external sites

By contrast, in the 2010s, the fragmentation of the fandom into so many Facebook groups and social media platforms and the rise of influencers producing a discourse favorable to Disney made the formation of a unified fan voice that could agree on a stance and subscribe to collective action a practical impossibility. Therefore, in answer to the question above, if social media platforms had been predominant in the 1990s, fan dissent would not have manifested to the same intensity or resolve. On the other hand, unlike the Usenet era of the 1990s, fan use in the 2010s of social media platforms, in addition to smartphones for mobile communication and organization, facilitated the creation of such an array of fan-organized events, meets, and clubs that almost any fan could find a complementary social group in the park. However, these social formations and activities emerged due to the strong desire and determined labor of highly motivated fans, because Disney has generally been unwilling to encourage and foster sociality at Disneyland.

CORPORATE SOCIAL UNPROFITABILITY

Since corporate inception as a small animation studio in Southern California in 1923, Disney has become a huge, global mass media and entertainment conglomerate. However, Disney and the legendary Southern California media entertainment industry were slow to adopt and adapt to the internet and online social platforms in the 1990s and 2000s. The Southern California media companies became dependent on the popular social media platforms owned by Northern California technology companies to reach, market, and interact with fans. The Disneyland apps, D23 fan club, and Disney Parks blog were tools not only to co-opt fan-created media but also were attempts to circumvent Silicon Valley social media companies and communicate directly with fans. The acquisition of the 21st Century Fox film and television studios not only gave Disney ownership of a vast array of intellectual property to add to an already expansive library but also, after eventually buying out Comcast's share, granted Disney ownership of over-the-top media service company Hulu, which, along with Disney+ as a new video on demand service, could compete directly with Netflix, Apple, and Amazon in the delivery of online television streaming. To further challenge Northern California technology companies, Disney could set out to buy or start a social media platform to bypass and compete with Facebook, Instagram, Twitter, and YouTube for not only Disney fans but the global public. However, Disney has shown no interest in co-opting the social functionality of MouseMingle, the fan-created dating app, or the member lounge in the MouseWait app within either of its official park apps. At official Disneyland themed night events such as the Halloween Oogie Boogie Bash or 90s Nite, Disney has not organized huge group photos in front of the castle, ride takeovers, scavenger hunts, or other activities that fan events have long used as icebreakers for participants to get to know each other. Unlike attractions that literally threw disparate people together at the early twentieth-century Coney Island amusement parks, Disneyland has generally eschewed anti-alienation rides and attractions that brought strangers into close proximity for sociality, with a telling recent example being the Legends of Frontierland live-action role-playing experience that Disney tried out for only a brief period in 2014.

For the three summer months of 2014, Disney presented Legends of Frontierland as a play test for games under consideration and development for the Galaxy's Edge land that would open in 2019.[1] The live-action role-playing experience allowed park visitors to pick a side between two rival towns and get a job, such as delivering messages, to earn in-game currency to buy land for their group. Frontierland locations were specially demarcated for the game, such as a talent agency and card table at the Golden Horseshoe Saloon, a sheriff's office and jail, a telegraph station for sending and receiving messages, and a trading post and hideout as home bases for the two feuding factions. Disney assigned cast members as daily characters for the game with deep back stories gradually revealed over the event's three months including family dramas and reunions, engagements and marriages, and professional and business aspirations fulfilled or dashed. The game concluded after three months of park play, with the two towns joining together to build a better future. Some annual passholders became avid fans of the game not just by attending regularly but actively participating in crafting their own personalized experiences with cast members by staging impromptu shows such as dance offs, establishing a portrait caricature illustration business to earn the in-game's currency of bits, engaging in fortune-telling, and hoisting the Frontierland flag on the Mark Twain riverboat. Participants received recognition by cast members for their great contributions to the game by being leveled up as heroes and legends in evening ceremonies at the Golden Horseshoe saloon. There was no upcharge to participate in the experience and merchandising was surprisingly minimal, with game bandanas sold for only US$2.50 and elixirs (flavored teas) that provided game boosts such as luck, knowledge, and charm available for just US$3 at an outdoor vending cart in Frontierland. The company gave cast members and participants a wide berth to do almost anything as long as it was in the spirit of the game and Disney. A MiceChat review of the game highlighted the strong storytelling and community-building aspect that fostered team-building, interpersonal speaking skills, and new friendships.[2] A commenter on the website article noted: "the best part was that I got to meet and now have so many Disney friends that we talk and now try to meet at the park to hang out," and "I hope Disney brings back this game for a new chapter." However, Disney has failed to revisit Legends of Frontierland, and the games of the new Galaxy's Edge land have all entailed using one's mobile device but no social interaction with fellow park visitors. Like most companies, Disney enjoys issuing public relations releases touting its corporate social responsibility, but there is little to no profit to be gained by promoting sociality among visitors to Disneyland, so it has been left up to fans to create their own social formations, activities, and experiences at the park. A notable exception had been the longstanding Disney-organized swing dancing on weekends adjacent to Sleeping Beauty Castle; but as of January 2024, that free event for locals had yet to return since the park reopened from the pandemic in April 2021.

Disney has customarily shied away from the delicate, thorny task of social and community management. In 1996 the company founded the master-planned community of Celebration, Florida, as a model of the New Urbanism movement featuring traditional town design. After residents began using the public sphere, including online social platforms, to complain about community issues such as property values, public education, and downtown shopping, Disney divested ownership and control of the town in 2004 to a New York investment firm specializing in residential and commercial developments.[3] However, in early 2022 Disney announced plans to build Storyliving by Disney residential communities in Riverside County in Southern California, though the community is being codeveloped with DMB Development LLC of Scottsdale, Arizona, to whom Disney could later sell the community as was done previously with the town of Celebration. In addition, with housing in the United States increasingly being bought out for investment holdings by corporations, private equity funds, and individual investors, Disney observer Niles expects "Storyliving by Cotino, when it opens, to be yet another investor-owned ghost town that serves only as temporary rental housing for Coachella and Stagecoach, or the occasional wealthy old Disney fan who just wants to check it out."[4]

For the most part, Disney has been satisfied engaging with fans at a safe distance, as evidenced by the low degree of social commitment required by peripatetic D23 club gatherings, ten-day ship cruises, and one-off themed Disneyland night events without social activities. Furthermore, the potential for lawsuits, such as the one between the two rival social clubs that named Disney as a defendant for failing to protect park visitors from each other, also likely constrains the company from directly bringing fans socially together with potential associated legal liabilities. Although it might be the wish of many fans, unless someone is well-connected to the company and willing to spend thousands of dollars for an overnight stay at the exclusive Dream Suite above the Pirates of the Caribbean attraction in New Orleans Square, one cannot spend the night in Disneyland. Visitors are only welcome for the day and must return to their home or hotel room every night. Considering the media and political opprobrium directed at Northern California technology companies for platform governance since the late 2010s, Disney prefers to leave the knotty online social management business to other corporations, as it already did in offline life at Celebration. Indeed, CEO Bob Iger recounted

Figure 7.4. Crowds in front of the Pirates of the Caribbean attraction in New Orleans Square on a nonholiday weekday afternoon, Disneyland, November 2017. Photo: Author.

in his autobiography that Disney almost bought Twitter in 2016 but backed out due to "the general rage and lack of civility" on the platform that "would become our problems . . . and be corrosive to the Disney brand."[5]

"DON'T FALL IN LOVE WITH DISNEYLAND, IT'LL BREAK YOUR HEART"

Chapter 2 demonstrated that Southern California fans had strong place attachment to Disneyland, but current and future developments could endanger the place's physical and social fabric and disrupt heretofore positive attachment sentiments. Since the rise of the AP program and online social platforms over three decades ago, total annual attendance at Disneyland (including DCA since 2001) increased from 11.6 million in 1992 to 28.6 million in 2019.[6] Unsurprisingly, 82 percent of survey respondents agreed the burgeoning crowds in the narrow walkways of a park designed in 1955 were having a negative impact on Disneyland as a social place (see Figure 7.4).

The pathways became so congested that Disney in late 2017 converted lucrative retail space in Adventureland to stroller parking. In 2018 and 2019 throughout the park, Disney removed grass and flower planters and benches to widen walkways. The 2017 launch of the fee-based digital Fastpass system on the Disneyland app for attractions led to even more visitors crowding the park's narrow walkways instead of the purpose-built attraction queues.

The overcrowding made poor behavior by other visitors even less tolerable because everyone in the park became tightly packed together. Guest misbehavior was cited by 74 percent of survey respondents as having a negative impact on Disneyland as a social place. When asked about favorite social areas in Disneyland, respondents most often cited the comparatively extensive walkways and roomy environs of New Orleans Square, Main Street, and Tomorrowland and rarely cited the narrow corridors and cramped spaces of Fantasyland and Adventureland. However, with the 2023 announcement by Disney of the removal of Magnolia Park and its old shady trees and fountain for an extension of the Haunted Mansion queue area, New Orleans Square will become increasingly cramped. Although Disney raises the price of admission every year, and sometimes twice a year, crowd levels have not receded. The price of one-day admission to Disneyland rose from US$43 in 2000 to a price in 2019 that varied by date of use from US$104 to US$149. A premium AP for everyday admission to Disneyland cost US$199 in 2000, while the early 2020 equivalent signature plus AP cost US$1,449. Fearing MiceChat members were being priced out of the park, Regan in 2018 modified the two-decade tradition of regular Sunday noon meets in the Disneyland hub to be the first Sunday of every month, with the remaining Sundays flexible for possible excursions to other Southern California destinations such as Knott's Berry Farm. Also in 2018, Bats Day founder and organizer Korda cited the increasing costs to participate as a factor in scaling back future events to only one day after being run for entire weekends for nearly twenty years.

Some fans, however, willingly paid any price for an AP since their social lives and emotional connections were intrinsically interconnected to physically being in the park.[7] Other fans took jobs at the resort with the express purpose of affording their families regular access to Disneyland through cast member sign-in admittance.[8] On discussion boards and Facebook groups, many fans declared they would simply visit the park even more often to justify paying the increased costs for their APs. Jenkins sees the fan experience as necessarily social and not only in isolation with a media fandom object such as a television show.[9] The object itself is the conversational currency to participate in the fandom. Since Disneyland as fandom object constitutes a physical place, to participate fully entails a need to show up regularly in the park. Unlike other media fandoms, vicarious enjoyment through the numerous fan podcasts, vlogs, videos, and photos readily available online feels insufficient when one can be a local passholder within driving distance of the physical place experience. Fan-produced online media about Disneyland just encourages locals to visit even more often for fear of missing out on new fan activities and Disney offerings that pop up on an almost weekly basis at the park.

The aggregate population of Southern California's ten counties comprises over twenty-three million people. Though totaling more than one million passholders by the mid-2010s, Disneyland has never been a democratic place allowing votes on which attractions get bulldozed for new ones or where to draw the fine line between cosplay (banned) and Disneybounding (allowed). There are no public meetings on Main Street for annual passholders and fans to assemble and air grievances, though there is a City Hall where one can register a complaint with the guest relations department. People need to believe they have a say in the direction of a place for attachment to endure.[10] Disneyland fans can experience profound emotional distress when Disney makes changes to the park.[11] Older fans, who have grown up with cherished memories of certain attractions or spots, have particularly felt a call to preserve Walt's legacy at Disneyland in an emotional attachment similar to Sullivan's observation of media fandoms struggling with parent companies to protect canon.[12] Citing Disney's penchant for making changes in the park, Regan cautioned, "don't fall in love with Disneyland, it'll break your heart."[13] Unlike longtime media fandoms devoted to television and film series such as Star Wars, Doctor Who, or Star Trek, in which a fan can simply ignore disliked new texts to still enjoy the old, immutable originals, Disneyland fans cannot return to the park of Walt Disney's time of the 1950s and '60s, or the early Eisner era of the late 1980s and early '90s. When parts of Disneyland are changed or removed, fans can never again personally experience those cherished physical settings gone to Yesterland (with a website so named as an archive devoted to the history of discontinued Disney theme park attractions). Television and film texts are predominantly stable over time in the presentation of their content (though audience readings can evolve and directors such as George Lucas and Steven Spielberg have digitally tinkered with their popular films), so viewers always have the opportunity to rewatch the exact same narrative at every screening.[14] Theme park fans do not enjoy this peace of mind with their fandom object. Alterations to favorite attractions, such as the replacement of the Hollywood Tower of Terror with a Guardians of the Galaxy attraction, were cited by 44 percent of survey respondents as having a negative impact on Disneyland as a social place. With nearly 30 percent expressing disapproval of the Disney company's handling of Walt Disney's legacy and vision, a major departure by current management was the 2018 decision to allow the public sale of alcoholic beverages at the park.

Since Disneyland's 1955 opening, Walt Disney famously dictated that alcohol would not be sold publicly in order to preserve a family atmosphere and keep out the rowdy element associated with seaside amusement parks. Nevertheless, in 2018, the company subtly announced on the Disney Parks blog that "libations for adults" would be available at Oga's Cantina in the then-under-construction Galaxy's Edge land. After Disney confirmed the euphemism meant alcoholic beverages, some fans strongly opposed the new policy in posts across social media; but the fragmented voice of fandom, as well as considerable fan support for the alcohol policy change, induced resignation to Disney's decision to reverse a notable element of Walt Disney's park legacy. Fans assumed the initial offering of alcohol in Galaxy's Edge would only be a prelude to the sale of "adult libations" throughout the park, similar to the Trojan Horse introduction of highly profitable alcohol sales at the new, in 2012, Beauty and the Beast restaurant at the Magic Kingdom at Walt Disney World that spread in a few short years to all table-service restaurants in the formerly alcohol-free Florida park. Indeed, when Disneyland reopened in April 2021 after being closed for over a year due to the pandemic, the Blue Bayou restaurant attached to the Pirates of the Caribbean attraction started to sell alcoholic beverages. And in September 2023, wine, beer, and specialty cocktails began to be sold in Disneyland's remaining table service restaurants of Carnation Café, River Belle Terrace, and Café Orleans. Perhaps by the end of the 2020s, Disneyland will roll out outdoor vending carts selling beer in yellow cups just as in DCA. As for Disney's international Magic Kingdoms, Paris was the first to break tradition and sell alcohol in 1993, but the three Disneylands in Asia continue not to sell alcohol publicly (the exclusive members-only Club 33 venues in Tokyo and Shanghai sell alcohol privately), thus honoring Walt Disney's conviction that alcohol does not belong at places where adults and children play together.

In addition to the introduction of alcohol, Disneyland and DCA in the 2010s started to pivot away from child-centric lands and attractions for young families. In 2018, Disney took the rare step of closing and bulldozing an entire land with "a bug's land" in DCA removed to create room for a Marvel superhero land called Avengers Campus that opened in 2021. Dedicated to the Pixar film *A Bug's Life*, the now-shuttered land used to be the most kid-friendly area of DCA, featuring four attractions and a water play area all designed for small children to enjoy with their families. Instead, Avengers Campus features an Ant-Man themed microbrewery with a giant beer can. The only two attractions in Galaxy's Edge (Rise of the Resistance and Millennium Falcon: Smuggler's Run) have minimum height requirements barring young children from going on the rides. In the pier section of DCA, a building next to the lagoon that previously housed a small bar on the top floor and a large princess meet-and-greet dining experience with Ariel from *The Little Mermaid* on the ground level became a massive bar on both levels in 2018 with the popular merfolk princess evicted. In the Downtown Disney district, Build-a-Bear Workshop and Ridermakerz (customizable toy car construction) were both shut down by Disney in 2018 to make way for two new restaurants featuring craft beers and cocktails. Disney's Grand Californian hotel started featuring a poolside bar for the first time in 2019. Except for the extensive refurbishment in 2022 of Disneyland's children-centered Toontown land, Disney's actions in the last decade have been predominantly in the direction of appealing to adult visitors.

In Disneyland's hub in front of Sleeping Beauty Castle stands the Partners statue featuring Walt Disney and Mickey Mouse holding hands. At the base rests an inlaid plaque quoting the park's founder on the raison d'etre for the park, "I think most of all what I want Disneyland to be is a happy place . . . where parents and children can have fun, together." Perhaps bowing to the steadily declining birth rate in the United States, the increasingly prohibitively high cost of a set of annual passes for families with children, and the allure of high-profit-margin alcohol sales, Disneyland has gradually and tacitly been positioning itself as a playground for adults, not unlike the seaside amusement parks of the first half of the twentieth century that Walt Disney disdained as antimodels for Disneyland. When the *New York Post* agreed with an anonymous mother's viral social media video shaming childless millennials for enjoying Disney theme parks, *CBS News* pointed out that Disney had been directly courting childless adult patrons for years, not only with alcohol in the parks but also adults-only cruises.[15] Besides theme parks and cruise ships, the Disneyification of the US film industry (Pixar, Marvel, Lucasfilm, and Fox) allowed Disney prepandemic to seize nearly half of US domestic box office receipts. In response, Manohla Dargis, cochief film critic of the *New York Times*, commented in 2019 that "Disney conquered childhood and has now managed to conquer adulthood."[16]

Fandoms often demonstrate a mix of fascination and frustration with their favorite texts, and are noted for being subversive in producing meaning and challenging power structures in a manner similar to Bakhtin's carnivalesque space.[17] Although fan communities are more dispersed, divided, and fragmented (especially with the emergence of social media platforms) than corporations in asserting their interests, media fandoms have a long history (stretching back to the Victorian era campaign to revive Sherlock Holmes) of organizing groups to form a base of consumer activism to speak back to producers.[18] Passholders are relatively powerless as individuals but, at times, have been able to use their collective strength online to have a voice with Disney. For almost twenty years, the MiceChat website has published a Disneyland Update column every Monday morning read not only by a large audience of fans but also by Disney management. When the column highlighted photographs of a small bridge with peeling paint next to the castle, Disneyland maintenance was on location a couple days later accompanied by printouts of the photographs from MiceChat to pinpoint the trouble spots with brushes and paint buckets in tow to do the necessary repairs. While Disney may continue to glance through MiceChat's Monday morning columns for park maintenance tips, the days of a unified fan voice online to resist Disney gradually faded away with the fragmented, acquiescent, and financially susceptible nature of each succeeding online social platform. Place attachment could then be threatened if local fans felt voiceless concerning continuous changes to the park and its legacy from Walt Disney. However, an entirely unforeseen and different threat emerged in March 2020 with the global pandemic. Would place attachment to Disneyland endure for local fans shut out of the park for over a year?

PARK CLOSURE IN 2020 AND REOPENING SINCE 2021

On March 14, 2020, Disneyland closed its doors to visitors due to the global pandemic. Jeff Reitz, the passholder who had visited Disneyland every day since January 11, 2012, live-streamed as the last visitor to exit the Disneyland gates that night. Many passholders online believed the park would reopen in only a few weeks or months, but this initially optimistic outlook dimmed as the closure continued month after month. The extended closure ruptured the sense of self and routines of many fans and their social world.[19] Fans who could no longer access and showcase the park in videos and photos found new ways to express their devotion to Disneyland with playful make-believe homemade Disney ride videos and park food cooked at home, hashtagged on social media platforms as #homemadeDisney.[20] While theme park fans since the beginning of YouTube have enjoyed posting and viewing first-person ride-through videos of themed attractions,[21] fans now turned their houses and backyards into makeshift park attractions such as the Haunted Mansion and Pirates of the Caribbean to record and post to social media. The sustained participatory culture of Disneyland fandom during the park closure further confirmed the sense of attachment to the theme park in the lives of fans; the hashtag #homemadeDisney "became a virtual communal space, the site of anxiety and brand loyalty but also invention and creation."[22] After taking note and highlighting the newly popular homemade ride videos on the company's social media accounts as a display of fans' affective attachment, Disney quickly co-opted the new fan practice by posting #homemadeDisney-style videos by cast members on its Instagram account and then on the official Disney Parks Blog. As with previous iterations of innovative fan practices co-opted by the company, Disney was able to offer subject matter beyond the capacity of fans, such as behind-the-scenes tours and genuine Disneyland content such as performances by the Dapper Dans Main Street barbershop quartet and recipes of fan favorite food and beverages from the park such as Dole Whip ice cream and churros. Many fans took to social media to express their longing to socialize once again with friends and cast members at Disneyland, as well as grieve over pandemic deaths of members from social clubs and Facebook groups. During the shutdown, there was little to discuss or share about a closed park, so the number of posts to web discussion boards saw a huge drop in August 2020, with no posts to Laughing Place, only twenty-two to MousePlanet, and 406 to MiceChat. Influencers also had much less content to post since the park trip reports that, for the most part, formed their social media personas were no longer possible. In the meantime, Disney tried to relieve the pent-up desire of locals to visit the park by opening parts of the Downtown Disney shopping district and Buena Vista shopping street of DCA when permitted by California state government pandemic policy. Disney also took the protracted time afforded by the shutdown to plan changes to the park's future regarding the annual passholder system, park overcrowding, and recouping of lost revenue due to the closure.

In January 2021, Disney announced the termination of the annual passholder program, refunded all existing passholders, and said a replacement program would be revealed at a later date. Local fans on online social platforms lamented the end of the passholder era but sanguinely anticipated Disney's announcement of a new pass system. After being shut down for over a year, on April 30, 2021, Disneyland reopened exclusively for California residents who had made an advance online reservation for a ticket. The limited number of tickets, due to occupancy limits set by California government policy, sold out quickly online, but the fortunate fans able to gain admission reported enjoying a pleasantly uncrowded park. Over several months, occupancy limits gradually increased, and the park started to return to a semblance of prepandemic normalcy, except for the absence of live entertainment, such as fireworks and shows, which usually create dense crowds. With a reopened Disneyland, web discussion boards in August 2021 rebounded with fifteen posts to Laughing Place and 248 to MousePlanet. MiceChat's 1,944 posts surpassed even its prepandemic 2019 number. The rebound in posting activity coincided with Disney's announcement of the replacement of APs with the new Magic Key program.

In most aspects, the Magic Key passes were similar to the old AP, with comparable price points at multi-tiered levels featuring the usual added benefits of free parking and discounts on merchandise and dining. However, one enormous difference was the retention of the reservation system instituted since the park's April reopening. This new system applied to all levels of Magic Key passes, and only a limited number of reservations could be held by one key at a time. Essentially, Disney eliminated the easy access that had enabled locals to come to the park on any day at any time without the need to preplan. Fans online speculated that Disney's name change from annual passes to Magic Keys was intended to signify locals would no longer be able to enjoy unlimited, at-will access to the park and instead henceforth would need a key controlled by the company to open the lock on the entrance gates. Due to the cost and limitation on sales of Magic Keys, as well as the reservation system, Regan in 2023 reduced MiceChat Sunday meets to a seasonal schedule of only four times per year. At WDW in Florida, which has a much smaller local fan base, annual passes continued to be called annual passes and the reservation system was slated to begin a phase-out process in early 2024. The new Magic Key program with an advance reservation system meant no future local Disneyland fan would ever be able to challenge Reitz's streak, reminiscent of US Major League Baseball's Lou Gehrig and Cal Ripken, of 2,995 continuous daily park visits. On online social platforms, local fans proclaimed disappointment but understanding of Disney's need to tackle park overcrowding and optimism that the reservation system would not too negatively affect their Disneyland experience.

Magic Key passes first became available to purchase and use for park admission on August 25, 2021. Locals quickly snagged the new passes to make reservations using the new system. However, with a ninety-day window, the two top-level passes, Dream and Believe, were restricted to only six reservations at one time, and the two low-level passes, Enchant and Imagine, were limited to just four and two reservations, respectively. Magic Key holders started to complain on web discussion boards and social media platforms that no reservations were available for weekends, even two months in advance. Criticism mounted that the top-level Magic Key passes were originally sold with the assurance of few or no weekend blockout dates, but in practice the reservation system made it very difficult to book plans to go to the park with friends and family on weekends when most fans had time off from work. Some Magic Key holders filed a class-action lawsuit against Disney for deceptive advertising due to the promise of no blockout dates when the reservation system actually created de facto weekend blockouts. Disney responded by stopping all new sales of the top-level Dream Pass in October 2021 and then the next level Believe Pass in November 2021. In May 2022, Disney even stopped new sales of the two low-level Magic Key passes. Sales resumed of all keys in January 2023 except for the only key with no blockout dates, the Dream Key, which was essentially replaced by a new top-level key called Inspire with blockout dates during the winter holiday period from December 21 to January 1. Therefore, for the first time since the 1984 advent of the AP program, Disney no longer sold a pass for the park with no blockout dates. In August 2023, Disney settled the class-action lawsuit with a US$67.41 payout each only to Dream Key holders, who numbered 107,736 members. As of early 2024 the program was in flux, with Disney constantly vacillating which keys would be available for purchase and/or renewal, thus leading to fan anxiety and uncertainty.

Fans also disliked Disney's elimination of free FastPasses in favor of the new Lightning Lane and Genie Plus systems that required Disneyland app payments when visitors wanted to skip standby queues for popular attractions. Some online fans irreverently expressed their displeasure with the Genie Plus system by dubbing it Jafar Plus. These new systems disrupted favorite fan rituals such as ride takeovers by social clubs, and event organizers now needed to assiduously coordinate their groups digitally and monetarily, whereas the older system was simply free paper passes distributed by kiosks adjacent to the attractions. The increasing cost of the keys and day tickets, as well as upcharges for skipping lines, prompted complaints that led returning CEO Iger, who replaced Chapek after his ouster by the Disney board in November 2022, to respond: "And I think that in our zeal to grow profits, we may have been a little too aggressive about some of our pricing. And I think there is a way to grow our business but be smarter about how we price so that we maintain that brand value of accessibility."[23]

However, in early October 2023, Disney once again raised prices for day tickets, Magic Keys, and Genie Plus. With Disney's stock price trading more than US$100 down from its 2021 high, Regan in a late October 2023 Monday morning Disneyland Update expressed the increasing concerns felt by many fans concerning the company's trajectory: "The endless optimism of Disney's most loyal fans is fraying. I've never seen so much hostility toward Disney and their decisions before. Even the foamers who are incapable of seeing any wrong in Disney are starting to grumble about price, the difficulties of park visits, and the lackluster content on Disney+ and at the movies."[24]

In the end, despite one year of closure due to the pandemic, increasing prices for park access, and frustrating changes to park admittance with reservations and attraction queueing with Lightning Lane and Genie Plus, place attachment to Disneyland has seemed to endure thus far into the early 2020s; locals continue to flock to the park, as evidenced by a frequently sold-out reservation system, an estimated one million Magic Key holders, and loads of trip reports on online social platforms by influencers, website owners, and fans calling out the persistently large crowds in the park.

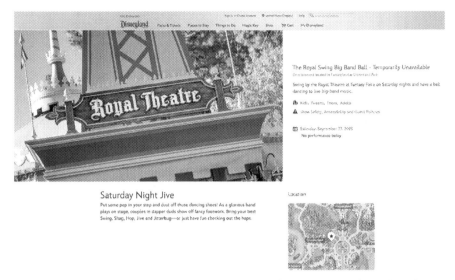

Figure 7.5. Disneyland website reporting the continued unavailability of Saturday night swing dancing. Screenshot taken on September 23, 2023.

DISNEYLAND FAN LEADERS AND SOCIAL MEDIA IN THE EARLY 2020s

Disneyland fan leaders have predominantly emerged from three types of participation: organizers of events and clubs, website discussion board owners, and social media influencers. Since the park reopening, the same organizers and website owners as before the pandemic have mostly picked up and continued their previously established roles. The largest fan events returned first with Gay Days in September 2021, Dapper Day in November 2021, MiceChat Gumball Rally in February 2022, and Bats Day in May 2022. By contrast, the organizers of the smaller-scale Lolita Day canceled plans for an October 2022 event due to the new reservation system and weekend blockout dates for lower-level keyholders that resulted in reduced park accessibility for event participants. The organizers announced on their website and social media accounts in August 2023 of their first postpandemic Lolita Day event subsequently held in January 2024. However, as of early 2024, Disney had yet to restore swing dancing to the park, with the venerable event chronically listed as "temporarily unavailable" on the Disneyland website (see Figure 7.5), though the administrator of the Disney Resort Swing Dance Band Schedule Facebook group has organized meets elsewhere in Southern California in the meantime. Social clubs returned to the park, but members acknowledged on Facebook the difficulty of gaining park admission for some associates due to the new reservation system. In a March 2022 accounting, the last before the Wix-hosted site disappeared in late 2023, the Social Clubs of Disneyland website (https://web.archive.org/web/20230929182120/https://socialclubsofdisney.com/list) listed 264 active clubs, twenty-one not yet fully established, seventeen inactive, 176 of unknown status, and 149 disbanded. The longstanding fan websites of MiceChat, Laughing Place, and Mouse Planet persevere while also looking to draw fans to their social media channels. MiceChat's Monday morning Disneyland update column continued into 2024 calling attention to park deficiencies, such as the often-broken animated windows at the Main Street Emporium. Consistent gains have been made on Instagram for Laughing Place at 26,900 followers, MiceChat at 40,100, and MousePlanet at 14,700 by January 2024. Since March 2019, MiceChat has intermittently uploaded videos to its YouTube channel while collecting a few thousand new subscribers to register above 12,000 in January 2024. On the other hand, Disneyland food vlogging channel Magic Journeys has regularly posted videos to increase its YouTube subscriber total from 75,600 in March 2019 to 268,000 by January 2024. Laughing Place has also been regularly uploading content to its YouTube channel about Disney and Universal theme parks worldwide to reach 177,000 subscribers, and some popular videos have amassed over one million views each. Although self-deprecatingly described in chapter 4 as being "old," Moseley's Laughing Place saw significant increases in audience to its channels on the two popular visual platforms by posting content on a regular schedule. These observations corroborate Cunningham and Craig's content creator commandment to regularly upload to YouTube to steadily realize audience gains.[25]

Instagram and YouTube were the primary visual platforms to build an audience until, in 2019 and 2020, TikTok emerged as the hot new visual social platform. While Disneyland does not have an official TikTok account, the Disney Parks account, which covers all Disney parks worldwide, had 12.7 million followers with over two thousand videos on the new platform by January 2024. With the staff and talent resources of a huge media corporation, Disney can be attentive to all popular and newly emergent online platforms. However, when a new platform suddenly takes off in popularity, labor costs increase for fan leaders who need to add yet another platform to a busy schedule of regular content uploads and audience relationship management. Therefore, it is unsurprising that longstanding fan website owners have been slow in establishing TikTok presences: MiceChat's account only had 120 followers and two videos, while Laughing Place had 52 videos with 1,148 followers as of January 2024. The commitment of fan event organizers to TikTok has been mixed, with Dapper Day having only 803 followers and forty-four videos, but Bats Day has built a sizable audience with over 300 videos and 12,000 followers. Just as was observed with early social media platforms, influencers, by far, have been the most active and successful in making the pivot to the new TikTok platform, with Sarah Sterling counting 22,700 followers from over 400 videos, Francis Dominic attracting 109,100 followers with over 600 videos, and former Thingamavlogs member Patrick Dougall amassing 378,800 followers with over 500 videos as of January 2024.

While the same event organizers and website owners have resumed their established practices and roles from prepandemic times, the Disneyland influencer scene has undergone considerable flux since the park closed. The high transaction costs of owning and maintaining a website necessitate continual investment in online engagement with fans by website owners, while the low transaction costs of free-to-use social media platforms afford influencers the luxury of intermittent commitment to online engagement with their audiences. Sarah Sterling fulfilled a common influencer goal of attaining work with Disney as a content specialist for the company's social media accounts and the Star Wars–themed hotel, Galactic Starcruiser, at WDW in Florida, which opened in March 2022 and closed a little over a year later in September 2023. Sterling's Instagram account, with 93,300 followers as of September 2023, noted in the bio section that the popular influencer was now a "retired YouTuber." Indeed, Sterling's YouTube account had 8,000 less subscribers in January 2024 compared to March 2019. After the relationship of Leo Camacho and Sterling ended, Camacho's content shifted focus to cosplay and graphic design rather than Disneyland. Camacho's main social media platform has always been Instagram, but the account went silent with no posting activity from July 2021 to September 2022. Followers fell during the long break to stand at 104,000 in January 2024, a drop of 19,000 from March 2019, but a sizable audience remained. Francis Dominic has continued to post regularly to Instagram with steady growth to 107,000 followers in January 2024, but added only a couple hundred new YouTube subscribers and, outside a few Shorts, has uploaded no new videos since Disneyland reopened. Patrick Dougall has regularly posted to YouTube since the park reopened, amassing 298,000 subscribers, and on Instagram had 101,000 followers as of January 2024. The fourth former member of Thingamavlogs, Tiffany Mink, had 26,700 subscribers on YouTube but has not posted to the platform since the park reopened. Mink is still active on Instagram with 44,700 followers as of January 2024, though the content has leaned toward Disney lifestyle more than focus on the park. Dougall has transformed from the Thingamavlogs member with the least subscribers and followers in 2017 to the most in 2024 by consistently posting content to the most popular visually oriented social media platforms of the 2010s, Instagram and YouTube, as well as enthusiastically embracing TikTok, the newly emergent popular visual platform of the 2020s. By also observing the commandment to regularly upload content to steadily build an audience, the YouTube channel of Fresh Baked grew from 111,000 subscribers in 2019 to 191,000 in January 2024 by focusing on park updates, history, tips, and commentary.

My discussion has focused on YouTube, TikTok, and Instagram because those platforms saw the greatest growth in audiences for all three types of fandom leaders. From March 2019 to January 2024, follower numbers on Twitter either increased or remained unchanged but Facebook witnessed anemic growth, stagnation, or even a downward trend in some cases. Gay Days Anaheim had almost no change in the number of Twitter followers but actually lost 3,000 on its primary platform of outreach, Facebook, to total 47,000. Sarah Sterling gained 1,500 more Twitter followers but lost 1,000 followers on Facebook by early 2024 compared to 2019. MiceChat gained over a thousand more Twitter followers and added almost 15,000 more on Facebook, its primary social platform, for a total of 81,000 in January 2024. Laughing Place not only gained almost 10,000 new Facebook followers to be slightly over 20,000 but doubled its Twitter audience to over 50,000 followers by January 2024. Event groups such as Steam Day and Lolita Day that have mostly been dormant since the park's closure have generally seen Facebook follower counts remain unchanged between 2019 and 2024, though Galliday shed a few hundred in the interim. Even the official Disneyland page on Facebook decreased by a million followers since 2019 to land at 16 million in 2024.

While Facebook remains an important platform for event organizers to communicate with potential attendees and web board owners to circulate news and moderate debates among fans in a primarily textual orientation, YouTube has become the leading platform for more recently established influencers. Since starting channels in the early 2010s, the newer influencers have foregrounded a visual orientation with vlogs such as Magic Journeys, which by January 2024 had only 13,000 Facebook followers compared to 268,000 on YouTube, and Fresh Baked with 23,000 on Facebook but 191,000 on YouTube. Launched only in 2017, Five Fires had 190,000 subscribers on YouTube as of January 2024 but has essentially ignored Facebook with only twenty-eight members. The Magic Journeys landing page on Facebook even features a YouTube logo on its cover photo and an intro section entreaty to "join me on YouTube as we learn the Secrets and History of the Magic Kingdom" (see Figure 7.6). Where Regan used Facebook in the late 2000s to drive traffic to the MiceChat website, newly established Disneyland influencers since the mid-2010s have used Facebook to divert and convert followers into subscribers to their YouTube

Figure 7.6. Magic Journeys Facebook landing page. Screenshot taken on March 5, 2023.

channels. Facebook, as Regan noted previously, has offered no economic value to group owners for creating content and governing users on the platform. By stark contrast, YouTube pays its influencer creators a share of the advertising revenue generated by a channel's videos. It is therefore unsurprising that influencers would try to divert traffic away from a platform such as Facebook that until recent years offered no direct generation of economic capital to one such as YouTube with the potential to earn a meaningful income stream. Furthermore, Disneyland influencers using YouTube as their primary platform, such as Fresh Baked and Five Fires, often offer critique with their long-form video commentaries, unlike the snapshots and short-form videos of the influencers using Instagram and TikTok as preferred platforms, thus further indicating the effect of platform nature and characteristics on a channel's disposition toward Disney. As fan leaders and Disney continue to develop their online social platform strategies with YouTube, Instagram, the newly emergent TikTok, and potential future platforms at the expense of an apparently declining Facebook, it will be telling to look back on the 2020s in the early 2030s to examine this fourth decade of the evolving intersection online and in-park compared with the previous three for new trends and developments.

Figure 7.7. Takeover of the Mad Tea Party attraction by Lolita Day participants, Disneyland, October 2017. Photo: Author.

INTERPLAY OF FANS, DISNEY, AND ONLINE SOCIAL PLATFORMS

Among the three types of fandom leaders, only event organizers hold some leverage with Disney because they bring economic value to the company in the form of visitors and commerce to the park. When Disney gave a major event organizer a hard time about the scheduling and assignment of ballrooms at the Disneyland hotel for a large annual fan event, the organizer shared spreadsheets with Disney management as a reminder of the large amount of revenue the popular event generated for the company. Disney promptly backed down. When the lead ride operator at the Mad Tea Party was initially uncooperative with Lolita Day participants doing a ride takeover for a group photo (see Figure 7.7), the organizers went to City Hall to voice their concerns. Guest relations pledged better coordination with the event organizers in the future. Just as in electoral politics, organized groups can apply pressure to make their voices heard, though the greater the amount of economic value generated by fan organizers likely determines the nature of Disney's response. Since the concerns of fan event organizers are usually limited to the event itself and not broadly to general park policies, plans, and management, and rarely are voiced online, Disney can discreetly deal with their issues on an ad hoc basis.

The nature of the relationships that organizers, website owners, and influencers form with Disney has relied in large measure on the characteristics of the different online social platforms and circulation of cultural, social, and economic capital. Outside of Gay Days and Dapper Day, fan organizers of in-park events, meets, and social clubs derive no economic value from their labor and instead pride themselves on the social value derived from establishing and sustaining a new friend group with shared interests at their cherished place of Disneyland. This characteristic profile of fan organizers resonates with Benkler's observation that the enabling of individuals to interact and share information through online networking outside previous institutional constraints was not for material gain but rather for a diverse set of motivations including self-gratification, well-being, and social connections.[26] Scott also observed fan community building as creating a gift economy driven by sharing, not profit.[27] Fannish outrage is often kindled when the ethos of fan gift economy has been violated in favor of profit, such as the case of the short-lived website FanLib monetizing archived fan fiction with adjoining advertisements.[28] Benkler believed this new decentralized, nonmarket transactional framework would result in social sharing and exchange. Interaction was no longer just for market production but rather a new kind of social production that could challenge incumbent industrial models. For example, Skype, peer-to-peer file sharing, and Wikipedia could threaten, and be threatened by, the telecommunication companies, the recording industry, and Encarta respectively. While fan event and social club organizers fulfill Benkler's rule, the website owners of the 2000s and social media influencers of the 2010s have been motivated to engage in information, knowledge, and social production to attract the cultural capital of status bestowal by Disney that in turn concomitantly builds social capital with fans. Social capital can then subsequently be parlayed into economic value that primarily benefits Disney and, to a lesser extent, website owners and influencers. Rather than challenging the incumbent industrial model as Benkler maintained, website owners and influencers are often motivated by the characteristics of their platforms to work together with Disney for mutual benefit in accruing all forms of capital.

Unlike Benkler's optimism in 2006 of a then-flourishing nonmarket sector of social production to challenge incumbents, van Dijck's 2013 analysis of Facebook, Twitter, Flickr, YouTube, and Wikipedia as the popular sociotechnical constructs of the time illustrated that all, except for Wikipedia, got consumed by a profit-driven social connectivity that became a normalized infrastructure affecting user values because "platform owners surreptitiously preempted the rhetoric of collaboration and gradually endowed concepts like sharing and friending with a different meaning."[29] Since status on Instagram derives in large part by showcasing a much greater number of followers than following fellow users, social media influencers cannot risk their cultural capital by reciprocating the likes, comments, follows, and subscribes received from everyday fans unless there is an evident self-interested benefit. On the other hand, the fan social formation organizers for events, clubs, and meets have mostly used the reciprocating platforms of Facebook and Messenger and generally embraced a socially productive motivation with no interest in financial benefit.

The divergent outlooks of the three types of fan leaders are tied into their online social platforms of choice to connect with fans. For web discussion board owners, high transaction costs necessitate a consistent revenue stream to pay the bills and, hence, a close relationship with Disney to access exclusive content to build site popularity and social capital with fans. The nature of being a social media influencer has entailed a persistent obligation to upload compelling photos and videos to followers and subscribers. This predicament has led influencers, similar to website owners beforehand, to form a close relationship with Disney for access to exclusive content in order to accrue nonreciprocated social capital with followers and subscribers. By contrast, fan social formation organizers need not form a relationship with Disney for their events and clubs to be popular. In addition, events such as Galliday, Lolita Day, and Steam Day are unconnected to Disney texts, so the company holds comparatively little cultural capital to offer as leverage to those fan event organizers who primarily measure success in social, not economic, capital. Jenkins et al. observed in 2013 that the commercial motivations of companies clashed with the social motivations of fans,[30] but this book's study of Disneyland has revealed prominent segments of the park's fandom, principally website owners and social media influencers, have accepted commercial values that not only align and liaise with Disney but have also been shaped by their choice of online social platforms.

CHAPTER 8

Platforms, Place, and Beyond

A common plot connecting the evolution of playful places from Roman Saturnalia to Disneyland and internet platforms from Usenet to social media has been the gradual commodification of both leisure places and online social platforms over their respective histories. While Saturnalia, festivals, and carnivals saw visitors participate in spontaneous activities within the crowd, the ephemeral nature, in terms of time and space, of early playful places precluded the formation of regular social groups among strangers. Pleasure gardens and amusement parks embraced longer operating seasons in fixed locations with large crowds of paying visitors but did not witness the creation of regular social formations among strangers at these playful places. Even though the AP program began in 1984, only the print-based fan clubs Disneyana and Mouse Club organized annual meets for members in the park through their print publications. No other fan-organized events, meets, or clubs at Disneyland formed until the popular diffusion of early online social platforms in the 1990s. With the Disney company and Disneyland both firmly rooted in Southern California culture, there were locals from the beginning of the park in the 1950s who developed an attachment to Disneyland and visited regularly for Disney organized events such as swing dancing or Date Nite. In the last three decades, the technology, business model, ownership, and architecture of both online social platforms and Disneyland have been purposefully designed by their corporate owners to extract as much economic value as possible from users and visitors. However, local fans have used online social platforms to discover fan-organized social activities in the park, and then attend and connect with strangers in person at events, meets, and clubs.

Early online social platforms combined with the AP program to super-charge the relationship between local fans and Disneyland. Fans who were previously strangers in the park logged onto a computer at their office or home to connect, interact, and organize together. In addition to exchanging information and knowledge, fans resisted the plans of the company and organized activities in the park without Disney's permission or supervision. Fans began to substitute Disney's rules-bound rides of constraining lap bars and routinized narratives for the free play of custom-designed apparel, Disneybounding, ride takeovers, socializing, staging photos and videos, gift giving, and simply having fun together. The sharing of text-based trip reports on Usenet (and later with photos and videos on web discussion boards and social media) encouraged other local fans to engage and share their own forms of in-park play. Disney saw its control of the discourse, commerce, and social formations related to Disneyland challenged by fans in the 1990s and early 2000s due to corporate technological torpidity and the nature of early online social platforms. However, the characteristics of subsequent online social platforms allowed Disney to wrest control over discourse and commerce by co-opting website owners and social media influencers, as well as fan-created media and practices.

The website owners and influencers of Disneyland fandom were comparatively more susceptible to co-option than their counterparts in other media fandoms because Disney could leverage the powerful reward of insider access to the place of Disneyland in exchange for positive coverage. By contrast, the settings of *The X-Files*, *Star Trek*, and other popular media properties filmed at studio soundstages and temporarily staged real-world locations fail to provide the persistent, fixed, emotionally resonant, physical place of Disneyland that a corporate owner can easily leverage as a recurring reward to fan website owners and influencers for persistent and reliable positive coverage. The Warner Bros. studio tour in Hollywood escorts visitors by tram to view the exteriors of soundstages with commemorative plaques listing the films and television shows that have been shot within the buildings for a century (see Figure 8.1). Although many of the films and shows named on the plaques are recognizable to visitors, there is little, if any, emotional resonance because there are no physical artefacts from the productions remaining inside or outside the soundstages to provide sensory modality. Other corporate media owners simply do not have the leverage of a fandom object with such enduring narrative power embodied in a physical, tangible place as Disneyland.

Contrary to admonitions by academics such as Turkle that digital screens are reducing human contact and warnings by major news

Figure 8.1. Commemorative plaque at Stage 15 on the Warner Bros. studio lot in Hollywood, California, November 2017. Photo: Author.

organizations such as the *New York Times* that human face-to-face contact is becoming a privilege for elites as the masses make do with screens,[1]
the intersection of online social platforms and smartphones for locals at
Disneyland has facilitated a continuous growth in fan-organized in-park
social formations and activities. The original fan-organized events of Gay
Days and Bats Day are still being celebrated in the park after twenty-five
years and a pandemic. However, the sustainability of any fan-organized
activity at Disneyland can be imperiled by three factors. First is the competition for participants from so many events, meets, and clubs in the park,
though the proliferation has afforded fans a much wider choice of social

associations. Second, the increasing costs of annual passes and one-day tickets and bureaucratic burden of the reservation system have limited and complicated fan access to the park. Bats Day has been truncated from a weekend of activities to one day, due in part to the first two factors, though the next final factor would not be applicable to the goth-themed event. Third is the threat of supplantation by Disney offering official park events substantially similar to already existing fan events such as, for example, a vintage fashion night comparable to Dapper Day. In June 2023, for the first time, Disneyland held After Dark events for Pride Nite to honor the LGBTQ+ community and allies with themed entertainment, food, and merchandise, iconic Disney characters in special costumes, and music and dancing. The events were held from 9 p.m. to 1 a.m. (early admission at 6 p.m.) with a ticket costing US$139. Fan organizers do not have the levels of economic and cultural capital to compete with Disney at Disneyland for an elaborately themed event, though, of course, fans could feel the more the merrier and attend both the official Disney event and fan version. However, a key persistent difference remains that Disney-organized themed events do not necessarily provide the ample opportunity for social mixing that fan-organized events have customarily offered with group photos, ride takeovers, and contests. In addition, fan events are predominantly free of charge with participation only contingent on possessing a ticket or annual pass to enter the park. Ultimately, the focus of Disney has been on economic capital, while most fan event organizers and participants have prioritized social capital.

Disneyland fans still critique the park online, but their views have fragmented across numerous social media platforms. In addition, the relatively equal voices of individual fans on Usenet became eclipsed in reach and prominence by fan website owners and influencers with cultural capital courtesy of cooperation with Disney. Only the fan-organized in-park social formations enabled by Facebook groups, Messenger (and also Facebook-owned WhatsApp by the late 2010s), and smartphones have remained outside Disney's sway for now, though a co-option strategy for the practice has seemingly started with official themed night events. Disney was slow to adapt to the online fan challenge of the 1990s and early 2000s, but the nature of online social platforms since the mid-2000s enabled the company, for the most part, to prevail over fans in the contest over discourse and commerce regarding Disneyland. This thirty-year arc of initial fan agency ultimately succumbing to corporate control mirrors the trajectory of online social platforms. Instagram, Flickr, and YouTube all started as self-regulating communities ultimately bought out by large media corporations that transformed their initial public social values into corporate commercial ones. An additional online example is the film and television review aggregation site Rotten Tomatoes, launched in 1998 by three students at the University of California, Berkeley, and then acquired by News Corp.'s Fox Interactive Media division in 2005. As of 2024, the site is jointly held by Warner Media and NBC Universal with 25 percent and 75 percent stakes, respectively. Rotten Tomatoes had originally allowed any fan who signed up for an account to post reviews until 2019, when a verification system was implemented to check first that a reviewer had purchased a ticket through Fandango and other ticketing sites for the film review being submitted. Conveniently, Fandango has the same corporate owners as Rotten Tomatoes, so fan reviewers essentially pay to post a critique within an integrated commercial ecosystem. In 2017, Rotten Tomatoes was accused of withholding early reviews on the site for the DC film *Justice League* until the Thursday night release to shield the movie from criticism and protect its corporate parent, Warner Bros., as the studio behind the film.[2] And in September 2023, entertainment news site *Vulture* reported reviews comprising a film's "Tomatometer" score had been manipulated by a public relations firm that paid off movie critics.[3]

Maxwell and Miller observe the evolutionary arc of the Internet as predictable since "the lesson of newer media technologies is the same as print, radio and television: each one is quickly dominated by centralized and centralizing corporations, regardless of its multi-dimensional potential."[4] As seen in the case of Disney and fans, the early democratic promise of many-to-many communication online gradually subsided in favor of the corporate-controlled model endemic to legacy media technologies. In the new digital one-to-many model, corporations speak not only through their official social media presences, apps, blogs, and websites but also through fan influencers and website owners with "authentic" voices touting the approved corporate-branded message. Participation in the online discourse regarding a fandom object is now constructed within an internet architecture that foregrounds and supports corporate commercial values over a public fan voice and critique. Chapter 3 noted the online uproar in 1996 when Disney replaced the metal cutlery and melamine plates with plastic and cardboard at Disneyland's French Market restaurant. Disney reversed the poorly implemented and environmentally malign change within forty-five days. As a sign of the change of the times over the last three decades, in January 2023 Disney once again swapped the metal and melamine for plastic and cardboard at the French Market but with almost no online outcry by fans.

FANS OUTSIDE SOUTHERN CALIFORNIA AND THEME PARKS BEYOND THE ORIGINAL DISNEYLAND

Although the scope of this book is restricted to residents of Southern California who visit Disneyland, research could also be done on park fan visitors who reside in other parts of the United States, or even around the world, to ascertain their sense of the original Disneyland as a place and use of online social platforms in comparison to the locals under study here. In particular, during fieldwork in the park and research online, I encountered annual passholders hailing from Northern California, Nevada, and Arizona who made monthly or bi-monthly visits and proclaimed a strong attachment to the park. In addition, I also met fans who were born and raised in Southern California but moved elsewhere in the United States for work or family but still returned to the region as often as possible to go to Disneyland. To continue to connect to Disneyland while living away from the region, forlorn fans watch fan-produced YouTube vlogs, such as Fresh Baked and Five Fires, that feature local fans uploading weekly park adventures with commentary. While at work or in the car, some fans listen to podcasts such as *The Sweep Spot*, hosted by former Disneyland custodians Ken Pellman and Lynn Barron, and *A Window to the Magic*, which since 2007 has simply consisted of a silent podcaster walking around and going on rides at Disneyland for the day while recording only the park soundscape.

Future research could plumb the quality and depth of the social relationships formed by locals at Disneyland using Oldenburg's concept of the third place, social network theory, or other community frameworks. Indeed, cast members at Disneyland have uniquely flipped Oldenburg's theory on its head by treating their second place (of work) as their third place (of leisure) and would gladly make the park their first place (of home) if permitted by Disney. In addition, since the study's survey, interviews, and participant observation were delimited to participants eighteen years of age and older, research could examine how local teenage fans navigate the intersection of online social platforms and Disneyland. A potential limitation of the study was the online survey's recruitment through Facebook and website fan groups and word-of-mouth during participant observation and fieldwork in the park, leading to annual passholders and cast members comprising 91 percent of total respondents. With adequate funding, a marketing firm could be retained to contact potential respondents in Southern California by phone to secure greater generalizability with a wider sample of respondents ranging from dedicated annual passholders to casual, infrequent park visitors. This book's model framework can be used to examine longitudinally the experience of other media fandoms and corporate intellectual property owners on online social platforms. Furthermore, citing Hill's call for more studies of cyclical fandom and Harrington and Bielby's appeal to examine fandoms over the duration of fan lifetimes, Click's longitudinal analysis of Martha Stewart fans could be a framework to study potential rises and falls in engagement by Disneyland locals throughout their lives.[5] And as mentioned in the previous chapter, this book's study could be updated in the early 2030s by continuing its longitudinal examination of the evolution of the online social platform landscape and Disneyland in the fourth decade of widespread internet usage, the 2020s. As the first longitudinal study of a fandom, place, and online social platforms, these updates could continue for decades to come.

Over the last few hundred years, pleasure gardens, mechanical amusement parks, and theme parks have often been derided by observers as frivolous, vacuous, antisocial spaces.[6] Eco and Baudrillard, in particular, have frequently been cited for their critiques of Disneyland as a spectacle of consumption.[7] However, this book not only illustrates that Disneyland is a meaningful place for many locals but also raises the question whether locals proximate to other Disney parks in Orlando, Tokyo, Paris, Hong Kong, and Shanghai exhibit the same cognitive, affective, and behavioral affinity as Southern California fans. Besides Disney, theme parks by Universal Studios, LEGOLAND, Dollywood, Busch Gardens, SeaWorld, and other themed entertainment venues could be examined for the intersection of online social platforms and place. Within this new research area, a 2023 study on De Efteling already revealed strong place attachment among locals to the esteemed Dutch theme park.[8] The growth of the themed entertainment industry continues apace as US domestic theme and amusement parks generate over US$50 billion in economic activity every year.[9] Six Flags in 2019 launched a new type of theme park rewards system for its annual passholders similar to airline loyalty programs with points earned for checking in to rides and shows, taking surveys, number of park visits, and every dollar spent at in-park restaurants and shops for perks including free tickets for friends, line-skip passes, and special experiences. The program is purpose-built to develop a base of local annual passholders similar to Disneyland. While Disney has already co-opted many of the functions of fan-created park apps, the company's Play app, launched in 2018, was designed to provide an augmented reality experience within the Star Wars milieu of the then new Galaxy's Edge land. The Play app afforded interaction with droids and light panels, scanning inside of crates, translation of signs and audio from Aurebesh (a Star Wars language) to English, tuning into antenna arrays to eavesdrop, and an overarching game where visitors could join a faction upon entering the land. Whereas locals have customarily used smartphones to facilitate fan-organized social activities in the park, Disney filled the interactive app with storytelling features to focus fan attention back on Disney organized and controlled activities with the potential for commercial tie-ins with park merchandise and replayable game scenarios to encourage repeat visits. However, it is doubtful fan-organized social activities can be displaced by a Disney Play app that has thus far failed to connect players socially with fellow park visitors.

In every formal interview and informal conversation with fans, all agreed that Disneyland possessed an incomparable magic, with Disney stories, themes, and characters a cut above in emotional resonance compared to almost anything at competing theme park chains (with the Wizarding World of Harry Potter at Universal Studios being the notable exception). The original Disneyland beckons visitors with the reassuring architecture of an idyllic Main Street, a fairy tale Fantasyland of Tudor-style structures, an elegant, jazz-imbued New Orleans Square, and a tranquil, rustic northwestern US backdrop of Critter Country. At Universal Studios Hollywood, Jurassic Park/World dinosaurs want to eat you, an actor playing Norman Bates from *Psycho* chases your tram wielding a large knife, the largest set of the famous studio tour features a huge and realistic plane crash site from *War of the Worlds*, and, until recently, the first attraction upon entering the park was a walkthrough with zombies from *The Walking Dead* shambling after you and your brains. Therefore, it was unsurprising to have locals often tell me that Universal was a great park to visit once every year or two, but Disneyland was their regular social place of choice. Scibelli believes the Disney theme park ". . . provides a reassuring dose of vicarious Prozac for stressed-out modern Americans. The original Disneyland Park in Anaheim illustrates this point. Within the attractions at the original Disneyland Park, one "theme" surfaces again and again, the desire for visitors to temporarily escape their everyday lives in the modern world."[10]

Disneyland was purposefully designed for visitors to transcend their everyday lives by stepping into a multi-dimensional experiential film.[11] Walt Disney's overriding emphasis on joy and laughter within an architecture of reassurance would seem to be by now a well-established formula in theme park design to attract and build a large local fan base for repeat visits, but many theme parks around the world have not necessarily abided by this winning precedent. The new Warner Bros. theme park that opened in 2018 in Abu Dhabi, United Arab Emirates, features DC comic book heroes such as Batman with a land dedicated to Gotham City including the following attractions: The Joker Funhouse, Scarecrow Scare Raid, Riddler Revolution, meet and greets with the Joker and Harley Quinn, and the Hall of Doom restaurant. The park's Gotham City is well themed to the source material by being dark, garish, eerie, and sinister, but hardly a place to visit on a regular basis to feel relaxed and reassured. The entrance to the Joker Funhouse recalls the "happy face" entrance of the

Figure 8.2. The Joker Funhouse in Gotham City land of the Warner Bros. World theme park in Abu Dhabi, United Arab Emirates, August 2018. Photo: Author.

early twentieth-century Coney Island parks while comprising a maze of scare-inducing mental and physical challenges themed to the Batman rogues gallery (see Figure 8.2). Even the Metropolis land, featuring superhero attractions and meet and greets with Superman, Aquaman, and Green Lantern, feels foreboding with dark lighting due in part to being an enclosed indoor park, though the Looney Tunes and Flintstones lands are much brighter and cheerier.

By contrast for superhero land design, the Marvel Avengers Campus of DCA features meet and greets almost exclusively with heroes such as Captain America, Black Widow, Doctor Strange, and Captain Marvel, and the Guardians of the Galaxy and Spiderman attractions are filled with humor and energetic, upbeat soundtracks. The emphasis on joy and laughter did not originate with Walt Disney and Disneyland but has been a key characteristic of playful places throughout history.[12] Walt Disney's overriding emphasis on the architecture of reassurance for the foundation of Disneyland and its original five lands is one of, if not the primary, reason for the park being so sticky a social glue as a place of attachment for locals to make regular visits.

Compared to other iterations of Disneyland around the world, the original in Anaheim might be uniquely designed and situated as a preternatural match to the fantasy penchant of the Southern Californian character,[13] and perhaps not replicable elsewhere to the same level of cognitive, affective, and behavioral effect. Matt Ouimet, who worked at Disney for seventeen years, including three as Disneyland president, believed:

Figure 8.3. Main Street Fire Station in Disneyland with lit lamp in the second-floor apartment window to signify the continuing spirit of Walt Disney in the park, October 2017. Photo: Author.

The reality of it is that there is a disproportionate amount of passionate guests here compared to any other park in the world. There is an emotional attachment, and Disneyland—because it is the original—has a heritage. I don't think you'll find people that passionate about Walt Disney World. These people grew up with it . . . this is the fabric of these people's lives. The intensity of it sometimes surprises me.[14]

As the only Disney park conceived and built by Walt Disney with his personal touch, élan, and discernment, Disneyland offers an intimate experience of interwoven attractions and architecture not manifest in later Disney parks that have incorporated greater distances between attractions and a larger scale to spread out crowds. Walt Disney's apartment above the Main Street Fire Station still exists more than fifty years after his death with a lit lamp (or Christmas tree during the winter holiday season) in the window to signify his continuing presence to the tens of thousands who walk by every day on their way in and out of his eponymous park (see Figure 8.3). No other Disney park contains such a personal and puissant semiotic overlooking the Town Square where Walt Disney delivered the July 17, 1955, dedication speech emphasizing the tangible physicality of the place and land by welcoming visitors, "To all who come to this happy place. Welcome. Disneyland is your land." On several late nights during my fieldwork, I stood next to the fire station observing visitors heading for the park exit gate with some acknowledging the second-floor window lamp by gazing upward to make eye contact, waving a hand goodbye, or murmuring a word of thanks.

DISNEYLAND IN 2155

This book began with a personal reflection on approaching Disneyland for the first time as an adult expecting to be overcome by commercialism and inauthenticity. Those elements can certainly be observed in the park, as many critics and observers have previously noted. However, by studying Southern California fans, a deeper layer emerged in which Disneyland and online social platforms intersected to create an extraordinarily meaningful, shared social place in fan lives. For example, fan web discussion boards and social media groups occasionally contain threads about locals who are frequently observed in the park. One local adored by fans is Peter Tu, a ninety-year-old Asian-American senior citizen who was initially dubbed "the clapper" due to repeatedly clapping hands and performing a special handshake with cast members and visitors during regular morning trips to the park. Tu's granddaughter discovered the online fan chatter and uploaded a YouTube video in 2015 of Tu's typical Disneyland day since starting his park visits in 1999.[15] The subsequent sharing of the video on online social platforms made Tu even more renowned among fans, who then looked for the nonagenarian in the park to perform the handshake or follow along and clap together. A couple years after the video was originally posted to YouTube, Tu's granddaughter, Jade Tu, posted the following comment:

> He really does appreciate the love y'all have for him. He loves when people go up to talk or take pictures with him. He was telling me the other day that this video made him so happy. He was saying that usually old people feel really sad because nobody ever talks to them or pays attention to them, but he doesn't feel that way at all. So, really, thank you all for the kindness you show him. I think the interactions he has with you guys is a major part of why he still goes there everyday.[16]

YouTuber commenters replied how much they loved seeing Tu in the park bringing joy to everyone he meets. After meeting Tu in Disneyland, fans have often uploaded photos and videos to YouTube, Instagram, Twitter, and Facebook, further establishing his fan celebrity. Tu did not initiate his park routine in 1999 contemplating fame as a local Disneyland fan. Instead, Tu reached this level of prominence through a continuous feedback loop of fans taking photos and videos with him in the park, and sharing the media to online social platforms, thereby increasing his fame and motivating more fans to seek him out in the park. Shirky highlighted this kind of feedback loop of personal and social motivations as a notable characteristic of social media that indulges a desire for greater connectedness.[17] Tu's carefree somatic expression of joy at just being in Disneyland is a kind of free play relatable to most fans. I can attest to meeting Tu one morning during my fieldwork at Disneyland, performing the special handshake while other visitors gathered around, and having a big smile on my face afterward. Unbridled joy is contagious within a shared interest social group, so it is quite understandable that locals search for fan events, meets, and clubs on online social platforms to offer every fan a multitude of different options almost every week to find a playful encounter or a steady social group. As Tu himself related in an April 2019 video, "I like Disneyland, because I make a lot of friends at Disneyland."[18]

Online social platforms have enabled disparate strangers with a shared interest to discover each other online through groups dedicated to that interest and then meet in person at a proximate shared place. However, Disneyland is a very particular social place that park visitors told me repeatedly was not transferrable on a cognitive, affective, and behavioral sense to any other locale in Southern California. When asked where they would be on a given Sunday if Disneyland did not exist, many simply replied, "home." Online social platforms have helped local fans find each other at Disneyland as a great social mixer; otherwise they might not have found each other at all. When Marty Sklar, a former president of Imagineering and Walt Disney confidant, was asked whether Disneyland would still be around on the 200th anniversary in 2155 or replaced by some virtual reality format, Sklar believed people would continue to seek out the physical experience of being in the park with other people.[19] Fans often cite Sklar's belief that "Disneyland will never be finished" because it is "something alive, something that keeps growing."[20] Indeed, Disney announced in September 2023 a planned investment of US$60 billion over the next ten years for its theme parks, cruise ships, and experiences, which includes a plan called Disneyland Forward to nearly double the size of the entire Southern California resort including a probable third theme park. With the announcement, Disney seems to be shifting focus away from its screen-based streaming services and film studios to the in-person experiences of theme parks and cruise ships that have traditionally been the most consistent and reliable revenue and profit generators for the company.

Playful places throughout history have witnessed people enjoying the communion of being part of a festive crowd while seeing and being seen, so new online platforms and technologies will probably continue to foster, complement, and evolve, and not displace or replace, the social activities and experiences created by fans in the park since the 1990s. Even before the internet, fandoms have long served as an alternative form of social community and will almost certainly continue to do so with whatever new mediums or platforms emerge in the future. This hitherto obscured level of fan organization, creativity, sociality, and play at the park, as exemplified by the many events, meets, and clubs afforded by online social platforms, is a development that previous observers of Disneyland did not note due to fixating on the mercantilist aspects often foregrounded by Disney itself. Although prognosticating to the year 2155 is nebulous, Southern California fans are likely to use any future online social platforms and technology to continue to connect with each other for knowledge, discussion, and creativity and form in-person groups and activities at Disneyland for social pursuits even as the Disney company continues to attempt to co-opt fan ingenuity and activities for commercial objectives. Putnam, in 2000, famously warned in the book *Bowling Alone* about the collapse of social capital with the demise of bowling leagues and other in-person communal locales and activities in the United States since 1950, but perhaps sociality has shifted to new local playful places such as theme parks that have been long derided and dismissed as placeless and synthetic. Together with assistance from online social platforms, Disneyland could represent a new model of in-person sociality to build upon and inspire the creation of more socially meaningful local places within an architecture of reassurance now and in the future.

ACKNOWLEDGMENTS

The journey to this book's publication has been long but filled with many wonderful people who must be thanked for their indispensable help, guidance, and support along the way. First, I want to express my deepest appreciation to all the interviewees who took time out from their busy lives to sit down and talk with me. I hope all of you find the book's account resonant and scrupulous because this study would not have been possible without your kind participation. Also, I want to thank all the survey respondents for their time providing invaluable input. Furthermore, I must thank the many, many fans I encountered and chatted up during almost three months of participant observation and fieldwork at Disneyland. And special thanks to all the fantastic cast members, particularly at the Opera House, Enchanted Tiki Room, and Main Street Magic Shop, who noticed my daily trips and greeted me like one of the regulars in a heartening exemplar of Oldenburg's third place. Although the Disney company receives a good deal of criticism in this book, I want to thank Disney and the Imagineers for creating a truly remarkable place that brings so many different people together publicly, socially, joyfully, and in-person at an expansive and engaging pedestrian oasis. I believe we need more places like Disneyland for a more gracious world. I was fortunate to find long-term affordable accommodation within a fifteen-minute walk to the park gate at Extended Stay America. A special thanks to Adrienne at the front desk who was not only a superb hotel manager but also an insightful sounding board.

Second, I need to express appreciation to the many people who helped and inspired me along the academic road. Thanks to Sal Humphreys, Kim Barbour, and Ming Cheung at the University of Adelaide; Toshio Kuroda and Kalevi Holsti at the International University of Japan; and Richard Maxwell, Walid Raad, Jonathan Buchsbaum, Ed Lenert, Morris Rossabi, Mayumi Itoh, and Pei-yi Wu at the City University of New York. Thanks to colleagues past and present at Zayed University including Filareti Kotsi, Marilyn Roberts, Dwight Brooks, Pam Creedon, Renee and Charlie Everett, Badran Badran,

Michael Mulnix, James Piecowye, Nadia Rahman, Russell Williams, Sevil Sönmez, Mian Asim, Kyung Sun Lee, and Andrea Juhasz. And, also, thank you to all the students I have taught over the years at Zayed University, you've been great. My apologies to so many others I am afraid I have neglected to call out for gratitude but please know all of you have been vital on this journey.

Third, thank you to the staff at University Press of Mississippi who have been so helpful and supportive along the way, and particularly to Emily Bandy for patiently answering my questions. Thank you to the anonymous reviewers for insightful feedback that strengthened the book. And, finally, I wish to thank all the doubters encountered through life's journey who relish declaring other people's dreams far-fetched to make a reality. Their doubts only get transformed into motivation fuel to prove them wrong, evoking Walt Disney's playful riposte: "It's kind of fun to do the impossible."

APPENDIX 1: LIST OF INTERVIEWEES

In total were eighteen interviewees, nine male and nine female:

Anonymous #1, local Disneyland fan who visits almost every day

Anonymous #2, founder and organizer of Steam Day and administrator of the event's Facebook group (uses handle on social media)

Anonymous #3, local Disneyland fan

Anonymous #4, administrator of the Facebook group for swing dancing at Disneyland

Anonymous #5, former cast member as well as social media influencer

Anonymous #6, coadministrator of the Facebook group for Disneyland social clubs as well as leader of a social club

Anonymous #7, local Disneyland fan

Anonymous #8, local Disneyland fan

Anonymous #9, cast member at time of interview as well as popular social media influencer

Bob Gurr, retired Imagineer and Disney Legend

Jim Hill, long-time media commentator on Disney and administrator of JimHillMedia.com

Noah Korda, founder and organizer of Bats Day and administrator of the event's website, social media, and Facebook group

Mike Marquez, organizer of approximately twenty park events and administrator of Facebook group One Big Disney Family Entertainment

Amy McCain, founder and organizer of Galliday and administrator of the event's website, social media, and Facebook group

Doobie Moseley, cofounder of the Laughing Place website and discussion board and coadministrator of its social media accounts

Ken Pellman, former Disneyland cast member from 1990s and 2000s and cohost of the podcast *The Sweep Spot*

Todd Regan (Internet handle: Dusty Sage), founder and CEO of MiceChat, organizer of the Gumball Rally event and Sunday hub meets, administrator of the MiceChat website and social media accounts

Hayley Ruszecki, cofounder and coorganizer of Lolita Day, and coadministrator of the event's website and social media accounts

APPENDIX 2: ONLINE SURVEY QUESTIONNAIRE

1) Do you consent to take the questionnaire? Yes / No
2) Are you 18 years old or over, have visited Disneyland in Anaheim, California, and your primary residence (where you spend most of the year) is in Southern California? Yes / No
3) In which Southern California county do you reside (where you spend most of the year)? Imperial / Kern / Los Angeles / Orange / Riverside / San Bernardino / San Diego / San Luis Obispo / Santa Barbara / Ventura / I do not live in Southern California
4) How old were you on your first visit to Disneyland? 0–5 years old / 6–12 / 13–17 / 18–21 / 22–29 / 30–39 / 40–49 / 50–59 / 60+
5) How many times have you visited Disneyland in your life (estimate if you do not remember exactly)? 1–10 times / 11–49 / 50–99 / 100–199 / 200–499 / 500–999 / 1000+
6) On average how often do you visit Disneyland? 1–10 days per year / 1 day per month / 2 or 3 days per month / 1 day per week / 2–3 days per week / 4–5 days per week / Almost every day
7) What type of Disneyland annual pass do you have? Signature Plus / Signature / Deluxe / Southern California / Southern California Select / Premier Passport / I do not own an annual pass
8) Do you have an annual pass to the following non-Disney theme parks in Southern California? Knott's Berry Farm / LEGOLAND / Sea World / Six Flags Magic Mountain / Universal Studios
9) Do you typically spend a day at Disneyland with (1 Never—7 Very often): Family / Friend(s) from school, work, neighborhood, etc. (not from Disneyland online boards or social media groups) / Friend(s) met through Disneyland online boards and social media groups / By myself
10) On a typical visit to Disneyland, how likely are you to do the following (1 Never—7 Very often)? Buy and/or trade Disney pins / DisneyBound (dress in Disney character inspired clothing) / Just enjoy walking around

and being in the park, and going on few, if any, rides / Post to my social media account(s) about my Disneyland visit

11) Is Disneyland your favorite place (outside of home) to socialize with family and/or friends? Yes / No

12) When participating in online forums and social media with Disneyland enthusiasts, how important is each of the following factors (1 Important—7 Very important)? Information and knowledge exchange / Being social and making friends / Relaxation and entertainment / Creative outlet / Giving my opinion and influencing debates

13) What was the FIRST online platform you used to connect with Disneyland enthusiasts? Internet Service Provider message boards (AOL, Prodigy, CompuServe, etc.) / Listserv email list / Usenet newsgroup (e.g., alt.disney.disneyland) / Web-based discussion board (e.g., MousePlanet, MiceChat, Laughing Place, etc.) / LiveJournal / Blog (e.g., Blogger, WordPress, etc.) / Podcast / MySpace / Facebook / Twitter / YouTube / Instagram / Tumblr / Meetup.com / Other (specify)

14) Check any of the following you have EVER used to connect with Disneyland enthusiasts online (you can check more than one): Internet Service Provider message boards (AOL, Prodigy, CompuServe, etc.) / Listserv email list / Usenet newsgroup (e.g., alt.disney.disneyland) / Web-based discussion board (e.g. MousePlanet, MiceChat, Laughing Place, etc.) / LiveJournal / Blog (e.g., Blogger, WordPress, etc.) / Podcast / MySpace / Facebook / Twitter / YouTube / Instagram / Tumblr / Meetup.com

15) Which is currently your favorite platform for connecting with Disneyland enthusiasts online? Web-based discussion board (e.g., MousePlanet, MiceChat, Laughing Place, etc.) / Facebook / Twitter / YouTube / Instagram / Tumblr / Meetup.com / Other (specify)

16) Based on your answer to the previous question, why did you choose that platform as your current favorite compared to the others? (specify)

17) Have you ever posted and shared online the following related to Disneyland? Video / Photography / Music or Song / Handmade painting and/or illustration / Computer graphic (e.g., Illustrator, Photoshop, etc.) / Arts, crafts and jewelry / Clothing design and creation / Story or fiction

18) To what extent has your use of online Disneyland discussion boards and social media had a positive effect on your in-park experience? (1 No effect—7 Very positive)

19) Have you gone swing dancing at the Royal Theater (next to Sleeping Beauty Castle)? Yes / No

20) Have you ever attended a fan-organized event in Disneyland (e.g., Gay Days, Dapper Day, Galliday, MiceChat meet, Gumball Rally, meetup .com, etc.)? Yes / No

21) Check the events you have ever attended (you can check more than one): Gay Days / Bats Day / Dapper Day / Galliday / Steam Day / Lolita Day (hara-juku) / It's a Ska World / Harry Potter Day / MiceChat anniversary weekend / MiceChat Gumball Rally / MiceChat Sunday hub meetup / Meetup.com Disneyland fan club / Other (specify)

22) Check how you learned of the events you attended (you can check more than one): Web-based discussion board (MousePlanet, MiceChat, Laughing Place, etc.) / Event website / Blog (Blogger, WordPress, etc.) / Podcast / Facebook / Twitter / YouTube / Instagram / Tumblr / Television, radio, newspaper, or magazine / Word of mouth from a friend, family member, coworker, etc. / Other (specify)

23) Did you ever make friends with another visitor (not in your group) while at Disneyland? Yes / No

24) Have you ever met up with someone in Disneyland that you first got to know in a Disneyland online discussion board or social media site? Yes / No

25) Are you a member of a Disneyland social club? Yes / No

26) What year did you join your social club? 2017 / 2016 / 2015 / 2014 / 2013 / 2012 / 2011 / 2010 or before

27) Which online platform does your social club primarily use to recruit and communicate with members, and plan activities? Website dedicated to the club / Meetup.com / Facebook / Tumblr / Twitter / Blog (Blogger, WordPress, etc.) / Other (specify)

28) What are the two things you enjoy most about being a member of a Disneyland social club? (specify)

29) What location is your favorite for being social with family and/or friends at the Disneyland Resort (e.g., an entire land, a ride, a restaurant, a seating area, etc.)? (specify)

30) For the social atmosphere at Disneyland, how important are each of the following (1 Unimportant—7 Very important)? Themed environment / Disneyland food and beverages / Shopping / Rides / Shows / Character meet and greets, and walkabouts / Cast members

31) While you are in line for an attraction at Disneyland, how likely are you to do the following (1 Never—7 Very often)? Chat with members of my group / Chat with other visitors (not part of my group) / Use social media (Snapchat, Twitter, Instagram, YouTube, etc.) and text messaging (SMS, WhatsApp, etc.) on my mobile / Listen to music and/or play a

game on my mobile / Read news, articles, books, etc. on my mobile / Read print (book, newspaper, magazine)

32) Have you ever done the following while at Disneyland? Helped another visitor (not in my group) with park directions, information, or take a photo. / Picked up trash (not mine) and put it in the trash bin. / Found lost property and returned it to a cast member. / Assisted a cast member in the park. / Tipped or bought a gift for a cast member (that was not a friend or relative) / Given a valid FastPass ticket to another park visitor not in your group (pre-June 2017 FP system change)

33) Have the following had a negative impact on Disneyland as a social place for you? Removal or changes to attractions and shows / High crowd levels / Behavior of other visitors / Premium up-charge experiences / The handling of Walt Disney's park vision and legacy by the Disney corporation / Neglectful and/or poor management of online fan websites and social media groups by owners/moderators / Fan websites, social media, and in-park events have become too commercial

34) Do you agree or disagree with the following statements (1 Strongly disagree—7 Strongly agree)? It would be very hard for me to move out of Southern California because of Disneyland. / Even if I visit Disneyland frequently, I do not get tired of the park. / Disneyland is a home away from home. / I feel trust and camaraderie with other visitors and cast members at Disneyland. / Disneyland is a force for good in American society.

35) Age: 18–25 years old / 26—35 / 36—45 / 46—55 / 56—65 / 66+

36) Gender: (specify)

37) Race / ethnicity: (specify)

38) Have you ever been a Disneyland cast member? Yes, I am currently Disneyland cast member. / Yes, I was a Disneyland cast member in the past. / No, I have never been a Disneyland cast member.

39) Are you a member of the official Disney fan club d23? Yes / No

NOTES

CHAPTER 1: NOT JUST CHILD'S PLAY

1. Eco, U. (1986). *Travels in hyperreality*. Picador.

2. Svonkin, C. (2011). A Southern California boyhood in the simu-southland shadows of Walt Disney's Enchanted Tiki Room. In K. M. Jackson & M. I. West (Eds.), *Disneyland and culture: Essays on the parks and their influence* (pp. 107–21). McFarland. 115.

3. Morris, J. A. (2019). Disney's influence on the modern theme park and the codi-fication of colorblind racism in the American amusement industry. In J. A. Kokai & T. Robson (Eds.), *Performance and the Disney theme park experience: The tourist as actor* (pp. 213–27). Palgrave Macmillan. 221.

4. Cresswell, T. (2015). *Place: An introduction* (2nd Ed.). Wiley Blackwell. 76–77.

5. Jenkins, H. (2006a). *Fans, bloggers, and gamers: Exploring participatory culture*. New York University Press; Jenkins, H. (2013). *Textual poachers: Television fans and participatory culture* (Twentieth anniversary ed.). Routledge.

6. Milman, A. (1991). The role of theme parks as a leisure activity for local communities. *Journal of Travel Research, 29*(3), 11–16.

7. Roberts, K. (2004). *The leisure industries*. Palgrave Macmillan. 159.

8. Bolter, J. D., & Grusin, R. (1999). *Remediation: Understanding new media*. MIT Press.

9. Lutz, A. (2009, October 13). Hello George and Starbucks. Good-bye Ed & easy parking, world of crowds, more . . . *MiceAge*. https://micechat.com/miceage/allutz/al101309a .htm; MacDonald, B. (2015, October 7). 7 reasons why Disneyland raised its annual pass prices. *Los Angeles Times*. http://www.latimes.com/travel/themeparks/la-trb-disneyland -annual-pass-prices-20151007-htmlstory.html; Martin, H. (2016, September 22). Disneyland brings back Southern California annual passes at a higher price, *Los Angeles Times*. http:// www.latimes.com/business/la-fi-disney-passes-20160922-snap-story.html

10. Rainie, L., & Wellman, B. (2012). *Networked: The new social operating system*. MIT Press.

11. Baym, N. K. (2015). *Personal connections in the digital age* (2nd Ed.). Polity.

12. Giroux, H. A., & Pollock, G. (2010). *The mouse that roared: Disney and the end of innocence*. Rowman & Littlefield. 8.

13. Bemis, B. (2022). *Disney theme parks and America's national narratives: Mirror, mirror, for us all*. Routledge. 61.

14. Baudrillard, J. (1983). *Simulacra and simulation*. University of Michigan Press.

15. Bernardini, J. (2014). The infantilization of the postmodern adult and the figure of kidult. *Postmodern Openings, 5*(2), 39–55.

16. Pierce, T. J. (2016). *Three years in wonderland: The Disney brothers, CV Wood, and the making of the great American theme park*. University Press of Mississippi. 182.

17. Karis, M. (2018). Between the lines: children's literature and the Disney theme parks. *Journal of Themed Experience and Attractions Studies, 1*(1), 69–71.

18. Svonkin (2011).

19. Cross, G., & Walton, J. (2005). *The playful crowd: Pleasure places in the twentieth century*. Columbia University Press. 169.

20. Davis, S. G. (1996). The theme park: global industry and cultural form. *Media, Culture & Society, 18*(3), 399–422; Williams, R. (2020). *Theme park fandom: Spatial transmedia, materiality and participatory cultures*. University of Amsterdam Press.

21. Pierce (2016); Bemis (2022); Snow, R. (2020). *Disney's land: Walt Disney and the invention of the amusement park that changed the world*. Scribner; Mittermeier, S. (2020). *A cultural history of the Disneyland theme parks: Middle class kingdoms*. Intellect.

22. Williams (2020).

23. Hirt, E. R., & Clarkson, J. J. (2011). The psychology of fandom: understanding the etiology, motives, and implications of fanship. In L. R. Kahle & A. G. Close (Eds.), *Consumer behavior knowledge for effective sports and event marketing* (pp. 93–120). Routledge; Wann, D.L. (2006). Understanding the positive social psychological benefits of sport team identification: The team identification-social psychological health model. *Group Dynamics: Theory, Research, and Practice, 10*(4), 272.

24. Wasko, J. (2020). *Understanding Disney*. Polity Press.

25. Jenkins (2013); Hills, M. (2003). *Fan cultures*. Routledge; Booth, P. (2017). *Digital Fandom 2.0*. Peter Lang.

26. Rowe, R. (2022). To act like a kid or not to act like a kid: Disneybounding in the parks. In S. Mittermeier (Ed.), *Fan Phenomena: Disney* (pp. 104–12). Intellect Books.

27. Koren-Kuik, M. (2013). Desiring the tangible: Disneyland, fandom and spatial immersion. In K. M. Barton & J. M. Lampley (Eds.), *fan CULTure: Essays on participatory fandom in the 21st century* (pp. 148–58). McFarland.

28. Hills (2003); Pearson, R. (2010). Fandom in the digital era. *Popular Communication, 8*(1), 84–95.

29. Bennett, L. (2014). Tracing textual poachers: Reflections on the development of fan studies and digital fandom. *Journal of Fandom Studies, 2*(1), 5–20.

30. van Dijck, J. (2013). *The culture of connectivity: A critical history of social media*. Oxford University Press.

31. Bourdieu, P. (1986). The forms of capital. In J. Richardson (Ed.), *Handbook of theory and research for the sociology of education* (pp. 241–58). Greenwood.

32. Foucault, M. (1980). *Power/knowledge: Selected interviews & other writings 1972–1977*. Pantheon.

33. Augé, M. (1995). *Non-places: An introduction to supermodernity*. Verso; Beatley, T. (2004). *Native to nowhere. Sustaining home and community in a global age*. Island Press;

Bellah, R. (1991). *The good society*. Knopf; Gratz, R. (1989). *The living city*. Simon & Schuster; Jacobs, J. (1961). *The death and life of great American cities*. Random House; Kunstler, J. H. (1993). *The geography of nowhere: The rise and decline of America's man-made landscape*. Simon & Schuster; Lanier, J. (2011). *You are not a gadget: A manifesto*. Vintage Books; Oldenburg, R. (1999). *The Great Good Place*. Da Capo Press; Putnam, R. D. (2000). *Bowling alone: The collapse and revival of American community*. Simon & Schuster; Sennett, R. (1977). *The fall of public man*. Knopf; Stein, M. (1960). *The eclipse of community*. Princeton University Press; Stoll, C. (1995). *Silicon snake oil: Second thoughts on the information highway*. Doubleday; Turkle, S. (2011). *Alone together: Why we expect more from technology and less from each other*. Basic Books; Virilio, P. (2000). *The information bomb*. Verso.

34. Oldenburg (1999); Findlay, J. (1992). *Magic lands: Western cityscapes and American culture after 1940*. University of California Press; Francaviglia, R. (1996). *Main Street revisited: Time, space, and image-building in small town America*. University of Iowa Press; Lerner, M. (1957). *America as a civilization: Life and thought in the United States today*. Simon & Schuster.

35. Oldenburg (1999); Putnam (2000); Shirky, C. (2010). *Cognitive surplus: Creativity and generosity in a connected age*. Penguin.

36. Wellman, B. (1992). Men in networks: Private communities, domestic friendships. In P. Nardi (Ed.), *Men's friendships* (pp. 74–114). Sage; Wellman, B. & Gulia, M. (1999). Netsurfers don't ride alone: Virtual communities as communities. In B. Wellman (Ed.), *Networks in the global village: Life in contemporary communities* (pp. 331–66). Westview Press.

37. Cross & Walton (2005); Cresswell (2015); Bryman, A. (2004). *The Disneyization of society*. Sage; Francaviglia, R. (1995, Autumn). History after Disney: The significance of "imagineered" historical places. *Public Historian, 17*(4), 69–74; Immerso, M. (2002). *Coney Island: The people's playground*. Rutgers University Press; Kasson, J. F. (1978). *Amusing the million: Coney Island at the turn of the century*. Hill and Wang; Parascandola, L. & Parascandola, J. (Eds.) (2015). *Coney Island reader: Through dizzy gates of illusion*. Columbia University Press; Peiss, K. (1986). *Cheap amusements: Working women and leisure in turn-of-the-century New York*. Temple University Press; Relph, E. (1976). *Place and placelessness*. Pion.

38. Oldenburg (1999).

39. Bondy, F. (2005). *Bleeding pinstripes: A season with the bleacher creatures at Yankee Stadium*. Sports Publishing LLC.

40. Edgell, S. & Jary, D. (1973). Football: A sociological eulogy. In M. Smith, S. Parker & C. Smith (Eds.), *Leisure and society in Britain* (pp. 214–29). Allen Lane. 221.

41. Telotte, J. P. (2008). *The mouse machine: Disney and technology*. University of Illinois Press. 117.

42. Kokai, J. A., & Robson, T. (2019). You're in the parade! Disney as immersive theatre and the tourist as actor. In J. A. Kokai & T. Robson (Eds.), *Performance and the Disney theme park experience: The tourist as actor* (pp. 3–20). Palgrave Macmillan.

43. Kokai & Robson (2019); Larkin, S., & Malone, T. B. (2022). "—yer a wizard." Immersion and agency in the Wizarding World of Harry Potter. In K. M. Jackson & M. I. West (Eds.) *Storybook worlds made real: Essays on the places inspired by children's narratives* (pp. 186–99). McFarland.

44. Williams (2020).

45. Relph (1976), 95.

46. Boorstin, D. J. (1964). *The image: A guide to pseudo-events in America*. Vintage. 103.

47. Sorkin, M. (1992). Introduction: Variations on a theme park. In M. Sorkin (Ed.), *Variations on a theme park* (pp. xi–xv). Hill and Wang. xiv.

48. Schickel, R. (1967). *The Disney version: the life, art, times and commerce of Walt Disney*. Simon & Schuster.

49. Giroux & Pollock (2010). 38.

50. Marin, L. (1984). *Utopics: The semiological play of textual spaces*. Humanities Press International. 240.

51. Bryman (2004).

52. Cross & Walton (2005); Jones, K. R., & Wills, J. (2005). *The invention of the park: Recreational landscapes from the Garden of Eden to Disney's Magic Kingdom*. Polity.

53. Tuan, Y.-F. (1997). Disneyland: Its place in world culture. In K. A. Marling (Ed.), *Designing Disney's theme parks: The architecture of reassurance* (pp. 191–200). Canadian Centre for Architecture.

54. Francaviglia (1995).

55. Lukas, S. A. (2007). How the theme park gets its power: Lived theming, social control, and the themed self. In S. Lukas (Ed.), *The themed space* (pp. 183–206). Lexington Books; Warren. S. (1996). Popular cultural practices in the "postmodern city." *Urban Geography, 17*(6), 545–67.

56. Fong, J., & Nunez, K. (2012). Disneyland: Still a world of strangers. *National Social Science Journal, 37*(2), 14–27.

57. Eco (1986).

58. Sparrman, A. (2022). The social aesthetics of family space: The visual heritage of Disney in a Swedish amusement park. In J. B. Metzler (Ed.), *On Disney: Deconstructing images, tropes and narratives* (pp. 229–47). Springer. 244.

59. Lewicka, M. (2011). Place attachment: How far have we come in the last 40 years? *Journal of Environmental Psychology, 31*(3), 207–30.

60. McCarthy, W. (2022). The pedigree of pixie dust: Disneyland and theme parks as a remediation of playful places throughout history. *Journal of Leisure Research, 53*(2), 253–71.

61. Jenkins (2013).

62. Urry, J. (2007). *Mobilities*. Polity.

63. Kelly, G., & Hosking, K. (2008). Nonpermanent residents, place attachment, and "sea change" communities. *Environment and Behavior, 40*, 575–94; Stedman, R. C. (2006). Understanding place attachment among second home owners. *American Behavioral Scientist, 50*, 187–205.

64. Laurier, E. (2004). Doing office work on the motorway. *Theory, Culture and Society, 21*(4/5), 261–77.

65. Manzo, L. C. (2005). For better or worse: Exploring multiple dimensions of place meaning. *Journal of Environmental Psychology, 25*(1), 67–86.

66. Moulay, A., & Ujang, N. (2021). Insight into the issue of underutilised parks: what triggers the process of place attachment? *International Journal of Urban Sustainable Development, 13*(2), 297–316.

67. Hwang, S. N., Lee, C., & Chen, H. J. (2005). The relationship among tourists' involvement, place attachment and interpretation satisfaction in Taiwan's national parks. *Tourism Management, 26*(2), 143–56; Ramkissoon, H., Mavondo, F., & Uysal, M. (2018). Social involvement and park citizenship as moderators for quality-of-life in a national park. *Journal of Sustainable Tourism, 26*(3), 341–61; Wolf, I. D., Stricker, H. K., & Hagenloh, G. (2015). Outcome-focused national park experience management: Transforming participants, promoting social well-being, and fostering place attachment. *Journal of Sustainable Tourism, 23*(3), 358–81.

68. Moore, R. L., & Graefe, A.R. (1994). Attachments to recreations settings. *Leisure Sciences, 16,* 17–31.

69. Hammitt, W. E., Backlund, E. A., & Bixler, R. D. (2006). Place bonding for recreation places: Conceptual and empirical development. *Leisure Studies, 25*(1), 17–41.

70. Tuan, Y.-F. (1977). *Space and place: The perspective of experience.* University of Minnesota Press. 33.

71. Relph (1976). 29.

72. Tuan, Y.-F. (1974). *Topophilia: A study of environmental perception, attitudes and values.* Prentice-Hall.

73. Altman, I., & Low, S. M. (Eds.) (2012). *Place attachment* (Vol. 12). Springer; Cuba, L., & Hummon, D. M. (1993). A place to call home: Identification with dwelling, community, and region. *Sociological Quarterly, 34*(1), 111–31; Laczko, L. S. (2005). National and local attachments in a changing world system: Evidence from an international survey. *International Review of Sociology, 15,* 517–28; Lewicka, M. (2005). Ways to make people active: Role of place attachment, cultural capital and neighborhood ties. *Journal of Environmental Psychology, 4,* 381–95; Scannell, L., & Gifford, R. (2014). Comparing the theories of interpersonal and place attachment. In L. C. Manzo & P. Devine-Wright (Eds.), *Place attachment: Advances in theory, methods and applications* (pp. 23–36). Routledge.

74. Massey, D. (1994). *Space, place and gender.* University of Minnesota Press; Wilken, R., & Goggin, G. (2012). *Mobile technology and place.* Routledge.

75. Seamon, D. (1980). Body-subject, time-space routines, and place-ballets. In A. Buttimer & D. Seamon (Eds.), *The human experience of space and place* (pp. 148–65). Croom Helm.

76. Lukas, S. A. (2008). *Theme park.* Reaktion Books.

77. Carlà, F., & Freitag, F. (2014). Ancient Greek culture and myth in the Terra Mítica theme park. *Classical Receptions Journal, 7*(2), 242–59. 244.

78. McCarthy (2022).

79. Lukas, S. A. (2013). *The immersive worlds handbook: Designing theme parks and consumer spaces.* Focal Press.

80. Alexander, C., Ishikawa, S., Silverstein, M., Jacobson, M., Fiksdahl-King, I., & Angel, S. (1977). *A pattern language.* Oxford University Press.

81. Oldenburg (1999). Benedikt, M. (2001). Reality and authenticity in the experience economy. *Architectural Record, 189*(11), 84–89.

82. Waysdorf, A., & Reijnders, S. (2016). Immersion, authenticity, and the theme park as a social space: Experiencing the wizarding world of Harry Potter. *International Journal of Cultural Studies, 21*(2), 173–88.

83. Nanjangud, A., & Reijnders, S. (2022) "I felt more homely over there . . .": Analysing tourists' experience of Indianness at Bollywood Parks Dubai. *Current Issues in Tourism*, 25(15), 2443–56.

84. Mitrašinović, M. (2006). *Total landscape, theme parks, public space*. Ashgate.

85. Aziz, N. A., Ariffin, A. A. M., Omar, N. A., & Evin, C. (2012). Examining the impact of visitors' emotions and perceived quality towards satisfaction and revisit intention to theme parks. *Jurnal Pengurusan*, 35, 97–109.

86. Scannell, L., & Gifford, R. (2010). Defining place attachment: A tripartite organizing framework. *Journal of Environmental Psychology*, 30(1), 1–10.

87. Twigger-Ross, C. L., & Uzzell, D. L. (1996). Place and identity processes. *Journal of Environmental Psychology*, 16(3), 205–20.

88. Manzo (2005).

89. Low, S. M. (1992). Symbolic ties that bind. In I. Altman & S. M. Low (Eds.), *Place attachment* (pp. 165–85). Plenum Press; Fried, M. (2018). Grieving for a lost home. In A. Kiev (Ed.), *Social Psychiatry* (pp. 335–59). Routledge; Mazumdar, S., & Mazumdar, S. (2004). Religion and place attachment: A study of sacred places. *Journal of Environmental Psychology*, 24(3), 385–97.

90. Manzo, L. C., & Perkins, D. D. (2006). Finding common ground: The importance of place attachment to community participation and planning. *Journal of Planning Literature*, 20(4), 335–50. 343.

91. Manzo (2005); Scannell & Gifford (2010); Twigger-Ross & Uzzell (1996).

92. Lewicka (2011); Hummon, D. M. (1992). Community attachment: Local sentiment and sense of place. In I. Altman & S. M. Low (Eds.), *Place attachment* (pp. 253–78). Plenum Press.

93. Hidalgo, M. C., & Hernández, B. (2001). Place attachment: Conceptual and empirical questions. *Journal of Environmental Psychology*, 21(3), 273–81.

94. Lewicka (2011); Kasarda, J. D., & Janowitz, M. (1974). Community attachment in mass society. *American Sociological Review*, 39, 328–39; Lalli, M. (1992). Urban-related identity: Theory, measurement, and empirical findings. *Journal of Environmental Psychology*, 12(4), 285–303; Lewicka, M. (2014). In search of roots: Memory as enabler of place attachment. In L. C. Manzo & P. Devine-Wright (Eds.), *Place attachment: Advances in theory, methods and applications* (pp. 49–60). Routledge.

95. Kaplan, S. (1984). Affect and cognition in the context of home: The quest for intangibles. *Population and Environment*, 7(2), 126–33.

96. Stedman, R. C. (2003). Is it really just a social construction? The contribution of the physical environment to sense of place. *Society & Natural Resources*, 16(8), 671–85.

97. Moore & Graefe (1994); Moulay & Ujang (2021); Kyle, G. T., Graefe, A., & Manning, R. E. (2005). Testing the dimensionality of place attachment in recreational settings. *Environment and Behavior*, 37, 153–77.

98. Scannell & Gifford (2010); McMillan, D. W., & Chavis, D. M. (1986). Sense of community: A definition and theory. *Journal of Community Psychology*, 14(1), 6–23; Nasar, J. L., & Julian, D. A. (1995). The psychological sense of community in the neighborhood. *Journal of the American Planning Association*, 61(2), 178–84.

99. Scannell & Gifford (2010). 5.

100. Meyrowitz. J. (1994). Medium theory. In D. Crowley & D. Mitchell (Eds.), *Communication theory today* (pp. 50–77). Stanford University Press.

101. Gillespie, T. (2010). The politics of "platforms." *new media & society, 12*(3), 347–64. 350.

102. Burnett, R., & Marshall, P. D. (2003). *Web theory: An introduction.* Routledge; Spurgeon, C. (2008). *Advertising and new media.* Routledge.

103. Spurgeon (2008); Jenkins, H. (2003). Digital cinema: Media convergence and participatory culture. In D. Thorburn & H. Jenkins (Eds.), *Rethinking media change: The aesthetics of transition* (pp. 281–312). MIT Press.

104. Hellekson, K., & Busse, K. (Eds.) (2006). *Fan fiction and fan communities in the age of the internet.* McFarland.

105. van Dijck (2013).

106. Langlois, G., & Elmer, G. (2013) The research politics of social media platforms. *Culture Machine, 14.* http://www.culturemachine.net/index.php/cm/article/view/505

107. Singer, J. B. (2014). User-generated visibility: Secondary gate-keeping in a shared media space. *new media & society, 16,* 55–73.

108. Cunningham, S., & Craig, D. (2019). *Social media entertainment.* New York University Press.

109. Kiriakou, O. (2019). Big name fandom and the (inevitable) failure of Disflix. *Transformative Works and Cultures, 30,* 1–16.

110. Fuchs, C. (2013). *Social media: A critical introduction.* Sage.

111. Coppa, F. (2014). Pop culture, fans, and social media. In J. Hunsinger & T. Senft, (Eds.), *The social media handbook* (76–92). Routledge.

112. Hills (2003). 46.

113. Bourdieu (1986).

114. Malaby, T. (2006). Parlaying value: Capital in and beyond virtual worlds. *Games and Culture, 1*(2), 141–62.

115. Thornton, S. (1995). *Club cultures: Music, media and subcultural capital.* Polity.

116. Hills (2003).

117. Ren, Y., Kraut, R., & Kiesler, S. (2007). Applying common identity and bond theory to design of online communities. *Organization Studies, 28*(3), 377–408.

118. Auslander, P. (1999). *Liveness: Performance in a mediatized culture.* Routledge.

119. Hills (2003). 57.

120. Fiske, J. (1992). The cultural economy of fandom. In L. A. Lewis (Ed.), *The adoring audience* (pp. 30–49). Routledge.

121. Malaby (2006). 146.

122. Bryman (2004); Wasko (2020); Adams, J. A. (1991). *The American amusement park industry.* Twayne Publishers; Fjellman, S. (1992). *Vinyl leaves: Walt Disney World and America.* Westview; Gutierrez-Dennehy, C. (2019). Taming the fairy tale: Performing affective medievalism in fantasyland. In J. A. Kokai & T. Robson (Eds.), *Performance and the Disney theme park experience: The tourist as actor,* 65–83. Palgrave Macmillan.

123. Hobbs, P. (2015). *Walt's utopia: Disneyland and American mythmaking.* McFarland. 60.

124. Foucault, M. (1991). *Discipline and punish: the birth of a prison.* Penguin.

125. Foucault, M. (1981). *The history of sexuality: Vol. 1. The will to knowledge.* Penguin. 94.

126. van Dijck (2013); Bourdieu (1986).

127. Malaby (2006). 144.

128. Bury, R. (2016). Technology, fandom and community in the second media age. *Convergence: The International Journal of Research into New Media Technologies.* 23(6), 627–42.

129. McCarthy, W. (2023). A drink on the terrace with Truus from Delft: Place attachment at De Efteling theme park. *Tourism Culture & Communication.* https://doi.org/10.37 27/109830422X16656826775912

130. Bengtsson, M. (2016). How to plan and perform a qualitative study using content analysis. *NursingPlus Open, 2, 8–14.*

131. Scannell & Gifford (2010).

132. Hidalgo & Hernández (2001); Lewicka (2005); Hammitt et al. (2006); Giuliani, M. V. (2003). Theory of attachment and place attachment. In M. Bonnes, T. Lee, & M. Bonaiuto (Eds.), *Psychological theories for environmental issues* (pp. 137–70). Ashgate.

CHAPTER 2: DISNEYLAND AS A PLACE FOR SOUTHERN CALIFORNIANS

1. Gurr, Bob. Interview with author. October 8, 2017.

2. Scannell & Gifford (2010).

3. Findlay (1992).

4. Gruen, V. (1964). *The heart of our cities: The urban crisis, diagnosis and cure.* Simon and Schuster. 22.

5. Whyte, W. H. (1988). *City: Rediscovering the center.* Doubleday.

6. Gruen (1964). 45.

7. Mannheim, S. (2002). *Walt Disney and the quest for community.* Routledge.

8. Gruen (1964).

9. Moore, C. (1965, January 1). You have to pay for the public life. *Perspecta, 9/10,* 57–106.

10. Gruen (1964).

11. Gruen.

12. Gruen, 202.

13. Gruen, 202.

14. Findlay (1992). 67.

15. Findlay (1992); Hench, J. (2003). *Designing Disney: Imagineering and the art of the show.* Disney.

16. Findlay (1992).

17. Mannheim (2002). 17.

18. Mannheim. 19.

19. Mannheim. 124.

20. Gottdiener, M. (2001). *The theming of America: American dreams, media fantasies, and themed environments* (2nd ed). Westview Press.

21. Findlay (1992).

22. Baudrillard (1983). 12.

23. Wyn, P. (1999, April 8). Mr. Pressler's wild ride. *OC Weekly.* https://ocweekly.com/mr-presslers-wild-ride-6395637/

24. Fjellman (1992); Wasko (2020); Bryman, A. (1995). *Disney and his worlds*. Routledge.

25. Regan, Todd. Interview with author. November 28, 2017.

26. Pimentel, J. (2015, September 15). Why planes, helicopters and drones can't fly over Disneyland. *Orange County Register*. https://www.ocregister.com/2015/09/24/why-planes-helicopters-and-drones-cant-flyover-disneyland/

27. Tuan (1997). 195.

28. Andersen, K. (2017). *Fantasyland: How America went haywire, a 500-year history*. Random House.

29. Duffett, M. (2013). *Understanding fandom: An introduction to the study of media fan culture*. Bloomsbury; Hills, M. (2012). "Twilight" fans represented in commercial paratexts and inter-fandoms: Resisting and repurposing negative fan stereotypes. In A. More (Ed.), *Genre, reception, and adaptation in the "Twilight" series* (pp. 113–31). Ashgate.

30. Adams (1991); Cross & Walton (2005).

31. Hutchins, A. L. (2022). Faith, trust and pixie dust: Disney's participatory publics and the cult of mouse. In S. Mittermeier (Ed.), *Fan phenomena: Disney* (pp. 188–97). Intellect Books. 193.

32. McCarthy (2022).

33. Moore, A. (1980). Walt Disney World: Bounded ritual space and the playful pilgrimage center. *Anthropological Quarterly*, 207–18, 211.

34. Pellman, Ken. Interview with author. October 21, 2017.

35. Hobbs (2015). 101.

36. Moore (1980). 215.

37. Hills (2003).

38. Sandvoss, C. (2005). *Fans: The mirror of consumption*. Polity.

39. Hills (2003).

40. Couldry, N. (1998). The view from inside the "simulacrum": Visitors tales from the set of Coronation Street, *Leisure Studies*, 17(2), 94–107.

41. Doss, E. (1999). *Elvis culture: Fans, faith, & image*. University of Kansas Press; Rodman, G. (1996). *Elvis after Elvis: The posthumous career of a living legend*. Routledge.

42. Hills (2003). 149.

43. Brooker, W. (2017). A sort of homecoming: Fan viewing and symbolic pilgrimage. In J. Gray, C. Sandvoss, & C. L. Harrington (Eds.), *Fandom: Identities and communities in a mediated world* (2nd ed.) (pp. 157–73). New York University Press. 172.

44. Doss (1999). 23.

45. Geraghty, L. (2018). Passing through: Popular media tourism, pilgrimage, and narratives of being a fan. In C. Lundberg & V. Ziakas (Eds.), *The Routledge handbook of popular culture and tourism* (pp. 203–13). Routledge. 204.

46. Geraghty. 205.

47. Geraghty.

48. Williams (2020). 166.

49. Findlay (1992); Gennawey, S. (2014). *The Disneyland story*. Keen Publications, LLC.

50. Jenkins (2013).

51. Geraghty, L. (2022). Fan tourism and conventions. In *The Routledge handbook of Star Trek* (pp. 258–63). Routledge. 258.

52. Hench (2003); Marling, K. A. (1997). Imagineering the Disney theme parks. In K. A. Marling (Ed.), *Designing Disney's theme parks: The architecture of reassurance* (pp. 29–177). Canadian Centre for Architecture.

53. Jones & Wills (2005).

54. Marling (1997). 85.

55. Themed Entertainment Association (TEA). (2021) Global Attractions Attendance Report 2020. https://www.teaconnect.org/images/files/TEA_408_543519_211001.pdf

56. Harris, K. (2017, November 30). These were the top 10 most-Instagrammed places in 2017. *BuzzFeed*. https://www.buzzfeed.com/kristinharris/these-were-the-top-10-most-instagrammed-places-in-2017

57. Lindquist, J. (2010). *In service to the mouse: My unexpected journey to becoming Disneyland's first president*. Neverland Media and Chapman University Press.

58. Shirky, C. (2008). *Here comes everybody*. Penguin.

59. Eco (1986); Jones & Wills (2005).

60. Manzo & Perkins (2006).

61. Koren-Kuik (2013). 152.

62. Martens, T. (2021, July 18). Why Disneyland's Jungle Cruise cultural changes aren't just "woke"—they're necessary, *Los Angeles Times*. https://www.latimes.comentertainment-arts/story/2021-07-18/disneyland-jungle-cruise-changes-woke-culture-vs-necessary-change-american-culture

63. Sandvoss, C., & Kearns, L. (2014). From interpretive communities to interpretative fairs. In L. Duits, K. Zwaan, & S. Reijnders (Eds.), *The Ashgate companion to fan cultures* (pp. 91–106). Ashgate. 101.

64. Sandvoss (2005). 96.

65. Sandvoss (2005); Relph (1976).

66. Frederickson, L. M., & Anderson, D. H. (1999). A qualitative exploration of the wilderness experience as a source of spiritual inspiration. *Journal of Environmental Psychology 19*(1), 21–39.

67. Manzo & Perkins (2006).

68. Korda, Noah. Interview with author. November 22, 2017.

69. McCain, Amy. Interview with author. October 31, 2017.

70. Jenkins (2013).

71. Baker, C. (2023). The prevalence of storyworlds and thematic landscapes in global theme parks. *Annals of Tourism Research Empirical Insights, 4*(1), 100080.

72. Milman, A. (2009). Evaluating the guest experience at theme parks: An empirical investigation of key attributes. *International Journal of Tourism Research, 11*(4), 373–87.

73. Duany, A., Plater-Zyberk, E., & Speck, J. (2000). *Suburban nation: The rise of sprawl and the decline of the American dream*. North Point Press. 63.

74. Anonymous #4. Interview with author. November 12, 2017.

75. Perkins, D. D., & Long, D. A. (2002). Neighborhood sense of community and social capital: A multi-level analysis. In A. Fisher, C. Sonn, & B. Bishop (Eds.), *Psychological sense of community: Research applications and implications* (pp. 291–316). Plenum.

76. Regan, Todd. Interview with author. November 28, 2017.

77. Wasko (2020).

78. Jenkins (2013). 282.

79. Hench (2003).

80. Regan, Todd. Interview with author. November 28, 2017.

81. Sandvoss (2005). 64.

82. Manzo & Perkins (2006).

83. Koren-Kuik (2013). 147.

84. Schiffler, E. (2019). The park as stage: Radical re-casting in Disneyland's social clubs. In J. A. Kokai & T. Robson (Eds.), *Performance and the Disney theme park experience: The tourist as actor* (pp. 247–64). Palgrave Macmillan.

85. Lam, C. (2014, February 27). The very merry un-gangs of Disneyland. *OC Weekly*. https://www.ocweekly.com/the-very-merry-un-gangs-of-disneyland-6429567/

86. Williams-Turkowski, S. (2023). Down the rabbit hole: Disneyland gangs, affective spaces, and Covid-19. In E. Champion, C. Lee, J. Stadler, & R. Peaslee (Eds.), *Screen tourism and affective landscapes* (pp. 180–98). Routledge.

87. Fraade-Blanar, Z., & Glazer, A. M. (2017). *Superfandom: How our obsessions are changing what we buy and who we are.* W.W. Norton. 124.

88. Manzo & Perkins (2006). 339.

89. Muniz Jr., A. M., & O'Guinn, T. C. (2001). Brand community. *Journal of Consumer Research*, *27*(4), 412–32.

90. Brown, B. B., Perkins, D., & Brown, G. (2003). Place attachment in a revitalizing neighbourhood: Individual and block levels of analysis. *Journal of Environmental Psychology*, 23, 259–71.

91. Ruszecki, Hayley. Interview with author. October 11, 2017; Marquez, Michael. Interview with author. October 16, 2017.

92. Regan, Todd. Interview with author. November 28, 2017.

93. Jenkins (2013); Sennett, R. (2008). *The craftsman.* Yale University Press.

94. Jenkins (2013).

95. Jenkins (2013); Pearson (2010).

96. Benkler, Y. (2006). *Wealth of networks: How social production transforms markets and freedom.* Yale University Press.

97. Gurr, Bob. Interview with author. October 8, 2017.

98. Gurr.

99. Baym, N. K. (2018). *Playing to the crowd: Musicians, audiences, and the intimate work of connection.* New York University Press. 179.

100. Gurr.

101. Muniz & O'Guinn (2001).

102. Gurr.

103. Jenkins (2013); Barthes, R. (1975). *S/Z.* Hill and Wang.

104. Barthes (1975).

105. Barthes.

106. Barthes.

107. Barthes.

108. Brooker (2017). 167.

109. Bielby, D. D., & Harrington, C. L. (2017). The lives of fandoms. In J. Gray, C. Sandvoss, & C. L. Harrington (Eds.), *Fandom: Identities and communities in a mediated world* (2nd ed.) (pp. 205–21). New York University Press.

110. Tuan (1997).

111. Disneyland, Inc. (1956). *The complete guide to Disneyland*. Western Printing and Lithography Company. 26.

112. Sandvoss (2005). 61.

CHAPTER 3: DISNEYLAND ONLINE FANDOM, 1990–2005—UNITY AND RESISTANCE

1. Coppa (2014). 77.

2. Jenkins (2013).

3. Korkis, J. (2016). *How to be a Disney historian*. Theme Park Press.

4. Korkis.

5. Coppa (2006).

6. Baym, N. K. (2000). *Tune in, log on: Soaps, fandom and online community*. Sage.

7. Duffett (2013). 239.

8. Muniz & O'Guinn (2001).

9. Kollock, P., & Smith, M. (1999). Communities in cyberspace. In M. Smith & P. Kollock (Eds.), *Communities in cyberspace* (pp. 3–25). Routledge. 16.

10. Coppa (2014); Jenkins, H. (2006a); Jenkins, H. (2006b). *Convergence culture: Where old and new media collide*. New York University Press.

11. Wellman & Gulia (1999).

12. Lutters, W. G., & Ackerman, M. S. (2003). Joining the backstage: locality and centrality in an online community. *Information Technology & People*, 16(2), 157–82.

13. Pellman, Ken. Interview with author. October 21, 2017.

14. Pellman.

15. Pellman.

16. Lutters & Ackerman (2003).

17. Lutters & Ackerman.

18. Lutters & Ackerman. 174.

19. Ackerman, M. S., & Starr, B. (1996). Social activity indicators for groupware. *IEEE Computer*, 29(6), 37–44.

20. Lutters & Ackerman (2003).

21. Regan, Todd. Interview with author. November 28, 2017.

22. Regan.

23. Regan.

24. Baym, N. K. (1994). The emergence of community in computer-mediated communication. In S. Jones (Ed.), *CyberSociety: Computer mediated communication and community* (pp. 138–63). Sage.

25. Baym (2000); Pfaffenberger, B. (2003). A standing wave in the web of our communications: Usenet and the socio-technical construction of cyberspace values. In C. Lueg & D. Fisher (Eds.), *From Usenets to cowebs: Interacting with social information spaces* (pp. 20–43). Springer.

26. Smith, M. A. (2003). Measures and maps of Usenet. In C. Lueg & D. Fisher (Eds.), *From Usenets to cowebs: Interacting with social information spaces* (pp. 47–78). Springer.

27. Nonnecke, B., & Preece, J. (2003). Silent participants: Getting to know lurkers better. In C. Lueg, & D. Fisher (Eds.), *From Usenets to cowebs: Interacting with social information spaces* (pp. 110–32). Springer; Whittaker, S., Terveen, L., Hill, W., & Cherny, L. (2003). The dynamics of mass interaction. In C. Lueg & D. Fisher (Eds.), *From Usenets to cowebs: Interacting with social information spaces* (pp. 78–91). Springer.

28. McLaughlin, M. L., Osborne, K. K., & Smith, C. B. (1995). Standards of conduct on Usenet. In S. G. Jones (Ed.). *CyberSociety: Computer-mediated communication and community* (pp. 90–111). Sage; Slouka, M. (1995). *War of the worlds: Cyberspace and the high-tech assault on reality.* Basic Books.

29. Rheingold, H. (1993). *The virtual community: Homesteading on the electronic frontier.* Harper. 118.

30. Rheingold. 130.

31. Ren et al. (2007).

32. McLaughlin et al. (1995). 107.

33. Jenkins (2013).

34. Shirky (2008).

35. Jenkins (2006a).

36. Pellman, Ken. Interview with author. October 21, 2017.

37. Jenkins (2013). 86.

38. Hill, Jim, Interview with author. October 24, 2017.

39. Moseley, Doobie, Interview with author. November 30, 2017.

40. Gardetta, D. (2005, November 1). Disnoidland. *Los Angeles Magazine.* https://www.lamag.com/longform/disnoidland/

41. Gee, J. P. (2005). Semiotic social spaces and affinity spaces: From the age of mythology to today's schools. In D. Barton & K. Tusting (Eds.), *Beyond communities of practice: Language, power and social context* (pp. 214–33). Cambridge University Press.

42. Jenkins (2013); Hills, M. (2010). *Triumph of a time lord.* I. B. Tauris.

43. Gardetta (2005).

44. Korkis (2016); Moseley, Doobie. Interview with author. November 30, 2017.

45. Korkis.

46. Jenkins (2013).

47. Dickerson, M. (1996b, December 18). Guests gong plastic utensils at Café Orleans. *Los Angeles Times.* https://www.latimes.com/archives/la-xpm-1996-12-18-fi-10234-story.html

48. Gardetta (2005).

49. Ren et al. (2007).

50. Granelli, J. (1997, October 15). Disneyland's Light Magic show falls on dark days. *Los Angeles Times.* http://articles.latimes.com/1997/oct/15/news/mn-43006

51. Pellman, Ken. Interview with author. October 21, 2017; Regan, Todd. Interview with author. October 28, 2017.

52. Niles, R. (2004, March 4). Revenge of the Internet: Disney dumps Eisner as chairman. *Theme Park Insider.* http://www.themeparkinsider.com/news/response.cfm?ID=1553

53. Available at the Wayback Machine archive: https://web.archive.org/web/19990427091849/http://members.aol.com/alweho/pressler/pressler.htm

54. Wyn (1999).

55. Sherr, I. (2019, June 6). Meet the angry gaming YouTubers who turn outrage into views. *CNET.* https://www.cnet.com/news/meet-the-angrygaming-youtuberwho-turn-outrage-into-views/

56. Pellman, Ken. Interview with author. October 21, 2017.

57. Dickerson, M. (1996a, September 12). Self-styled keepers of the Magic Kingdom. *Los Angeles Times.* http://articles.latimes.com/1996-09-12/news/mn-42945_1_magic-kingdom

58. Gardetta (2005).

59. CAL/OSHA (1999, March 25). CAL/OSHA cites Disneyland for December accident. https://www.dir.ca.gov/dirnews/1999/IR99-02.html

60. Gardetta (2005).

61. Regan, Todd. Interview with author. November 28, 2017.

62. Bruns, A., & Burgess, J. (2015). Twitter hashtags from ad hoc to calculated Publics. In N. Rambukkana (Ed.), *HashtagPublics: The power and politics of discursive networks* (pp. 13–28). Peter Lang.

63. Jenkins (2013).

64. Baym (2018).

65. Segan, S. (2008, July 31). R.I.P. Usenet: 1980–2008. *PC Magazine.* http://archive.is/20120909001021/http://www.pcmag.com/article2/0,2817,2326849,00.asp

66. Forum Software Reviews (2011). Forum Software Timeline 1994–2012. https://www.forum-software.org/forum-software-timeline-from-1994-to-today

67. Postill, J. (2011). *Localizing the Internet: An anthropological account.* Berghahn Books.

68. Postill.

69. Kozinets, R.V. (2015). *Netnography: Redefined.* Sage. 10.

70. Pellman, Ken. Interview with author. October 21, 2017; Regan, Todd. Interview with author. October 28, 2017.

71. Regan, Todd. Interview with author. October 28, 2017.

72. Regan, Todd. Interview with author. October 28, 2017.

73. Regan, Todd. Interview with author. October 28, 2017.

74. Pellman, Ken. Interview with author. October 21, 2017.

75. Moseley, Doobie. Interview with author. November 30, 2017.

76. Moseley, Doobie. Interview with author. November 30, 2017.

77. Regan, Todd. Interview with author. October 28, 2017.

78. Regan, Todd. Interview with author. October 28, 2017.

79. Doctorow, C. (2004, August 22). Imagineering's decline and fall. *BoingBoing.* https://boingboing.net/2004/08/22/imagineerings-declin.html

80. Niles (2004).

81. Doctorow (2004).

82. Britt, R. (2001, April 20). No gold rush for California Adventure. MarketWatch. https://www.marketwatch.com/story/no-gold-rush-for-california-adventure

83. Aitken, Aitken & Cohn. (2009). Wrongful death of son on Disney's Big Thunder Mountain Railroad. https://web.archive.org/web/20090315051823/http://www.aitkenlaw.com/verdicts_settlements/disneys_big_thunder_mountain.html

84. Korkis (2016). 61.

85. Regan, Todd. Interview with author. October 28, 2017.

86. Disney, R. (2003, November 30). Letter of resignation, dated 11/30/03, from Roy E. Disney to Michael D. Eisner. U.S. Securities and Exchange Commission. https://www.sec.gov/Archives/edgar/data/1001039/000119312503090215/dex991.htm

87. Stewart, J. (2005). *Disney war*. Simon & Schuster. 493.

88. Stewart. 494.

89. Niles (2004).

CHAPTER 4: DISNEYLAND ONLINE FANDOM, 2006–2020 —FRAGMENTATION AND RESIGNATION

1. Moseley, Doobie. Interview with author. November 30, 2017.

2. Regan, Todd. Interview with author. November 28, 2017.

3. Anonymous #4. Interview with author. November 12, 2017.

4. Moseley, Doobie. Interview with author. November 30, 2017.

5. Moseley, Doobie. Interview with author. November 30, 2017.

6. Regan, Todd. Interview with author. November 28, 2017.

7. Regan, Todd. Interview with author. October 28, 2017.

8. Regan, Todd. Interview with author. October 28, 2017.

9. Edidin, R. (2014, January 27). How to get away with dressing like a superhero at work. *Wired*. https://www.wired.com/2014/01/stealth-cosplay/

10. Torres, K. (2022). Disney's social media moms. In S. Mittermeier (Ed.), *Fan phenomena: Disney* (pp. 198–206). Intellect Books.

11. Torres.

12. Archived by the Wayback Machine at: https://web.archive.org/web/20200815160238/https//www.awesomeretreat.com/

13. Kiriakou (2019).

14. Anonymous #6, Interview with author. November 6, 2017.

15. Marquez, Michael. Interview with author. October 16, 2017.

16. Jenkins (2013).

17. Moseley, Doobie. Interview with author. November 30, 2017.

18. Regan, Todd. Interview with author. November 28, 2017.

19. Shirky (2008).

20. Meyrowitz (1994).

21. Fraade-Blanar & Glazer (2017). 75.

22. Moseley, Doobie. Interview with author. November 30, 2017.

23. Sandvoss & Kearns (2014).

24. Korda, Noah. Interview with author. November 22, 2017.

25. Bury, R., Deller, R. A., Greenwood, A., & Jones, B. (2013). From Usenet to Tumblr: The changing role of social media. *Participations: Journal of Audience and Reception Studies, 10*(1), 299–318.

26. Baym (2018).

27. Marquez, Michael. Interview with author. October 16, 2017.

28. Marquez, Michael. Interview with author. October 16, 2017.

29. Marquez, Michael. Interview with author. October 16, 2017.

30. Regan, Todd. Interview with author. November 28, 2017.

31. Regan, Todd. Interview with author. November 28, 2017.

32. Regan, Todd. Interview with author. November 28, 2017.

33. Regan, Todd. Interview with author. November 28, 2017.

34. Bury et al. (2013).

35. Howard Rheingold Episode [Audio podcast]. (2016, October 17). http://www
.communitysignal.com/the-howard-rheingold-episode/

36. Moseley, Doobie. Interview with author. November 30, 2017.

37. Moseley, Doobie. Interview with author. November 30, 2017.

38. Moseley, Doobie. Interview with author. November 30, 2017.

39. Marquez, Michael. Interview with author. October 16, 2017.

40. Anonymous #2. Interview with author. November 14, 2017; Ruszecki, Hayley.
Interview with author. October 11, 2017; Marquez, Michael. Interview with author.
October 16, 2017.

41. Regan, Todd. Interview with author. November 28, 2017.

42. Regan, Todd. Interview with author. November 28, 2017.

43. Anonymous #1. Interview with author. October 17, 2017.

44. Regan, Todd. Interview with author. November 28, 2017.

45. Anonymous #5. Interview with author. October 17, 2017; Anonymous #9. Interview
with author. November 16, 2017.

46. Regan, Todd. Interview with author. November 28, 2017.

47. Soto-Vásquez, A. D. (2022). YouTube and TikTok as platforms for learning about
others: The case of non-Chinese travel videos in Shanghai Disneyland. *Online Media and
Global Communication*, 1–24. https://doi.org/10.1515/omgc-2022-0012

48. Anonymous #5. Interview with author. October 17, 2017; Anonymous #9. Interview
with author. November 16, 2017.

49. Pett, Emma (2021). Experiencing cinema: Participatory film cultures, immersive
media and the experience economy. Bloomsbury Publishing USA.

50. Regan, Todd. Interview with author. November 28, 2017.

51. Bury et al. (2013).

52. Anonymous #5. Interview with author. October 17, 2017.

53. Anonymous #5. Interview with author. October 17, 2017.

54. Anonymous #5. Interview with author. October 17, 2017.

55. Duffy, B. (2015). Amateur, autonomous, and collaborative: Myths of aspiring
female cultural producers in web 2.0. *Critical Studies in Media Communication*. 32(1),
48–64; Kuehn, K., & Corrigan, T. F. (2013). Hope labor: The role of employment prospects
in online social production. *The Political Economy of Communication*, 1, 9–25.

56. Anonymous #5. Interview with author. October 17, 2017.

57. Anonymous #5. Interview with author. October 17, 2017.

58. Anonymous #9. Interview with author. November 16, 2017.

59. Bricker, T. (2011). Pixiedusters v. doom & gloomers: What's wrong with Disney fans.
Disney Tourist Blog. https://www.disneytouristblog.com/disney-fancommunity-criticism/

60. Regan, Todd. Interview with author. November 28, 2017.

61. Anonymous #9. Interview with author. November 16, 2017.

62. Amon, M. P. (2019). The Royal Theatre presents: Echoes of melodrama in the Magic Kingdom. In J. A. Kokai & T. Robson (Eds.), *Performance and the Disney theme park experience: The tourist as actor* (pp. 193–210). Palgrave Macmillan.

63. Amon, 208.

64. Korda, Noah. Interview with author. November 22, 2017.

65. Anonymous #7. Interview with author. October 27, 2017.

66. Bolter & Grusin (1999).

67. Booth (2017).

68. Weinberger, M. (2016, October 14). How Disneyland is taking cues from Uber and Apple to make sure everybody enjoys their holiday more. *Business Insider*. https://www.businessinsider.com/disneyland-disney-app-2016-10?r=US&IR=T

69. Fickley-Baker, J. (2017, November 1). 9 "walls" Disney parks super fans deem Instagram worthy. *Disney Parks Blog*. https://disneyparks.disney.go.com/blog/2017/11/9-walls-disney-parks-super-fans-deem-instagram-worthy/

70. Lobo, T. (2023). Selfie and world: On Instagrammable places and technologies for capturing them. *Journal of Human-Technology Relations*, *1*(1), 1–11. 2.

71. Anonymous #7. Interview with author. October 27, 2017.

72. Regan, Todd. Interview with author. November 28, 2017.

73. Anonymous #7. Interview with author. October 27, 2017.

74. Anonymous #7. Interview with author. October 27, 2017.

75. Anonymous #8. Interview with author. October 29, 2017.

76. Gurr, Bob. Interview with author. October 8, 2017.

77. Anonymous #1. Interview with author. October 17, 2017.

78. Gurr, Bob. Interview with author. October 8, 2017.

79. Gurr, Bob. Interview with author. October 8, 2017.

80. WDW *News Today* (2022, September 18). CNBC reporter calls Bob Chapek "BOB PAYCHECK" on live television. https://wdwnt.com/2022/09/cnbc-reporter-calls-bob-chapek-bob-paycheck-on-live-tv/

81. Regan, Todd. Interview with author. November 28, 2017.

82. Regan, Todd. Interview with author. November 28, 2017.

83. Tully, S. (2012, June 19). Disney California Adventure breaks attendance record, blog says. *Orange County Register*. https://www.ocregister.com/2012/06/19/disney-california-adventure-breaks-attendance-record-blog-says/

84. Regan, Todd. Interview with author. November 28, 2017.

85. Hill, Jim. Interview with author. October 24, 2017.

86. Hill, Jim. Interview with author. October 24, 2017; Regan, Todd. Interview with author. November 28, 2017.

87. Johnson, D. (2017). Fantagonism: Factions, institutions, and constitutive hegemonies of fandom. In J. Gray, C. Sandvoss, & C. L. Harrington (Eds.), *Fandom: Identities and communities in a mediated world* (2nd ed.) (pp. 369–86). New York University Press. 379.

CHAPTER 5: FAN EVENTS, MEETS, AND CLUBS AT DISNEYLAND: FROM A FEW TO A MULTITUDE, 1990–2020

1. Parrish, J. J. (2013). Metaphors we read by: People, process, and fan fiction. *Transformative Works and Cultures, 14*, 1–16. Para. 4.8.

2. Regan, Todd. Interview with author. November 28, 2017.

3. Pellman, Ken. Interview with author. October 21, 2017.

4. Schrader, E. (1997, September 22). Disneyland, police combat troublesome teens. *Los Angeles Times.* http://articles.latimes.com/1997/sep/22/local/me-35085

5. Schrader.

6. Lam (2014).

7. Schrader (1997); Pellman, Ken. Interview with author. October 21, 2017.

8. Pellman, Ken. Interview with author. October 21, 2017.

9. Tully, S. (2013, June 12). Swing dancing returns to Disneyland. *Orange County Register.* https://www.ocregister.com/2013/06/12/swing-dancing-returns-to-disneyland/

10. Anonymous #4. Interview with author. November 12, 2017.

11. Anonymous #4. Interview with author. November 12, 2017.

12. Anonymous #4. Interview with author. November 12, 2017.

13. Bemis (2022).

14. Shady, J. (2011, September 22). Q&A: Gay Days Anaheim co-founder event producer Eddie Shapiro. *OC Weekly.* https://www.ocweekly.com/qanda-gay-days-anaheim-co-founder-event-producer-eddie-shapiro-6457122/

15. Shady.

16. Kinser, J. (2015, September 20). This year's Gay Days Weekend at Disney will be the most thrilling yet. *Queerty.* https://www.queerty.com/gay-days-disney-is-coming-and-it-will-be-more-fun-than-ever-20150920

17. Martin, H. (2019, May 28). Disneyland Paris takes over its gay pride event. Will U.S. parks do the same? *Los Angeles Times.* https://www.latimes.com/business/la-fi-disney-theme-park-gay-pride-20190528-story.html

18. Martin.

19. Korda, Noah. Interview with author. November 22, 2017.

20. Korda, Noah. Interview with author. November 22, 2017.

21. Korda, Noah. Interview with author. November 22, 2017.

22. Korda, Noah. Interview with author. November 22, 2017.

23. Ruszecki, Hayley. Interview with author. October 11, 2017.

24. Ruszecki, Hayley. Interview with author. October 11, 2017.

25. McCain, Amy. Interview with author. October 31, 2017.

26. Anonymous #2. Interview with author. November 14, 2017.

27. Ruszecki, Hayley. Interview with author. October 11, 2017; Marquez, Michael. Interview with author. October 16, 2017.

28. Anonymous #6. Interview with author. November 6, 2017.

29. Anonymous #6. Interview with author. November 6, 2017.

30. van Meter, C. (2014, March 11). The young, tattooed, obsessive fans roaming Disneyland. *VICE*. https://www.vice.com/en_au/article/8gdqy5/the-punks-of-the-magic -kingdom

31. Anonymous #3. Interview with author. October 29, 2017; Anonymous #8. Interview with author. October 29, 2017.

32. Anonymous #3. Interview with author. October 29, 2017.

33. Anonymous #3. Interview with author. October 29, 2017.

34. Anonymous #3. Interview with author. October 29, 2017.

35. Korda, Noah. Interview with author. November 22, 2017.

36. Korda, Noah. Interview with author. November 22, 2017.

37. McCain, Amy. Interview with author. October 31, 2017.

38. Anonymous #6. Interview with author. November 6, 2017.

39. Anonymous #8. Interview with author. October 29, 2017; Lam (2014).

40. Anonymous #8. Interview with author. October 29, 2017.

41. Shirky (2008).

42. Jones, G. L. (2010). The social fabric of civil war reenacting. In J. Schlehe, M. Uike-Bormann, C. Oesterle, & W. Hochbruck (Eds.), *Staging the past: Themed environments in transcultural perspectives* (pp. 219–34). Transcript Verlag.

43. Williams-Turkowski (2023).

44. Anonymous #6. Interview with author. November 6, 2017.

45. Anonymous #8. Interview with author. October 29, 2017.

46. Anonymous #6. Interview with author. November 6, 2017.

47. Anonymous #1. Interview with author. October 17, 2017; Lam (2014).

48. Williams-Turkowski (2023).

49. Anonymous #7. Interview with author. October 27, 2017.

50. Anonymous #7. Interview with author. October 27, 2017.

51. Korda, Noah. Interview with author. November 22, 2017.

52. Regan, Todd. Interview with author. November 28, 2017.

53. Duffy, B. E. (2017). *(Not) getting paid to do what you love: Gender, social media, and aspirational work.* Yale University Press.

54. McCain, Amy. Interview with author. October 31, 2017.

55. McCain, Amy. Interview with author. October 31, 2017.

56. Anonymous #2. Interview with author. November 14, 2017.

57. Anonymous #8. Interview with author. October 29, 2017.

58. Pearson (2010); Busse, K. (2015). Fan labor and feminism: Capitalizing on the fannish labor of love. *Cinema Journal, 54*(3), 110–15; Stanfill, M., & Condis, M. (2014). Fandom and/as labor. *Transformative Works and Cultures, 15*, 130–57.

59. Korda, Noah. Interview with author. November 22, 2017.

60. Korda, Noah. Interview with author. November 22, 2017.

61. Regan, Todd. Interview with author. November 28, 2017.

62. Marquez, Michael. Interview with author. October 16, 2017.

63. Anonymous #4. Interview with author. November 12, 2017.

64. Anonymous #4. Interview with author. November 12, 2017.

65. Jenkins (2013).

CHAPTER 6: CONTESTATION OF DISNEY AND FAN POWER
ONLINE AND AT DISNEYLAND, 1990–2020

1. Adams (1991); Bryman (2004); Cross & Walton (2005); Fjellman (1992); Wasko (2020); Schlehe, J., & Uike-Bormann, M. (2010). Staging the past in cultural theme parks: Representations of self and other in Asia and Europe. In J. Schlehe, M. Uike-Bormann, C. Oesterle, & W. Hochbruck (Eds.), *Staging the past: Themed environments in transcultural perspectives* (pp. 57–91). Transcript Verlag.

2. Pellman, Ken. Interview with author. October 21, 2017.

3. Pellman, Ken. Interview with author. October 21, 2017.

4. Pellman, Ken. Interview with author. October 21, 2017.

5. Lutters & Ackerman (2003).

6. Moseley, Doobie. Interview with author. November 30, 2017.

7. Moseley, Doobie. Interview with author. November 30, 2017.

8. Regan, Todd. Interview with author. November 28, 2017.

9. Regan, Todd. Interview with author. November 28, 2017.

10. Regan, Todd. Interview with author. November 28, 2017.

11. Regan, Todd. Interview with author. November 28, 2017.

12. Korda, Noah. Interview with author. November 22, 2017.

13. Moseley, Doobie. Interview with author. November 30, 2017.

14. Anonymous #5. Interview with author. October 17, 2017.

15. Anonymous #5. Interview with author. October 17, 2017.

16. Anonymous #5. Interview with author. October 17, 2017.

17. Maheshwari, S. (2018, November 11). Are you ready for the nanoinfluencers? *New York Times*. https://www.nytimes.com/2018/11/11/business/media/nanoinfluencers-instagram-influencers.html; Melas, C. (2018, July 24). One of Instagram's biggest influencers wants influencers to know the end is near. *CNN*. https://money.cnn.com/2018/07/24/technology/fat-jewish-swish-beverage-canned-wine/index.html

18. Anonymous #5. Interview with author. October 17, 2017; Seemayer, Z. (2017, September 8). "The Mickey Mouse Club" is back with Todrick Hall and all-new Mouseketeers! Yahoo! Entertainment. https://www.yahoo.com/entertainment/apos-mickey-mouse-club-apos-130001068.html

19. Barnes, B. (2014, March 24). Disney buys Maker Studios, Video supplier for YouTube. *New York Times*. https://www.nytimes.com/2014/03/25/business/media/disney-buys-maker-studios-video-supplier-for-youtube.html

20. Ingram, M. (2017, February 23). Disney scales back the dream at its Maker Studios video unit. *Fortune*. http://fortune.com/2017/02/23/disney-maker-studios/

21. Anonymous #7. Interview with author. October 27, 2017; Pellman, Ken. Interview with author. October 21, 2017.

22. Pedicini, S. (2015, June 4). Disney policy requiring character confidentiality comes under fire. *Orlando Sentinel*. https://www.orlandosentinel.com/business/os-disney-characters-20150604-story.html; Walt Disney Company (2016). *Employee Policy Manual*. https://cepfranco.files.wordpress.com/2016/04/employee-policy-manual-02-2016.pdf

23. Anonymous #9. Interview with author. November 16, 2017.

24. Anonymous #8. Interview with author. October 29, 2017.

25. Martin, H. (2018, February 28). Three quarters of employees surveyed at Disney's Anaheim resort say they can't afford basic living expenses. *Los Angeles Times*. https://www.latimes.com/business/la-fi-disneyland-study-20180228-story.html

26. Kiriakou (2019).

27. Anonymous #7. Interview with author. October 27, 2017; Anonymous #8. Interview with author. October 29, 2017.

28. Regan, Todd. Interview with author. November 28, 2017.

29. Martens, T. (2019, February 27). Star Wars: Galaxy's Edge will be Disneyland's most interactive experience. Let's play. *Los Angeles Times*. https://www.latimes.com/entertainment/herocomplex/la-et-ms-disneyland-star-warsgalaxys-edge-20190227-story.html

30. Niles, R. (2019a, January 22). Get your cheese on at Disneyland's Mickey Mouse festival. *Theme Park Insider*. https://www.themeparkinsider.com/flume/201901/6560/

31. Soto-Vásquez, A. D. (2021). Mediating the Magic Kingdom: Instagram, fantasy, and identity. *Western Journal of Communication, 85*(5), 588–608.

32. Villamor, N. (2019, March 21). Disneyland resort spring update: Fox in the mouse house. *MiceChat*. https://www.micechat.com/220295-disneyland-resort-spring-update-fox-in-the-mouse-house/

33. Jenkins, H., Ford, S., & Green, J. (2013). *Spreadable media: Creating value and meaning in a networked culture*. New York University Press.

34. Anonymous #3. Interview with author. October 29, 2017.

35. Regan, Todd. Interview with author. November 28, 2017.

36. Cunningham & Craig (2019); Jenkins, et al. (2013).

37. Anonymous #5. Interview with author. October 17, 2017; Anonymous #9. Interview with author. November 16, 2017.

38. Williams (2020).

39. Regan, Todd. Interview with author. November 28, 2017.

40. Regan, Todd. Interview with author. November 28, 2017.

41. Chmlelewski, D. C., & Patten, D. (2017, November 3). Disney slams "biased" L.A. Times; No word that boycott is over—update. *Deadline*. https://deadline.com/2017/11/disney-los-angeles-times-battle-anaheim-coverage-boycott-1202201260/

42. Chmlelewski & Patten.

43. Ember, S., & Barnes, B. (2017, November 7). Disney ends ban on Los Angeles Times amid fierce backlash. *New York Times*. https://www.nytimes.com/2017/11/07/business/disney-la-times.html

44. Ruszecki, Hayley. Interview with author. October 11, 2017.

45. Korda, Noah. Interview with author. November 22, 2017.

46. Korda, Noah. Interview with author. November 22, 2017.

47. Anonymous #4. Interview with author. November 12, 2017; Marquez, Michael. Interview with author. October 16, 2017; Regan, Todd. Interview with author. November 28, 2017.

48. Anonymous #5. Interview with author. October 17, 2017.

49. Anonymous #5. Interview with author. October 17, 2017.

50. Anonymous #5. Interview with author. October 17, 2017; Anonymous #8. Interview with author. October 29, 2017.

51. Marquez, Michael. Interview with author. October 16, 2017.

52. Anonymous #4. Interview with author. November 12, 2017.

53. McCain, Amy. Interview with author. October 31, 2017.

54. McCain, Amy. Interview with author. October 31, 2017.

55. McCain, Amy. Interview with author. October 31, 2017; Anonymous #2. Interview with author. November 14, 2017.

56. Necrosis, Z. (2016, January 18). 2006–2014 Harry Potter at Disneyland. http://www.potterday.org/

57. Necrosis, Z. (2015, June 13). What happened. http://acrimoniousdiatribes.blogspot.com/2015/06/what-happened.html

58. Necrosis, Z. (2015).

59. Hench (2003). 35.

60. Koren-Kuik (2013). 147.

61. Gray, J., Sandvoss, C., & Harrington, C. L. (2007). Introduction: Why study fans? In J. Gray, C. Sandvoss, & C. L. Harrington (Eds.), *Fandom: Identities and communities in a mediated world* (pp. 1–16). New York University Press.

62. Koenig, D. (2017, December 7). The not-so-social clubs of Disneyland. *MiceChat*. https://micechat.com/179550-david-koenig-disneyland-social-clubs/

63. Koenig.

64. Kiriakou (2019).

65. Jenkins (2013).

66. Hutchins (2022).

67. Regan, Todd. Interview with author. November 28, 2017.

68. Lee, D., Kim, H. S., & Kim, J. K. (2011). The impact of online brand community type on consumer's community engagement behaviors: Consumer-created vs. marketer-created online brand community in online social-networking web sites. *Cyberpsychology, Behavior, and Social Networking, 14*(1–2), 59–63.

69. Hill, Jim. Interview with author. October 24, 2017.

70. Regan, Todd. Interview with author. November 28, 2017.

71. Baker, C. A. (2016). Creative choices and fan practices in the transformation of theme park space. *Transformative Works and Cultures, 22*, 1–15.

72. Koren-Kuik (2013). 152.

73. Baker (2016); Koren-Kuik (2013). 152.

74. Sage, D. (2023, March 1). UPDATED: Everything You Need To Know About Disneyland MagicBand+. *MiceChat*. https://www.micechat.com/334202-disneyland-magicband-plus-essential-guide/

75. Baker (2016). 2–3.

76. Anonymous #3. Interview with author. October 29, 2017; Anonymous #8. Interview with author. October 29, 2017.

77. Niles, R. (2019b, May 9). Here's how the virtual queue will work for Star Wars: Galaxy's Edge. *Theme Park Insider*. https://www.themeparkinsider.com/flume/201905/6766/

78. Williams (2020).

79. Karmali, S. (2012, October 23). Harrods' Designer Disney Princess Dresses Unveiled. *Vogue UK*. http://www.vogue.co.uk/gallery/harrods-disney-princess-designer-dresses -christmas-window-display

80. Gabbana, S. [Vogue]. (2016, February 28). *Dolce & Gabbana Fall 2016 Ready-to-Wear | Milan Fashion Week* [Video File]. https://www.youtube.com/watch?v=EBJptIH4vio

81. Archived at the Wayback Machine: https://web.archive.org/web/20180204213157/ https://danielle-nicole.myshopify.com/collections/disney-dn

82. Martin (2019); Petter, O. (2019, February 7). Disneyland Paris to host first-ever LGBTQ+ event. *Independent*. https://www.independent.co.uk/life-style/disneyland-paris -lgbt-pride-event-magical-june-2019-a8767206.html

83. Regan, Todd. Interview with author. November 28, 2017.

84. Bordewijk, J. L., & van Kaam, B. (1986). Towards a new classification of tele-information services. *Intermedia*, *14*(1): 16–21.

CHAPTER 7: THE EVOLVING INTERSECTION OF FANS AND DISNEY ON ONLINE SOCIAL PLATFORMS AND AT DISNEYLAND

1. Martens, T. (2014, July 26). From the archives: Disneyland's live-action game is a fun dose of the Old West. *Los Angeles Times*. https://www.latimes.com/entertainment/music/ la-et-ms-disneyland-legends-frontierland-20140726-story.html

2. Zylstra, H. (2014, September 2). Legends of Frontierland: Get in the game. *MiceChat*. https://www.micechat.com/78929-legends-of-frontierland-fun-in-the-frontier-and -an-extension/

3. Ross, A. (1999). *The Celebration chronicles*. Ballantine; Clavé, S. A. (2007). *The global theme park industry*. CABI.

4. Niles, R. (2023, September 13). Disney reveals more plans for its new California community. *Theme Park Insider*. https://www.themeparkinsider.com/flume/202309/9774/

5. Iger, R. (2019). *The ride of a lifetime: Lessons learned from 15 years as CEO of the Walt Disney Company*. Random House. 191.

6. Themed Entertainment Association (TEA). (2020) Global Attractions Attendance Report 2019. https://www.teaconnect.org/images/files/TEA_369_18301_201201.pdf

7. Pellman, Ken. Interview with author. October 21, 2017; Regan, Todd. Interview with author. November 28, 2017.

8. Pellman, Ken. Interview with author. October 21, 2017.

9. Jenkins (2013).

10. Manzo & Perkins (2006); Shumaker, S. A., & Taylor, R. B. (1983). Toward a clarification of people-place relationships: A model of attachment to place. In N. R. Reimer & E. S. Geller (Eds.), *Environmental psychology: Directions and perspectives* (pp. 219–51). Praeger.

11. Dickerson (1996a); Kiriakou (2017). "Ricky, this is amazing!": Disney nostalgia, new media users, and the extreme fans of the WDW Kingdomcast. *Journal of Fandom Studies*, *5*(1), 99–112.

12. Sullivan, J. L. (2019). *Media audiences: effects, users, institutions, and power.* Sage.

13. Regan, Todd. Interview with author. November 28, 2017.

14. Kiriakou (2017).

15. Oleksinski, J. (2019, July 26). Sorry, childless millennials going to Disney World is weird. *New York Post.* https://nypost.com/2019/07/26/sorry-childless-millennials-going-to-disney-world-is-weird/; Min, S. (2019, July 29). Childless millennials should be banned from Disney World, tired mom rants. *CBS News.* https://www.cbsnews.com/news/disney-world-rant-mom-criticizes-childless-couples-at-happiest-place-on-earth-insists-its-for-kids-and-parents-only/

16. Dargis, M. (2019, May 1). The Avengers just took over our world. We need to talk. *New York Times.* https://www.nytimes.com/2019/05/01/movies/avengers-endgame-critics.html

17. Jenkins (2013); Sandvoss (2005).

18. Jenkins et al. (2013); Jenkins (2013).

19. Williams, R. (2022). Creativity and connection: How Disney parks' fans responded during the Coronavirus closures. In S. Mittermeier (Ed.), *Fan Phenomena: Disney* (pp. 93–103). Intellect Books.

20. Baker, C. (2022). Creating virtual homes during COVID-19: #HomemadeDisney and theme park fandom's response to crisis. *Popular Communication, 20*(4), 260–73; Schweizer, B. (2021). Playing make-believe with #homemadeDisney pandemic ride videos. *Eludamos: Journal for Computer Game Culture, 12*(1), 199–218.

21. Meikle, K. (2022). Time for the theme park ride-through video. *Transformative Works and Cultures, 37,* 1–11.

22. Baker (2022). 260.

23. Goldsmith, J. (2023, March 9). Bob Iger says Disney theme parks were priced too high in "zeal to grow profit"—It's "a brand that needs to be accessible." *Deadline.* https://deadline.com/2023/03/bob-iger-says-disney-theme-parks-priced-high-brand-needs-to-be-accessible-1235283912/

24. Sage, D. (2023, October 23). Disneyland update—Snowfall, pumpkins & missed opportunities. *MiceChat.* https://www.micechat.com/371000-disneyland-update-snowfall-pumpkins-missed-opportunities/

25. Cunningham & Craig (2019).

26. Benkler (2006).

27. Scott, S. (2009). Repackaging fan culture: The regifting economy of ancillary content models. *Transformative Works and Cultures, 3*(1.6), 1–11.

28. Pearson (2010).

29. van Dijck (2013). 158.

30. Jenkins et al. (2013).

CHAPTER 8: PLATFORMS, PLACE, AND BEYOND

1. Bowles, N. (2019, March 23). Human contact is now a luxury good. *New York Times.* https://www.nytimes.com/2019/03/23/sunday-review/human-contact-luxury-screens.html; Turkle (2011).

2. Raftery, B. (2017, November 20). *Justice League*, Rotten Tomatoes, and DC fans' persecution complex. *Wired*. https://www.wired.com/story/justice-league-rotten-tomatoes-fans/

3. Brown, L. (2023, September 6). The decomposition of Rotten Tomatoes. *Vulture*. https://www.vulture.com/article/rotten-tomatoes-movie-rating.html

4. Maxwell, R., & Miller, T. (2011). Old, new and middle-aged media convergence. *Cultural Studies, 25*(4–5), 585–603. 594.

5. Bielby & Harrington (2017); Click, M. (2017). Do all "good things" come to an end? In J. Gray, C. Sandvoss, & C. L. Harrington (Eds.), *Fandom: Identities and communities in a mediated world* (2nd ed.) (pp. 191–204). New York University Press; Hills, M. (2005). Patterns of surprise: The "aleatory object" in psychoanalytic ethnography and cyclical fandom. *American Behavioral Scientist, 48*(7), 801–21.

6. Adams (1991); Cross & Walton (2005); Lukas (2008); Parascandola & Parascandola (2015); Conlin, J. (Ed.). (2013). *The pleasure garden, from Vauxhall to Coney Island*. University of Pennsylvania Press.

7. Baudrillard (1983); Eco (1986.

8. McCarthy (2023).

9. Johnson, S. (2016). *Wonderland: How play made the modern world*. Pan Macmillan.

10. Scibelli, C. (2011). Forget the Prozac, give me a dose of Disney. In K. Jackson & M. West (Eds.), *Disneyland and culture: Essays on the parks and their influence* (pp. 215–22). McFarland & Company. 216.

11. Hench (2003); Snow (2020).

12. McCarthy (2022).

13. Andersen (2017); Gurr, Bob. Interview with author. October 8, 2017.

14. Gardetta (2005).

15. Tu, J. [Jade Tu]. (2015, March 8). A Day in a Life of Peter Tu [Video file]. https://youtu.be/BjvmAjQNuPs

16. Tu (2015, March 8).

17. Shirky (2010).

18. Tu, J. [Jade Tu]. (2019, April 6). Disneyland's Clapping Man: Peter Tu [Video file]. https://youtu.be/hKHltoyh65M

19. Mannheim (2002).

20. Snow (2020). 324.

INDEX

Figures and tables are indicated by *f* and *t* following page numbers.

ABOUT THE AUTHOR

Photo courtesy of the author

William McCarthy is an assistant professor in the College of Communication and Media Sciences at Zayed University in Dubai, United Arab
Emirates. His work has appeared in publications including *Social Semiot-
ics, Tourism Geographies, Semiotica, Quarterly Review of Film and Video,*
and *Journal of Leisure Research.*

Printed in the United States
by Baker & Taylor Publisher Services